The Escape of the Mind

The Escape of the Mind

HOWARD RACHLIN

OXFORD
UNIVERSITY PRESS

OXFORD
UNIVERSITY PRESS

Oxford University Press is a department of the University of
Oxford. It furthers the University's objective of excellence in research,
scholarship, and education by publishing worldwide.

Oxford   New York

Auckland   Cape Town   Dar es Salaam   Hong Kong   Karachi
Kuala Lumpur   Madrid   Melbourne   Mexico City   Nairobi
New Delhi   Shanghai   Taipei   Toronto

With offices in

Argentina   Austria   Brazil   Chile   Czech Republic   France   Greece
Guatemala   Hungary   Italy   Japan   Poland   Portugal   Singapore
South Korea   Switzerland   Thailand   Turkey   Ukraine   Vietnam

Oxford is a registered trademark of Oxford University Press
in the UK and certain other countries.

Published in the United States of America by
Oxford University Press
198 Madison Avenue, New York, NY 10016

Library of Congress Cataloging-in-Publication Data
Rachlin, Howard, 1935–
The escape of the mind / by Howard Rachlin.
pages cm
Includes bibliographical references and index.
ISBN 978-0-19-932235-0 (alk. paper)
1. Mind and body.   2. Self-control.   3. Philosophy of mind.
4. Cognitive psychology.   I. Title.
BF161.R2293 2014
150—dc23   2013046958

1 3 5 7 9 8 6 4 2
Printed in the United States of America
on acid-free paper

For Nahid, Leila, Greg, and Ethan

If one sees the behavior of a living thing, one sees its soul.
— Ludwig Wittgenstein

CONTENTS

ACKNOWLEDGMENTS

I thank my friend, Marvin Frankel, whose contribution to this book goes far beyond the co-authored chapter reprinted here. I am grateful for the valuable comments and discussions with William Baum, Diane Barthel-Boucher, Jasper Brener, Leonard Green, Edward Katkin, John Malone, and Rohit Parikh and two anonymous reviewers.

Many of the ideas expressed in this book, especially regarding behavioral interpretation of ancient philosophy, owe a great debt to J. R. Kantor (1963, 1969).

Preparation of the book was supported by grants from the US National Institute of Health.

PREFACE

These chapters are arranged to tell a story (not necessarily *the* story) in the history and present state of philosophy and psychology of thinking about thinking. There are as many threads in this material as in a Persian carpet. The particular one I will try to pick out opens up questions that most people regard as settled: What does it mean to have a mind, to think, to be conscious of something? And, when we think, where do we do it? In my story, the history of thought about thought is really the history about how people relate to objects in the world and to each other. I believe that when we relate to objects and other people narrowly, wholly in the present and in the particular, we are not thinking. When we relate to objects and people widely, when our present actions depend on abstract relationships, widespread in both the past and future, we are thinking. This way of thinking about thinking applies to conscious as well as unconscious thought.

In my story, the ancient Athenian philosophers, Plato (who is said to have invented the mind) and Aristotle, both tended to think about thought in the above way. Our minds in this conception are not only active minds but, as long as we are conscious, are in continuous contact with the world—especially with each other. In my story, a person's mind and the world, and the minds of other people, were originally bound up together, each inconceivable without the other. But in the course of history, in my story, they became separated. In the name of ethics and religion, great thinkers, represented here by Saint Augustine and Descartes, teased apart the mind and the world and began to conceive of the mind as wholly contained within the body. In their conception, the mind, isolated from the world in the brain and served by millions of nerves (like a general, safe in his headquarters) continuously receives messages from the sense organs and sends messages to the muscles, but is never in direct contact with the world. This is the view of the mind that dominates current thought about thought—that most people regard as settled, as axiomatic. This is the view of the mind taken by the sort of common-sense folk psychology that refers to an *inner* life, as you might say, "The characters in this novel seem to have no inner lives."

Only recently, in the twenty-first century, have a few philosophers and psychologists come to conceive once again of the mind as active in the world. The main purpose of this book is to tell some of that story, of the escape of the mind, and to argue as strongly as possible for its usefulness and its relevance to modern times. The chapters are based on a series of articles that I and my colleagues have published over the years (in which this view was developed and refined), rewritten so as to tell a continuous story.

The Escape of the Mind

The Invention of the Mind (Plato)

The ancient Greek philosopher, Plato, tells an allegory of prisoners in a cave chained so they cannot move. They see only shadows projected on a wall. One prisoner is temporarily released and interacts with real objects and other people. When he returns to the cave, he cannot convince the others that their world is only a shadow of reality.

The freed prisoner learns about the real world by interacting with objects and people; analogously, we may learn about an ideal world by interacting not with objects and people but with the abstract patterns of their movement. Plato's conception of the mind (like the modern biological conception of an ecological niche) is a framework of interacting behavioral-environmental patterns. For him, the good life and the happiness that it entails in the soul are one and the same thing—a harmonious pattern of behavior in society and the world.

Philosophers occasionally say that Plato (427–347 B.C.) "invented the mind." According to one website (http://www.hermes-press.com/plato_thought.htm), "…the powers of mind that we call 'rational intelligence' were actually invented by Plato and the thinkers who followed in his path. When it comes to *critical thinking*, we find it hard to understand that at one time this capability of the human mind did not exist and had to be deliberately invented." You do not have to go as far as this to understand that the ideas formulated in Plato's writings have had a tremendous influence on our concepts of intelligence and rational thought.

Plato's Allegory of the Cave

In his most famous dialogue, *The Republic*, Plato considers "our nature in respect of education and its lack." (*Republic* VII, 514 a). As part of his philosophy of education, of what it means to acquire knowledge, he imagines prisoners in a cave chained to their seats and able to view only shadows (two-dimensional projections of objects) on a wall. Then he imagines what it would be like for one of these prisoners to be freed and brought out of the dark cave and into

the bright sunlight of our world. He describes the initial blindness and the subsequent enlightenment that the freed prisoner would experience. Then, in the
allegory, the same person goes back into the cave, where it takes him a while to
re-adapt. He tries to explain to the prisoners what the shadows really represent.
The unfreed prisoners cannot understand. They see him as a fool at best and, at
worst, a grave danger. Of course, an allegory invites all sorts of interpretation.
However, a critical point is that the prisoners in the cave do not see "*anything
of themselves or of one another.*" (*Republic* VII, 515 a; italics added). The man who
journeys out of the cave and becomes enlightened learns about his own reality at
the same time that he learns about the reality of other people and of the world.
Plato is saying that all of us learn about ourselves in the same way that we learn
about other people and about the world.

To give the reader a sense of Plato's allegory, here is the core of it:

> *Socrates: And now, let me show in a figure how far our nature is enlightened
> or unenlightened: —Behold! human beings living in an underground den,
> which has a mouth open towards the light and reaching all along the den;
> here they have been from their childhood, and have their legs and necks
> chained so that they cannot move, and can only see before them, being pre-
> vented by the chains from turning round their heads. Above and behind
> them a fire is blazing at a distance, and between the fire and the prisoners
> there is a raised way; and you will see, if you look, a low wall built along the
> way, like the screen which marionette players have in front of them, over
> which they show the puppets.*
>
> Glaucon: I see.
> *S: And do you see men passing along the wall carrying all sorts of vessels, and
> statues and figures of animals made of wood and stone and various materi-
> als, which appear over the wall? Some of them are talking, others silent.*
> G: You have shown me a strange image, and they are strange prisoners.
> *S: Like ourselves; and they see only their own shadows, or the shadows of one
> another, which the fire throws on the opposite wall of the cave?*

[Note that the same limitation applies to their vision of themselves and their
vision of others.]

> G: True; how could they see anything but the shadows if they were never
> allowed to move their heads?
> *S: And of the objects which are being carried in like manner they would only see
> the shadows?*
> G: Yes.
> *S: And if they were able to converse with one another, would they not suppose
> that they were naming what was actually before them?*
> G: Very true.

S: And suppose further that the prison had an echo which came from the other side, would they not be sure to fancy when one of the passers-by spoke that the voice which they heard came from the passing shadow?

G; No question.

S: To them, the truth would be literally nothing but the shadows of the images.

G: That is certain.

S: And now look again, and see what will naturally follow if the prisoners are released and disabused of their error. At first, when any of them is liberated and compelled suddenly to stand up and turn his neck round and walk and look towards the light, he will suffer sharp pains; the glare will distress him, and he will be unable to see the realities of which in his former state he had seen the shadows; and then conceive someone saying to him, that what he saw before was an illusion, but that now, when he is approaching nearer to being and his eye is turned towards more real existence, he has a clearer vision—what will be his reply? And you may further imagine that his instructor is pointing to the objects as they pass and requiring him to name them—will he not be perplexed? Will he not fancy that the shadows which he formerly saw are truer than the objects which are now shown to him?

G: Far truer.

S: And if he is compelled to look straight at the light, will he not have a pain in his eyes which will make him turn away to take in the objects of vision which he can see, and which he will conceive to be in reality clearer than the things which are now being shown to him?

[To the prisoner the shadows will be clear and real; what we conceive of as real objects will to him be vague images.]

G: True.

S: And suppose once more, that he is reluctantly dragged up a steep and rugged ascent, and held fast until he's forced into the presence of the sun himself, is he not likely to be pained and irritated? When he approaches the light his eyes will be dazzled, and he will not be able to see anything at all of what are now called realities.

G: Not all in a moment.

S: He will require to grow accustomed to the sight of the upper world. And first he will see the shadows best, next the reflections of men and other objects in the water, and then the objects themselves; then he will gaze upon the light of the moon and the stars and the spangled heaven; and he will see the sky and the stars by night better than the sun or the light of the sun by day?

G: Certainly.

S: Last of all he will be able to see the sun, and not mere reflections of him in the water, but he will see him in his own proper place, and not in another; and he will contemplate him as he is.

G: Certainly.

S: *He will then proceed to argue that this is he who gives the season and the years, and is the guardian of all that is in the visible world, and in a certain way the cause of all things which he and his fellows have been accustomed to behold?*

G: Clearly, he would first see the sun and then reason about him.

S: *And when he remembered his old habitation, and the wisdom of the den and his fellow-prisoners, do you not suppose that he would felicitate himself on the change, and pity them?*

G: Certainly, he would.

S: *And if they were in the habit of conferring honors among themselves on those who were quickest to observe the passing shadows and to remark which of them went before, and which followed after, and which were together; and who were therefore best able to draw conclusions as to the future, do you think that he would care for such honors and glories, or envy the possessors of them? Would he not say with Homer,*

Better to be the poor servant of a poor master, and to endure anything, rather than think as they do and live after their manner?

G: Yes, I think that he would rather suffer anything than entertain these false notions and live in this miserable manner.

S: *Imagine once more, such a one coming suddenly out of the sun to be replaced in his old situation; would he not be certain to have his eyes full of darkness?*

G: To be sure.

S: *And if there were a contest, and he had to compete in measuring the shadows with the prisoners who had never moved out of the den, while his sight was still weak, and before his eyes had become steady (and the time which would be needed to acquire this new habit of sight might be very consider-able) would he not be ridiculous? Men would say of him that up he went and down he came without his eyes; and that it was better not even to think of ascending; and if any one tried to loose another and lead him up to the light, let them only catch the offender, and they would put him to death.*

[How could they put him to death if they are in chains? But Plato is willing to stretch the terms of his allegory in order to rebuke his fellow Athenians for condemning to death his own teacher, Socrates. Socrates was condemned to death for "impiety and corrupting the youth of Athens." Plato is saying that they put Socrates to death because of his greater knowledge and their own ignorance. Plato's depiction of Socrates' final moments in his earlier dialogue, *Phaedo*, presented that knowledge and that ignorance as contrasting patterns of behavior.]

G: No question.

S: *This entire allegory, you may now append, dear Glaucon, to the previous argument; the prison-house is the world of sight, the light of the fire is the sun, and you will not misapprehend me if you interpret the journey upwards to be the ascent of the soul into the intellectual world according to my poor belief, which, at your desire, I have expressed whether rightly or wrongly God knows.*

[The allegory illustrates an analogy: The world of the prisoners is to our world as our world is to "the intellectual world."]

But, whether true or false, my opinion is that in the world of knowledge the idea of good appears last of all, and is seen only with an effort; and, when seen, is also inferred to be the universal author of all things beautiful and right, parent of light and of the lord of light in this visible world, and the immediate source of reason and truth in the intellectual; and that this is the power upon which he who would act rationally, either in public or private life must have his eye fixed.

[From Plato (tr. 1874), *The Republic*, B. Jowett (trans.), http://classics.mit.edu/ Plato/republic.html]

Note the final emphasis on rational *action*. Plato's "invention of the mind" is sometimes thought to imply that our "inner lives" are somehow more important than how we actually behave. You could conceivably interpret Plato's reference to "public or private life" in terms of overt versus covert behavior. And, as we shall see in the rest of this book, this is how many people do conceive it. But I believe that this allegory and all of Plato's writings imply the more usual distinction between public and private life—life in the outside world versus life among close family and intimate friends—overt behavior in either case.

The point of the allegory, according to Plato, is to distinguish between "education and its lack." As regards education, Plato objects to what, in modern terms, would be called the storehouse theory of knowledge. Education is "not like inserting vision into blind eyes," he says. It is not, in fact, an internal change at all. It is a change of behavior in the whole body: "The true analogy for this indwelling power of the soul and the instrument whereby each of us apprehends [learns] is that of an eye that could not be converted to the light from the darkness except by turning *the whole body*" (*Republic* VI, 518 c; italics added). This passage is important because it is Plato's own explanation of the meaning of the allegory of the cave. That a mental process (learning) corresponds to an interaction of *the whole body* with its environment rather than an interaction among parts of the body indicates that the freed prisoner learns because he can now engage in a functional relation with the environment. The gaining of knowledge is an active, not a passive, exercise. The distinction between the prisoners and the freed man in the allegory is not just

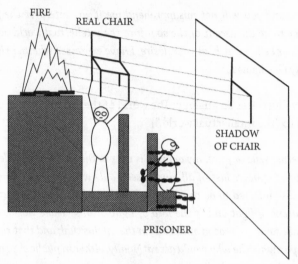

Figure 1.1 Plato's allegory of the cave. The fire casts shadows of objects held up by slaves on the wall of the cave. The prisoners are chained so tightly that they cannot see the objects, the other prisoners, or even themselves. (Only one slave, one object, and one prisoner are shown, but Plato supposed that there were many of each.)

that they see the world in two dimensions and he sees it in three, but that they are chained and completely passive, and he can *interact* with the environment, including other people.

What does the allegory of the cave *really* mean? Plato's dialogues are plays of a sort with a drama of their own (Friedlander, 1958, 1964, 1969). Each interpreter approaches them with his own purposes. Below I will discuss several distinctions and dimensions. They are my attempt to use Plato to further my own purpose—to portray him as the inventor of a concept of mind as an interaction of people with the world that has, over the years, become distorted. In later chapters I will argue that the distortion has permeated our way of thinking about the mind to the point where Plato's original conception may seem absurd. Nevertheless, I will show that some recent theories of mind in philosophy and psychology have begun to approach Plato's original conception.

Shadow of a Thing (Prisoner) versus Thing Itself (Free Man)

The literal difference between a prisoner and the freed man is that the prisoner sees only a single projection of objects, whereas the freed man may see whole objects from many different viewpoints. The freed man may walk around objects (and other people) and interact with them (as we do), whereas the prisoner may not.

Particular (Prisoner) versus Abstract (Free Man)

The relation between a prisoner's view of a single projection of a chair, for instance, and the freed man's view of a real chair is that of a particular (a particular viewpoint) to an abstract conception of a chair. When we non-prisoners see a chair from one viewpoint, we see a whole chair, not just the projection now in front of our eyes. The back and sides of the chair may not be within our visual scope, but we behave as if they were there. We confidently sit down on a chair, even though we may have had the merest glimpse of it. Our relation to chairs is a functional one.

The allegory of the cave asks us to consider three worlds:

A. The world of the prisoners.
B. The world outside the cave—our own world.
C. The ideal world.

By analogy, the world of the prisoners is to our world as our world is to the ideal world. We see the chair only as it exists in our world. But the "educated" person, who has expended the necessary intellectual effort, may come to interact with something approximating the *ideal* chair. According to Plato, you can know ideal objects, and you can live in the ideal world, if (a) you are intelligent enough and (b) you expend the necessary effort.

Perception (Prisoner) versus Reason (Free Man)

For Plato, the goal of philosophy was to enable a person to live a good life, to live the best possible life. The freed man in the allegory is forcibly dragged out of the cave and brought into the sun. But in our world no one will drag us to The Good. We may have teachers to point the way (as Plato had Socrates), but the effort and the intelligence must be our own. Anyone, even an animal, can understand the world through sensation and perception and behave so as to attain pleasure. But only the intelligent elite who spend the effort to use their reason are capable of knowing truth, which is located in the ideal world. Humans have the option of interacting with the world (including other people) with their intelligence as well as with their senses.

Animal (Prisoner) versus Ecological Niche (Free Man)

A modern analog to Plato's ideal world is the concept of the ecological niche. According to *The Free Dictionary*, an ecological niche is "...the status of an organism within its environment and community." Imagine then the Serengeti savannah. Together, all the animals and plants, along with the topography and the weather, form an ecological system. Each animal and plant plays its part in delicate balance with the rest. As the weather and topography change, the various species adapt. New ones are formed, others go extinct. But now imagine that one species is entirely removed—say, the giraffes—while (contrary to possibility) all else is held constant. The giraffes' removal would create a perceptible ecological niche, a sort of hole in the system formerly filled by giraffes—like a jigsaw puzzle with one piece missing. Without the giraffes: the leaves at the top of the trees would go uneaten and the seeds produced there would not be spread as widely as they are now; the various parasites living on and around the giraffe would have no host; no animal would be able to spot lions from far off and start to run, thus signaling the others; the actual physical area occupied by the giraffes would be less populated, perhaps underpopulated; the giraffes' predators would have less food. A gap would thus exist where actual giraffes existed before.

As long as all the giraffes were gone, and as long as the rest of the ecological system remained as it was, the system would contain the niche where the giraffes were. No actual group of giraffes could perfectly occupy this niche. It is the nature of real giraffes that they are not perfect. Sometimes they would not spot the lions, sometimes they would not spread the seeds from the high trees, sometimes they would not reproduce enough to feed the lions and the lions would die. But, without real giraffes, the giraffes' *functions* in the ecological system essentially define an ideal species. In practice it is of course impossible to remove a species from an ecological system while keeping everything else constant. Other species would evolve to fill the suddenly empty niche. But the niche itself (the ideal giraffe) may be known up to a point—say, by an ecologist who has spent her life studying the ecological system that the giraffe occupies—even while actual giraffes are still there. When a neophyte walks in the jungle he does not see ecological niches. He sees trees, plants, individual animals, bugs. But when an ecologist walks in the jungle she may see the niches because through intelligence and effort she has attained an abstract view. She "sees" this niche; she sees this ideal giraffe species, in terms of its "status. . . within its environment and community." Eyes, ears, smell, touch, and taste may be necessary for her to make the discrimination, but they are not sufficient. Also necessary are intelligence and hard work. *The niche, the ideal species, exists as such not inside the brain of the ecologist (no more than an actual giraffe exists in the brain of the ecologist), and not someplace in heaven, but in the world, in the ecological system itself. The ecologist's interaction with the niche (verbal and non-verbal) and her knowledge of it (I will argue in this book) are one and the same thing.*

Similarly, within human society there is a kind of niche for a chair—a set of needs that chairs fulfill. Chairs are manufactured, not grown, but they evolve no less to fill the need we have for them (aesthetic and symbolic as well as supportive). Plato sometimes did tentatively speculate that ideal forms may have some

CHAIR'S FUNCTIONS

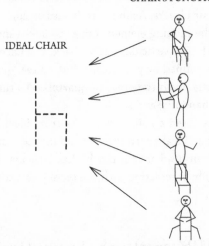

IDEAL CHAIR

Figure 1.2 The ideal chair (dashed lines) is the function of the chair in human behavior (symbolized by the diagrammatic figures); if it exists as such anywhere, it exists in the world (perhaps in heaven, according to Plato). But it does *not* exist inside any person.

kind of existence somewhere in heaven. But that is not because the form does not exist on earth. Rather, it is because the truly ideal chair would meet the needs of ideal humans in an ideal society in an ideal cosmos. Figure 1.2 illustrates this conception. For Plato, the ideal chair (dashed-line "chair-symbol") is to a real chair as a real chair is to the shadow of a chair in Plato's allegorical cave (see Figure 1.1). The ideal chair exists, as an ecological niche exists, in the world (symbolized by the human icons interacting with chairs), not anywhere inside a person.

Plato's invention of the mind is not an invention of a representation in the ecologist's brain. In Plato's allegory, the journey of the freed man out of the cave is a metaphor for an intellectual journey, a teasing out from the environment of ideal forms defined by their function within their environment and community. Of course, Plato was no biologist and did not think in terms of ecological systems. But he did think a lot about how individual people relate to each other in a human society. So let us abandon ecological niches for the moment and take, as another example, a human system.

Particular Player (Prisoner) versus Football Team (Free Man)

Suppose you are a billionaire (pleasant to imagine) and have just bought a football team. You own a stadium, with all its appurtenances; you have hired a coach, assistant coaches, trainers, cheerleaders, and so on. You have signed on dozens of offensive and defensive players. But you have not yet signed on a first-string quarterback. Certainly you need a quarterback—one whose skills will fit with those of the rest of your players. As in a giraffe-less ecological system, there is a sort of hole where the missing element ought to be—a missing piece of the puzzle. So long as you lack a particular quarterback, you have, in a sense, a perfect quarterback—one defined by your needs. But no real quarterback will satisfy your needs perfectly. Even the greatest quarterbacks throw interceptions, fumble balls, mess up handoffs, and so on.

Even after you have hired a real, perhaps far from ideal, quarterback, it is possible to know what an ideal quarterback would be like. But that quarterback would not then be in your head or your coach's head. He may be known (that is, defined and discussed) by interacting with the team—as a coach may do—with intelligence and effort.

Individual (Prisoner) versus Society (Free Man)

Note, however, that, no matter how rich you may be, you do not have an ideal team. The players are all too real. A perfectly ideal quarterback would be playing in the context of perfectly ideal teammates on a perfectly ideal team. In turn, a perfectly ideal team could exist only in a perfectly ideal league, and a perfectly ideal league, in a perfectly ideal sports culture, and a perfectly ideal sports culture in a perfectly ideal state. Thus, before it becomes possible to know (to talk about and discriminate) what constitutes a truly ideal quarterback, you would need to know what constitutes a perfect state. And, before an individual can know what it means to behave perfectly in society (to attain The Good), she needs to know what constitutes an ideal state. This, according to Friedlander (1964), was Plato's reason for writing *The Republic*—which presents his version of an ideal state. According to Plato, without such a conception it is impossible to conceive of ideal individual behavior. About the ideal city-state described in *The Republic*, Plato says, "...it makes no difference whether it exists now or will ever come into being. The politics of this city only will be his [the wise man's] and of none other" (*Republic* IX, 592 b).

In the dialogues prior to *The Republic*, no firm conclusions are reached about individual behavior. Only after an ideal context of individual behavior is established is ethical behavior definable. The prisoners in the cave live in a drastically impoverished society relative to our society. But our society, Plato argues, is just as impoverished relative to the perfect society that *The Republic* attempts to describe.

Selfish Behavior (Prisoner) versus Ethical Behavior (Free Man)

Within the analogy: prisoners' world/our world = our world/ideal world is another analogy: prisoners' behavior/our behavior = our behavior/ideal behavior. The state serves for Plato as a model of the individual writ large. As individual people are to the ideal state, individual actions are to an ethical pattern of actions. In *The Republic*, Plato allows no political analysis to go very far without turning back to its ethical implications.

Concern for individual behavior permeates *The Republic*. For example, near the beginning: "Do you think it a small matter that you are attempting to determine and not the entire conduct of life that for each of us would make living most worthwhile?" (*Republic* I, 344 e); and "Is it true that the just have a better life than the unjust and are happier?. . . It appears even now that they are, I think, from what has already been said. But all the same we must examine it more carefully. For it is no ordinary matter that we are discussing, but the right conduct of life" (*Republic* IX, 578c). *The Republic* takes its place among the dialogues as an essential step in describing how a person should live; it attempts to describe an ideal context (an ecological niche) for individual behavior.

Plato emphasizes that the main difference between selfish behavior and ethical behavior is not that ethical behavior is controlled by an inner moral sense whereas selfish behavior is controlled by external rewards and punishment. Both are controlled by external factors. The difference is that ethical behavior is controlled by an ideal environment (including but not limited to other people) whereas selfish behavior is controlled by particular and temporally constricted aspects of our real environment.

For Plato, the first, last, and most essential question is: How should a person live? Plato deals with this question by considering life as a series of choices between the merely pleasant and the good. But the very acts of distinguishing between the pleasant and the good are those that are called (in our language) virtuous. There is no difference, for him, between ethical understanding and ethical action. In other words, knowledge of the good cannot be separated from good behavior. Knowledge of the good (a potential result of our efforts analogous to the freed prisoner's journey) is difficult because many (but not all) actions that give us pleasure are not good. Pleasure confuses us. Eventually, the bad person will be unhappy, especially when permitted by social circumstances to live a life of pure pleasure. Furthermore, a person who lives such a life is like a lower animal—an oyster (*Philebus*, 21 c).

What abilities do you need to tell the difference between pleasure and good? In the long run, for Plato, good behavior is intrinsically harmonious, while bad behavior is not (however pleasant it may be in the short run). Ultimately, the ability to discriminate between the pleasurable and the good is an aesthetic ability; it is absolute—there are better and worse patterns of individual behavior that cut across societies—and it is rare. The best we can do is to try to create a society in which goodness will be fostered and, failing that, we ought to behave (we will thereby be happiest) as if such a society existed. Plato's view of the soul, his theory of ideal forms, his dialectical method, and all other aspects of his philosophy revolve around this argument.

In Book X, the last book of *The Republic*, Socrates says:

> It should be our main concern that each of us, neglecting all other stud-
> ies, should seek after and study this thing—if in any way he may be able
> to learn of and discover the man who will give him the ability and the
> knowledge to distinguish the life that is good from that which is bad,
> and *always and everywhere to choose the best that conditions allow*. . . so
> that he may make a reasoned choice between the better and the worse
> life. (*Republic* X, 618c; italics added)

A theme that runs through all of Plato's dialogues is that perception not
guided by intellect is a poor guide to reality. Furthermore, a person who knows
which alternative is better *cannot* choose the worse alternative. If he does, he has
by definition calculated wrongly. Thus, "no one ever willingly goes to meet evil"
(*Protagoras*, 358 c). A person's knowledge, for Plato, *necessarily* corresponds to
the choices he makes. In *The Republic* (IX, 587 c, d, e) the dimension of comparison between pleasure and good is temporal—how long-lasting are the benefits
of each? The comparison, Plato says, "is. . . pertinent to the lives of men if days
and nights and months and years apply to them" (*Republic* IX, 588 a). The essential difference between The Good and the pleasurable, then, lies in their relative
durations (days, nights, months, and years).

Impulsive Act (Prisoner) versus Self-Control (Free Man)

Just as the individual person is an element within the state, so the individual
act is an element within that person's broader pattern of acts. Plato character-
izes acts and patterns of acts along the dimension: pleasure—intelligence. Some
particular acts or narrow patterns of acts are explicable only in terms of gaining pleasure and avoiding pain. A life consisting of such acts is, according to
Plato, the life of an oyster. Some extended patterns of acts (giving up smoking
cigarettes, for a modern example) are explicable only in terms of larger, more
abstract goals—success, health, social approval, and so on. Some still more
extended patterns (a life of study, for example) are explicable only in terms of
attaining The Good.

Self-control for Plato is *not* an action of an *internal* will, not a squeezing of
some kind of muscle in the brain, but a behavioral pattern consisting of a harmonious mixture of intelligence and pleasure. Plato defines such a pattern as
wisdom. In one of the later dialogues, Plato says: "Why it's just as if we were supplying drinks, with two fountains at our disposal; one would be of honey, standing for pleasure, the other standing for intelligence, a sobering, unintoxicating
fountain of plain salubrious water. We must go to work and make a really good

mixture" (*Philebus*, 61 c). The answer to the question of how one should live is to choose a balanced or well-mixed or harmonious life, "always to choose the life that is seated in the mean and shun the excess in either direction, both in this world so far as may be and in all the life to come. . . this is the greatest happiness for man" (*Republic* X, 619 b).

Body (Prisoner) versus Mind (Free Man)

Near the end of *The Republic* Plato discusses how to evaluate the happiness of a tyrant. The tyrant is rich and powerful. But is he happy? To answer this question, Plato rejects the validity of the tyrant's own view—his introspection. Instead, he claims, the best—the ideal—way to evaluate the tyrant's happiness is as follows: "The man to whom we ought to listen [about the tyrant's happiness] is he who has this capacity of judgment [not to be overawed] and who has lived under the same roof with a tyrant and has witnessed his conduct in his own home and observed in person his dealings with his intimates in each instance where he would best be seen stripped of his vesture of tragedy, [who has observed him in his private life] and who likewise observed his behavior in the hazards of his public life" (*Republic* IX, 577 b).

The fundamental difference between the prisoners and the freed man is a difference in their actions. The freed man attains knowledge, but that knowledge consists of the way he behaves. Let us extend the allegory a bit and say that the freed man, disgusted with the attitude of his erstwhile fellow prisoners, gives up trying to convince them of the true nature of things, and comes to live permanently in the outside world. He gets married, has children, and lives a normal middle-class life in Athens. Does he love his family? Plato would say, I think, that to definitively answer this question we should ask them, not him. A man's love for his family, Plato would say, is a pattern in his overt behavior and theirs. There exists an ideal pattern of loving behavior (like an ecological niche). No real group of people can love each other perfectly. To the extent that their pattern comes to resemble the ideal pattern, it is loving behavior.

I am not a professional classicist and cannot claim that this is the way Plato actually thought about thought. All I am claiming is that one reasonable interpretation of the allegory of the cave is that the journey out of the cave, the journey in pursuit of knowledge, consists of a pattern of behavior conforming to a sort of ecological niche—not the ecological niche in the necessarily imperfect society that exists, but the ecological niche in (what Plato considered to be) a perfect society, the one outlined in *The Republic*.

That the good life and the happiness that it entails in the soul are one and the same thing—a harmonious pattern of behavior (i.e., a series of choices) is stated quite specifically in *Theaetetus*, the dialogue that Friedlander (1964) places immediately after *The Republic*:

> There are two patterns, my friend, in the unchangeable nature of things, one of divine happiness, the other of godless misery—a truth to which their [unjust peoples'] folly makes them utterly blind, unaware that in doing injustice they are growing less like one of these patterns and more like the other. The penalty they pay is the life they lead, answering to the pattern they resemble. (*Theaetetus*, 176 e–177 a)

Then Plato goes on to question whether even private sensations, "what the individual experiences at the moment," (*Theaetetus*, 179 c), are valid knowledge. For Plato, what is private is not knowledge and what is knowledge is not private. The reason for insistence on this is that for Plato a person's mind (and soul) do not reside inside the person; they are actions of the whole person in the world and are observable to others; actions of a whole person (like the actions of a state) cannot be intrinsically private. With our intelligence and effort another person's pattern of particular acts may become transparent, and we will perceive that pattern abstractly as a mental state. Of what does such perception consist? We will discuss that in the next chapter.

Acknowledgment

Chapter 1 contains material from Rachlin (1985) and Rachlin (1992). Unless otherwise indicated, quotes from Plato come from Plato (trans. 1961). They are referenced by book and section rather than page number.

|| 2 ||

Body and Mind (Aristotle)

This chapter says that mind is behavior on a higher level of abstraction. The mind stands to behavior as a more abstract pattern (such as a dance) stands to its own particular elements (the steps of the dance). For Aristotle (the chapter argues), the more abstract pattern is what he called the final cause of its particular components; that is, the mind is a final cause of behavior. Final causes answer the question: WHY did this or that action occur? Q. Why did you take that step? A. Because I was doing that dance. (Our more familiar efficient causes are answers to the question: HOW did this or that action occur.) A science of final causes is called a teleological science; the book's approach to the mind (its theory of mind) is teleological behaviorism. The remainder of the book will work out the implications of teleological behaviorism for contemporary philosophy of mind, for the science of psychology, and for everyday human life.

Just as the thread of my story picks out one episode in Plato's philosophy, his allegory of the cave, so it winds through one aspect of the philosophy of the second great pillar of ancient Greek philosophy, Aristotle (384–322 B.C.). That aspect is his analysis of the relation of mind to bodily movement.

Aristotle was a Platonist in his early years. His philosophy may be seen as a development and continuation of Plato's philosophy (Gadamer, 1986). For Aristotle, the relation of mind to bodily movement was as a final cause to its effect. To modern ears, this sounds like the mind must be inside the body and controlling it, as a driver controls the motion of a car. But that is not at all the way Aristotle saw the distinction. The reason for the confusion is that for modern science a cause is usually what Aristotle called an *efficient* cause—like one billiard ball hitting another and causing it to move. However, this is far from always the case in modern science. According to Max Planck, the founder of quantum theory: "The *cause efficiens*, which operates from the present into the future and makes future situations appear as determined by earlier ones, is joined by the *cause finalis* for which, inversely, the future—namely a definite goal—serves as the premise from which there can be deduced the development of the processes which lead to this goal" (cited in Yourgrau & Mandelstam, 1968, p. 165).

Moreover, the utility functions that serve as the basic predictive tool of modern microeconomic theory are essentially final causes (Rachlin, 1994, pp. 148–149). For Aristotle, the mind is not an efficient cause but a *final* cause of bodily movement (Randall, 1960, p. 124). Philosophers call the explanation of something in terms of final causes a *teleological* explanation.

I call myself a "teleological behaviorist" (Rachlin, 1992, 1995). Also, teleological explanation has recently been in the air in both philosophy (Nagel, 2013) and psychology (Seligman et al., 2013); Chapters 7 and 8 of this book will apply teleological thinking to issues of self-control and social cooperation. However, the purpose of the present chapter is quite narrow—to present a coherent view of final causes (teleological explanation) and to show in what sense the mind is the final cause of bodily movement.

[Aristotle referred to four types of causes: material, formal, efficient, and final. Material and formal causes explain the nature of *substances* (what we would call *objects* or *things*); efficient and final causes explain *motions*—the movement of objects (inanimate objects as well as organisms). Although we are mainly concerned here with efficient and final causes, it is worth noting the relation between material and formal causes. For Aristotle, a substance consisted of matter taking on a certain form. Thus, a circular piece of cardboard (a substance) might be said to consist of cardboard (its material cause) taking on the form of a locus of points equidistant from a single point (its formal cause). It is odd for us to think of cardboard or a circular form as a cause of something, but remember, Aristotle used the concept of cause in a much more general way than we do. Either cardboard alone or circularity alone cannot be a substance. An actual substance (a cardboard circle) is matter (cardboard) taking on a certain form (a circle). However, no material object ever perfectly fits its form (no piece of cardboard can be a perfect circle).]

Final Causes

Aristotle's concept of cause was much wider than the modern one. For him, a causal explanation of a process was an answer to a question about the process—what might follow the word "because" in a sentence (Hocutt, 1974). Efficient causes, the causes we are familiar with, are answers to the question, HOW. . .? *Question:* How does the elevator get you up to your office? *Answer:* A motor winds a wire rope around a spool with a weight at the other end, the rope is attached to the elevator car, and the rope pulls the car up. As the car goes up, the weight goes down, and so on. Final causes, on the other hand, are answers to the question, WHY. . .? *Question:* Why are you buying that coloring book? *Answer:* It's a present for my niece.

In our everyday way of thinking, causes precede their effects. Aristotle's efficient causes do precede their effects. When discussing the effects of objects on sense organs Aristotle used efficient-cause explanations. For instance, Aristotle stated in *De Anima* (Book II, chap. 12, 424a) that our sense organs are affected by forms of objects "the way in which a piece of wax [the organ] takes on the impress of a signet ring [the form of the object] without the iron or gold [the matter]." However, most of *De Anima* (*On the Soul*) is devoted not to how the forms of objects make their way into the body but to the relation between objects in the environment and the behavior (the movement) of whole organisms. It is movement of whole bodies rather than the transmission of forms within the body that Aristotle labeled with the familiar terms *sensation, perception, imagination,* and *thought.* And movements of whole bodies were explained by Aristotle in terms of final rather than efficient causes.

Let us at this point abandon the attempt to be faithful to Aristotle and just consider how the concept of final causes might be applicable to contemporary psychology and to our daily life. To do this, we need to distinguish between two ways to look at final causes: narrow and wide.

The Narrow View of Final Causes

Suppose that you put a dollar into a candy machine, press a button, and get a candy bar. The narrow view says that getting the candy bar is the final cause of the sequence: put dollar in slot, press button. Note that putting the dollar in the slot is *extrinsic* to eating the candy; they are separate events happening at different times.

Narrow final causes act in the opposite direction to efficient causes. Inserting the dollar and pressing the button cause the candy to appear in the tray (*efficient* cause). And the future appearance of the candy causes you to insert the dollar (*final* cause).

In a behavioral laboratory, a pigeon pecks an illuminated button and gets a food pellet. Subsequently, the pigeon pecks the button faster. The food (or rather eating the food) may be thought of as the (narrow) final cause of the peck. As with pressing the button and getting the candy bar, pecking the button and eating the food are separate events happening at different times. The peck causes the food delivery (*efficient* cause). And the future food delivery causes the peck (*final* cause). Similarly, you need a bat in order to play baseball. Therefore, playing baseball would be the final cause of buying the bat.

Efficient causes work forward in time; narrow final causes work backward in time. Eating a candy bar, which happens after you insert the dollar into the machine, would be the final cause of inserting the dollar. Playing baseball, which can only happen after you obtain a bat, is the cause of buying the bat. This concept is so alien to our sense of what a cause should be, and what we use causes for in science (to predict future events), that we are tempted to translate such narrowly conceived final causes into (more comfortable) efficient causes. Rather than saying that a future candy bar causes the current dollar insertion, or the future baseball game causes the current bat buying, we are tempted to postulate current states within the actor—your desire for a candy bar and knowledge that inserting a dollar into the machine and pressing the button will cause the candy bar to appear; the bat buyer's desire to play baseball and knowledge that she needs a bat in order do so—and to suppose that it is the internal desire and internal knowledge rather than the candy bar delivery or the baseball playing that *actually* causes you to insert the dollar or the player to buy the bat.

[The narrow view of final causes matches nicely with the behavioral concept of *reinforcement* (response at t_1, reinforcer at t_2). Psychologists attribute behavioral change to a particular reinforcer (such as eating a candy bar) acting on a particular response sequence (such as inserting a dollar into a machine and pressing a button). A particular reinforcer may be delayed or may be symbolic or conditional (money, or a pat on the back) but, to work, it is commonly thought, a particular reinforcer must follow a particular response. Where behavior change is observed but no particular reinforcer is observed in the *external* environment, reinforcement is often assumed to occur in the *internal* environment (an internal pat on the back, so to speak). There is nothing intrinsically wrong with such internal explanations, but they usually end up as explanations in terms of efficient rather than final causes.]

The Wide View of Final Causes

On the other hand, the wide view of final causes says that the cause of putting the dollar in the slot and pressing the button is not the appearance of the candy bar as such, but the *relationship* between putting the dollar in the slot, pressing the button, and getting the candy bar. That is, the entire sequence of actions—the pattern of actions—is the cause of each individual component of the pattern. From the wide view, the *relationship* (the contingency) between bat buying and baseball playing is the final cause of the increase in bat buying. The wide view alters the traditional concept of reinforcement in a subtle way. From the wide view, the reinforcer (the cause) of the bat buying is no longer just playing baseball but is the (more abstract) *relationship* between buying a bat and playing baseball. Thus, with the wider view, in order to determine the (final) cause of bat buying, it is not necessary to find a reinforcer for each instance of bat buying; the overall contingency of baseball playing on bat buying is both necessary and sufficient to count as a cause. When no particular event, such as a baseball game, follows a given act, such as buying a bat, it is therefore *not* necessary to postulate an inner "satisfaction" of owning the bat to explain the purchase. It is not necessary, for example, to suppose that after each dessert refusal the dieter inwardly pats herself on the back; the overall relationship between dessert refusals and weight (hence social approval, better health, job performance, etc.) is sufficient.

Such abstract relationships gain control over behavior only with difficulty (that's why dieting is so hard to do successfully) but from the wide view, when dieting is successful, that abstract relationship is the actual cause of the dessert refusal. (See Chapters 7 and 8 in this volume, and Rachlin, 1989, 2000, for applications of the wide view in decision making and self-control.)

The effects of a wide final cause are *intrinsic* to their cause; the effects of a narrow final cause are *extrinsic* to their cause. To take another baseball example, running bases is intrinsic to playing baseball, whereas buying a bat is extrinsic to playing baseball. From both wide and narrow views, playing baseball may be a final cause: From the wide view, playing baseball is a final cause of running bases; from the narrow view, playing baseball is a final cause of buying a bat. Figure 2.1 illustrates this distinction.

From the wide view, a dance is a final cause (but not the only one) of a step; a program of dances is a final cause of a specific dance; a dance career is a final cause of a dance program; a happy life is a final cause of a dance career. Each more abstract and temporally extended pattern is a final cause of its narrower component. A final cause, such as dancing a dance or playing a game of baseball or playing a sonata on the piano, may be said to "embrace" its particular effects (steps, shots, themes). From the wide view, the relationship between a cause and its effect need not be 1:1. For example, living a healthy life may be a final cause of regular exercise, but no particular positive consequence may follow from each pushup. I believe that the wide view (incorporating economic utility functions as well as contingencies between responses and consequences as final causes of behavior) is more useful. From now on, when I speak of final causes I will be taking the wide view.

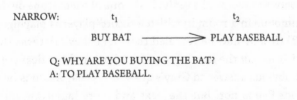

NARROW: t_1 t_2

BUY BAT   ⟶   PLAY BASEBALL

Q: WHY ARE YOU BUYING THE BAT?
A: TO PLAY BASEBALL.

WIDE: PLAY BASEBALL

HIT RUN BASES FIELD   PITCH CATCH

Q: WHY ARE YOU RUNNING THE BASES?
A: I'M PLAYING BASEBALL, AND IT'S PART OF THE GAME.

Figure 2.1 TWO KINDS OF FINAL CAUSES: The effect (buying a bat) of a narrow final cause (playing baseball) is extrinsic to its cause. The effect (running the bases) of a wide final cause (playing baseball) is intrinsic to its cause.

Analysis of final causes (widely conceived) yields *ends*—ends that consist of patterns of the movements that comprise them, ends that embrace those movements. Wide final causes are not simply efficient causes in reverse. An effect of an efficient cause follows its cause, but an effect of a final cause does not strictly precede its cause; it *fits into* its cause. In a sense, a particular movement must occur first in order for a pattern of movements to emerge, just as the movements of a symphony have to be played (the effects) before the symphony is played (the cause), or nine innings have to be played (the effects) before a baseball game is played (the cause). In that sense and in that sense only, a final cause follows its effects.

Remember, efficient causes are answers to the question: HOW does this or that movement occur? Analysis of efficient causes ultimately yields mechanisms that may range from simple billiard-ball-like interactions to complex computer circuits to complex neurochemical processes (Staddon, 1973). Correspondingly, final-cause analyses are attempts to answer the question: WHY does this or that movement occur? Of what more abstract process does this particular movement form a part? Answers to the *how* question, regardless of their completeness, do not automatically answer the *why* question. Knowing how a person crosses the street does not tell you why he crosses the street. To illustrate how final causes apply to mental terms, let us return to Aristotle, and consider his accounts of sensation, perception, and imagination.

Jeffrey Gray and the Behaviorist

The following question was posed to a behaviorist by the British psychologist Jeffrey Gray (2004, p. 123, and as quoted by Staddon, 2001, p. 177): "What is the difference between two awake individuals, one of them stone deaf, who are both sitting immobile in a room in which a record-player is playing a Mozart string quartet?" (It may now be revealed that the behaviorist was the author of this book.) Let us call the hearing person Adam, and the deaf person Eve. The trivial and obvious answer to Gray's question is that Adam is hearing the quartet and poor Eve is not. But the next and more important question is, "What does it mean for Adam to be able to hear and what does it mean for Eve to be stone deaf?" The crucial difference between Adam and Eve is that Adam may do different things when sounds are present than when they are absent, while Eve generally does not do different things in the presence and absence of sounds.

As illustrated in Figure 2.2, you could take most of Adam's actions and divide them into two classes, one class for sounds and one class for no sounds. You could further parse Adam's actions into sub-classes for different sorts of sounds. You could not do this for Eve. Figure 2.2 illustrates each action as a point in a

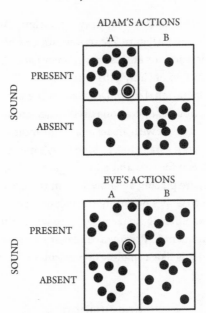

Figure 2.2 The crucial difference between a hearing person (Adam) and a deaf person (Eve) shown in terms of actions (black dots) discriminating between the presence and absence of sounds.

2 × 2 grid. For Adam (who by assumption can hear) there will be some actions (in the category labeled *A*) that are much more likely in the presence or expectation of sounds than in their absence. Examples of such actions would be buying tickets to a concert and engaging in an oral conversation. Similarly, there will be some actions (in the category labeled *B*) that are more likely in the absence of sounds than in their presence. An example might be Adam's saying, "Gee, it's awfully quiet here." Consistent with a wide concept of final cause, Adam's long-term pattern of discrimination of sounds from silences is the final cause of his sensation of sound at this particular time. And (still wider) Adam's long-term pattern of musical discrimination is the final cause of his perception of this particular quartet.

For Eve (by assumption, deaf) no matter how hard you tried, there would be no way to separate *A*-actions from *B*-actions. She would be equally likely to do any act in the presence or absence of actual sounds. Eve almost never says, "I hear a strange noise," and she is just as unlikely to say it in the absence as in the presence of strange noises. That is what it *means* to say that Adam can hear while Eve cannot. Although there are differences between Adam's and Eve's internal auditory mechanisms, neural differences, underlying the psychological differences between Adam and Eve, the *psychological* difference itself (hearing versus not hearing) rests in Adam's actual behavior over time (his discrimination) and Eve's actual behavior over time (her failure to discriminate), diagramed in Figure 2.2. At this very moment (in Gray's question), Adam and Eve happen to be doing the same thing. (Figure 2.2 represents this by the circled points in the two grids.) But their actions at this very moment are merely one corresponding step, as it were, in two entirely different dances. [This is a behavioral view of deafness, not an operational view. Deafness is the zero correlation between behavior and sounds, not the operations used to determine that correlation.]

Identifying a mental event with an act at a single moment in time is like identifying a spot of color with a painting. Asking Gray's question is like asking what the difference is between Picasso and a kindergarten child, both of whom, at a certain point in time, are placing a yellow spot in the upper left-hand corner of a painting. In answer to Gray's question, the behaviorist should have pointed to the differing patterns, differing final causes, into which this particular moment fits. Returning for a moment to Plato's cave allegory, a final cause is like an object, whereas a particular act is like a shadow (a particular projection) of an object.

Imagination

The teleological conception of imagination follows from the teleological conception of sensation. (Aristotle says, "Imagination must be a movement resulting from an actual exercise of a power of sense"; *De Anima*, Book III, chap. 3, 429a.) As far as the overt speech and action of a person are concerned, imagination is the same as sensation. If I am doing a good job of imagining that I smell a rose, I will behave, for a moment, just as I would behave if I actually smelled a rose. The difference is that an object being sensed is present in the world during sensation (the rose is there when you are sensing it), whereas during imagination the object is not present in the world (the rose is not there when you are imagining it). It is not necessary to infer that the rose I am imagining (that would be present in the world if I were sensing it) is present *inside* me (as a representation, an internal image, a neural discharge, or anything else) when I am imagining a rose. When I imagine a rose, my overt movements with the rose absent are the same as those I would make if there were a real rose present. In other words, all is the same in sensation and imagination except that when I imagine the rose it is not present.

If you generally behave one way in the presence of, and another way in the absence of, red lights, you are discriminating between red lights and other things. However, if, on occasion, you behave in the absence of a red light as you normally do in its presence, you are on that occasion imagining a red light. In Figure 2.2, the three occasions on which Adam behaves in the absence of a sound as he normally does when the sound is present are instances of imagination. Because imagination depends so strongly on sensation, Eve would not be imagining a sound in corresponding instances (the seven dots in the lower left quadrant of her grid).

Imagining is acting and not dreaming: Vividness of imagination is not vividness of interior image but of overt behavior. Suppose two people are asked to imagine a lion present in the room. One closes her eyes and says, "Yes, I see it, a mane and a tail, that's right, it's walking around," and so on. The other runs screaming for the door. The first person is not really imagining the lion but just striking a pose (as bad actors do) or imagining a picture of a lion. The second person is really imagining the lion. The location, intensity, orientation, or even the existence of an image in her head would be entirely irrelevant to the process. A good imagination is not just an aid or a tool in good acting. Rather, good acting *is* good imagining.

As the rest of this book will illustrate, teleological analyses of perception, thought, consciousness, self-control, social cooperation, and altruism follow a similar path: A particular act is identified as a particular perception or thought, as free or unfree, as good or bad, not on the basis of the particular *internal* acts (spiritual, cognitive, or neural) that may efficiently cause it, but rather on the basis of the temporally extended pattern of overt behavior into which the particular act fits, that is, on the basis of its wide final cause.

Imagination is a necessary part of perception. If perception (as distinct from sensation) is current discrimination among complex, temporally extended sequences of stimuli (as distinct from simpler, immediate stimuli), then the immediate discriminative response, especially if made early in the sequence, involves a sort of gamble—behaving as if the extended sequence had occurred. For example, at any given moment I treat my wife as the person she is in the long run, not as the particular bundle of sensations she presents to me at that moment. It is in connection with such premature but necessary discrimination (the universal arising out of particular instances) that Aristotle gives his famous analogy of soldiers turning and making a stand: "It is like a rout in battle stopped by first one man making a stand and then another, until the original formation has been restored" (*Posterior Analytics*, II, 19, 100a). The function of the soldiers' behavior is to create an abstraction (the renewed formation) out of individual actions. The first soldier to turn is behaving as he would if all the others had already turned; he is imagining that they had already turned. His imagination is what *he* does, not what his nervous system is doing. The function of our ordinary imagination is to allow us to get around in the world on the basis of partial information. We do not have to carefully test the floor of every room we walk into.

As regards introspective knowledge of one's own mental states, one Aristotelian interpreter stated, "Aristotle has no reason to think that psychic states—perceptions, beliefs, desires—must be transparently accessible to the subject, and to him alone. Even if there are such states, this feature of them is not the feature that makes them psychic states. Psychic states, for human souls as for others, are those that are causally relevant to a teleological explanation of the movements of a living organism" (Irwin, 1980, p. 43).

Acknowledgment

Chapter 2 contains material from Rachlin (1992) and Rachlin (1994). All Aristotle quotes are from McKeon, R. (1941). As with Plato quotes, citations refer to book and paragraph rather than page.

The Division of Mind and Body (Saint Augustine)

Saint Augustine's main philosophical problem was the reconciliation of Plato's intellectual elitism with the inclusiveness of Christianity. According to Augustine a person can, by an effort of will, turn his soul inward. By looking inward (introspecting), Augustine declared, a person of ordinary intelligence may live in an ideal (Platonic) world and know Truth (with a capital T). Thus, for Augustine, our minds are firmly ensconced inside us. Nevertheless, for him, the mind's inside view was a common view. When we look inside us, according to Augustine, we all see the very same Truth. Although Augustine believed that the mind existed within the body, it was not a prisoner there, but rather was in the place where its greatest happiness lay.

Now we jump ahead about 750 years from the golden age of Greece (~350 B.C.), through the ascendency of the Roman Empire, to the point in time (~400 A.D.) when the Goths and Vandals were overrunning the Italian peninsula and were beginning to threaten North Africa where Augustine lived. Augustine was not yet a saint, of course, but he was soon to become a bishop in the Christian church. In his youth he had abandoned his mother's Christian faith and had become a follower of the Neo-Platonist philosopher Plotinus. Neo-Platonism was an amalgam of Plato's philosophy and Eastern mysticism. When he became a Christian, Augustine abandoned Neo-Platonism in turn, but there are strong strains of Neo-Platonic thought in all of his subsequent works, especially his earlier Christian writings. I shall focus on one particular work, *On Free Will* (FW), written as a dialogue between Augustine and a follower, Evodius, which J. H. S. Burleigh (1953, p. 107) regards as "the high water mark of [Augustine's] earlier works, and the best and fullest exposition of what may be called the peculiarly Augustinian brand of Neoplatonism."

As a Christian, Augustine was concerned with how to behave—how to lead a good, or Godly, life. In this respect, he was very much like Plato. But there was one sticking point—and it was a big one. For Plato, a good life could be lived only with (a) high intelligence and (b) great effort. Living a good life was for Plato the equivalent of rocket science. How could the intellectual elitism of Platonism be reconciled with the inclusiveness of Christianity? This was Augustine's main philosophical problem. *On Free Will* makes the lines of Augustine's solution clear. Living a good life, which both Augustine and Plato identify with knowing the truth, was for Augustine purely a moral problem—not an intellectual problem at all. As I showed in the first chapter, Plato considered the ideal forms to be discriminable abstractions of real-world objects and events (like ecological niches); Augustine, however, considered the ideal forms to exist entirely in another place than the perceptible world (in the "City of God," as opposed to the "City of Man," as he called them in a later work). He believed that you could come to understand the truth, and live in the City of God, not by being smart and working hard, but by an act of faith—what he called "good will." To have good will, you did not have to be very intelligent, you did not even have to be literate. In *On Free Will*, Augustine set about to specify what exactly constitutes good will (a person's proper use of his free will).

Let us consider how Augustine might have interpreted Plato's allegory of the cave. Recall that for Plato (in my interpretation) the crucial aspect of the freed prisoner's journey was his release from the chains that bound him, that forbade him even to turn his head. The freed prisoner, by his newfound ability to interact with the three-dimensional world and with other people, gained a rounded perception of what had previously been flat—only shadows. The prisoner who escaped from Plato's cave learned to distinguish real chairs from shadows of chairs, by interacting with them in three dimensions. Analogously, according to Plato, we may learn to distinguish the ideal world from the sensible world by interacting with the temporally extended and abstract (multidimensional) properties of things (extension in time, social distance, probability, utility, etc.) in our world. The journey that we may take, analogous to the prisoner's journey, is an intellectual one. Plato emphasized over and over again that living in the ideal world takes intelligence and effort. A person living in the ideal world, for Plato, is not living in *another* world; he is living in *this* world but in a different way—in contact with the multidimensional envelopes (the ecological niches) of things and other people. The journey to enlightenment, for Plato, would be outward, into the world, gaining a wider perspective on that world—seeing it in all of its dimensions.

Augustine saw things differently. Figure 3.1 illustrates Augustine's view of how human behavior may be guided. By nature, like other animals, we tend to look at the world through our senses. If a soul looks leftward at the material world, as in Figure 3.1a, through the senses, it will see only chaotic objects (Plato's "shadows," symbolized in Figure 3.1a by chairs in various projections) whose true nature is obscured, according to Augustine, by bodily pleasures and pains. The soul, looking leftward in the diagram, as it naturally does, may attempt to use reason to analyze what it sees. But reason can see the world only through the filter of the untrustworthy senses. On the other hand, according

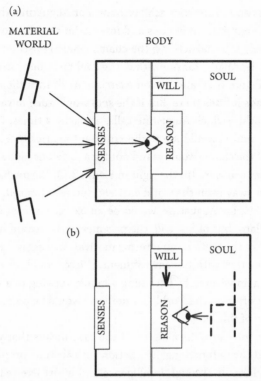

Figure 3.1 Augustine's conception of a person's interaction with (a) the material world, and (b) the spiritual world (the person's own soul). Reason is normally turned outward where it sees, through the senses, chaotic material objects, different from each perspective (Plato's shadows). However, if the will turns reason inward (heavy vertical arrow), it sees the ideal world (a higher reality).

to Augustine, by means of our will, we humans are free to turn our souls right-ward in the diagram and to look at the spiritual world inside ourselves—to introspect (as in Figure 3.1b). This spiritual view is filtered not by our senses but only by reason itself. If our soul looks rightward we will see things as they really and truly are, symbolized in Figure 3.1b (as in the figures of Chapter 1) by a dashed-lined chair. In other words, says Augustine, our God-given free will, unique to humans, may, if it is strong enough (the downward pointing arrow in Figure 3.1b), turn our reason toward reality and away from its natural proclivity to face the senses and bodily pleasures and pains.

For Augustine (if he had considered Plato's allegory), the freed prisoner's journey would be purely internal. For Augustine, the prisoners' chains would stand not for constraints on our bodies and actions but for constraints on our ability to turn our reason to the right. The compelling nature of our senses chains our soul, which Augustine saw as a spiritual entity within our bodies. Our soul can be released from its chains by means of our *will*, which turns our reason to the right. This is an *introspective* achievement. For Augustine, the chains would stand not for constraints on actions and interactions in the world but for constraints on purely internal actions; the chains would constrain not our bodies but our reason. Normally, for Augustine, the soul faces outward into the world (to the left in Figure 3.1), and reason exercises itself in futile efforts to make sense of the chaos it finds there. But if the soul would turn inward it would face the spiritual world—which Augustine calls, at various times, Truth, Wisdom, God, or Christ, and it would know the truth automatically. Plato's prisoner's breaking free of the chains would stand not for a different mode of acting in the world, but a *turning* inward (to the right in Figure 3.1). The unchained prisoner's soul would turn away from the world entirely, and into himself. The act of casting off our chains, for Augustine, would be an exercise not of our intelligence (as it was for Plato) but of our *will*; the prisoner would attain his freedom and gain knowledge of the truth by an internal motivational act rather than an overt pattern of interaction with the environment. [Plato would never have thought that you could gain wisdom by becoming a monk, retiring to a monastery, and closing yourself off from the world, but doing so would be perfectly in line with Augustine's way of thinking.]

In summary, for Plato, the allegory of the cave means that you could know truth (you could have a functional interaction with abstract properties of objects and other people) only through intelligence and effort exerted in an outward direction (which I call "outsight"). For Augustine (in my conceptualization of his interpretation of Plato's allegory), you could know truth (absolute and identified with God) only by an effort of will to turn your soul in an inward direction ("insight"). Once you did turn inward, your behavior would automatically be good. You would be living in what Augustine later called the "City of God," rather than in the "City of Man."

Since, for Augustine, *will* exercised freely was the means by which a person could come to know truth, it was very important to him to understand the purpose and nature of free will. According to Augustine, God's highest creation is a person who is good of his own free will—a person who voluntarily turns his soul toward the spiritual world. But people who are free to be good must also be free to be bad. The possibility of evil behavior is thus, for Augustine, a necessary consequence of human free will.

Let me try to summarize his position: Free will is a break in the normal chain of efficient causation. Human voluntary behavior does not have a chain of efficient causes traceable to God in the sense that a stone does. God is the ultimate cause of all motion in the universe *except* voluntary human behavior. Thus, the chain of causation of voluntary human behavior is traceable backward only as far as the free will of the behaving person: "It is not in the power of a stone to arrest its downward motion, while if the soul is not willing it cannot be moved to abandon what is higher and to love what is lower" (FW, III, i, 2). On the other hand, all voluntary human behavior does have what Aristotle had called a *final cause*. Human final causes are divisible into two main categories: virtue and sin. Virtuous final causes are identified by Augustine with God; sinful final causes are identified with the pleasures and pains of worldly objects. The critical question then becomes: How, in practice, does a person aim his soul "upward" (to the right in Figure 3.1) so as to achieve goodness and avoid sin?

Like Plato, Augustine identifies wisdom with the highest virtue (he uses Wisdom as another name for Christ). For Augustine, however, as opposed to Plato, wisdom and virtue are separable from the world, not only in the sense that abstract behavioral patterns are separable from particular acts, but also in essence. Both Plato and Augustine use visual analogies to make the distinction clear. In Plato's allegory of the cave, the freed prisoner comes to see the world as it really is; he sees the world differently from the way the chained prisoners see it; moreover, it is something outside himself that he sees. For Plato, wisdom is analogous to a better view of something, but not a view of a different thing. Plato's freed prisoner could not gain knowledge by closing his eyes; on the contrary, his eyes take in more than those of the prisoners. But Augustine separates wisdom and virtue entirely from the world. He identifies them, in substance, with God and locates them inside the person. For Augustine, the wise person does not just see better or see more dimensions of something than does the foolish person; the wise person sees something else entirely; the wise person looks for truth in a different direction, away from the world, and into herself. For Augustine, the analogy to upward movement is interior vision. Reason, uncluttered by sensual input, may look inward on itself as in a mirror. To put it another way, for Plato, the wise man perceives (behaves in accordance with) the abstract nature of the world. For Augustine, the wise man perceives (behaves in accordance with) his own reason: "Does reason comprehend reason by any other means than by reason itself? Would you know that you possess reason otherwise than by reason?... Surely not" (FW, II, 9).

In Augustine's view, God stands for all abstract truths—all known rules—ranging from mathematical rules ("the science of numbers") to social rules. The rule that $7 + 3 = 10$ and the rule that "each man should be given his due" are, according to him, not true because they are useful; they are not empirical rules at all; *they are absolutely and eternally true* and are identified as "wisdom" (FW, II, ×, 28). According to Augustine, such abstract truths are observable in only one way: by internal observation (introspection). Augustine considers whether mathematical truth might be empirical and rejects it:

> *Augustine: Suppose someone said that numbers make their impression on our minds not in their own right but rather as images of visible things, springing from our contacts by bodily sense with corporeal objects, what would you reply? Would you agree?*

Evodius: I could never agree to that. Even if I did perceive numbers with the bodily senses I could not in the same way perceive their divisions and relations. By referring to these *mental operations* [emphasis added] I show anyone to be wrong in his counting who gives a wrong answer when he adds or subtracts. Moreover, all that I contact with a bodily sense, such as this sky and this earth and whatever I perceive to be in them, I do not know how long it will last. But seven and three make ten not only now but always. . . . So I maintain that the unchanging science of numbers is common to me and to every reasoning being.

Augustine: I do not deny that your reply is certainly most true. (FW, II, viii, 21, 22)

Because the concept of introspective knowledge is so familiar to us, it is important to emphasize how Augustine's conception of introspection differs from ours. Despite everything said above, despite how the soul is depicted in Figure 3.1, totally contained within the body, the soul is *not*, in Augustine's conception, actually a prisoner within the body. In the modern conception, introspection gives us *private* knowledge, available to ourselves alone. For Augustine, however (in this early essay on free will), what we see when we turn our vision inward is not private and subjective at all, but *public* and *objective*—more truly objective (because unchangeable and the same from all perspectives) than what we see when we look outward.

As Figure 3.1 illustrates, Augustine conceived of two sorts of vision—external and internal. A person's reason, a spiritual entity within his body, is normally oriented leftward, as in Figure 3.1a. Particular objects affect the sense organs, which act as a window to the external, material world. Reason then attempts to organize that information and use it to guide behavior (not shown in the diagram). This system, according to Augustine, is highly unreliable. First, our reason is separated from the world by the intermediation and limitations of our senses. Second, pleasure and pain confuse our reason. Third, and most important, objects may appear differently to different people. John may be looking at the front of the chair while Martha is looking at the back. Like the blind men with respect to the elephant, they may see different aspects of the same objects. It is as if they were Plato's prisoners, watching different shadows of the same things. These differences in perspective, Augustine believed, isolate people from each other and make social cooperation difficult.

But Augustine believed that human beings need not be limited by any deficiencies of their sensations. By an act of their free will (the heavy vertical arrow in Figure 3.1b) they may orient their reason inward and away from the outer world. (Think of the soul as normally facing left and receiving messages from the outer world via the senses, but capable, by means of free will, of turning around and facing rightward.) This turning by force of will brings reason into contact with the spiritual world—with God. [To use modern psychological terms, for Plato, the effort required to know the truth was a *cognitive* effort; for Augustine, the effort required to know the truth was a *motivational* effort.] For Augustine, once a person makes this effort of will she will be able to perceive the truth without any intellectual effort at all. This turning inward is Augustine's version of reflection or introspection. According to Augustine, such inward vision has none of the disadvantages of outward vision and can be used to guide behavior in the world much better than outward vision possibly could. Moreover, for Augustine, when one person looks inward, he sees precisely the same reality that another person sees by turning inward. It is not as if a carbon copy of the truth is implanted in each person's soul individually. Rather, there is just one truth, the original truth; when we look inward, that very same original truth is what each of us sees. *Inward vision, or introspection, is for Augustine not private at all.* How can that be? How is it possible to look inward and yet see something that is public?

When I took plane geometry in high school many years ago, it was recommended that we read a slim volume called *Flatland* by the pseudonymous "A. Square" (1886). *Flatland* is about a world that exists wholly in two dimensions. The characters are triangles, squares, pentagons, circles, and so on, of different sizes and with a rigid class system—the more sides, as I remember, the higher the class. The characters can move, but only within the plane. Since all of the characters live on the same flat plane, they cannot directly see their own shapes or those of anyone else. All they can see in their two-dimensional world are lines. So when two of them meet, they take turns rotating around their central axis. From a single viewpoint within the plane, the line formed by the edge of a polygon will change in length, becoming wider and narrower, as it rotates— the more sides, the less change. At the extreme, the length of the highest-class circle does not change at all as it rotates around its center. By this process, time within the two spatial dimensions is essentially substituted for our third spatial dimension. That is, an aspect of the two-dimensional world that cannot be known directly by the flatlanders (the shape of a flat object seen edge-on) can be inferred from temporally extended patterns over time. [I ask the reader to keep this in mind. Why? Because the true analogy in our world to the freeing of Plato's prisoner is the patterning of our overt behavior over time. These patterns (corresponding to the flatlanders' rotations) add an extra dimension—a mental dimension—to *our* world.] The characters in *Flatland* live their lives within the two-dimensional world and believe that no other world exists. Toward the end of the book, in what has to be a reference to Plato's allegory of the cave, one character is lifted out of a prison (a large square surrounding the two-dimensional prisoners) into the third dimension, is allowed to see the others, as they are, from above, and then is placed back down in the plane (but out of prison). Of course, as in Plato's allegory, when he goes back to the plane and tries to describe the third dimension, and tells them how he escaped, they cannot understand him. It seems like magic.

As A. Square points out, it is possible for two separate and distinct individuals in two dimensions to be connected in the third dimension. Figure 3.2 shows such an arrangement. Imagine a donut cut into two U-shaped halves and one of the halves placed on end against a piece of paper. The donut is oily, so the two circles against the paper show through to the other side. The front view to the left shows the two circular stains on the paper with the donut invisible behind it. The circles seem unconnected. But the side view to the right shows that they are connected (by the half-donut) in the third dimension. If the donut were flexible, the circles would be able to move around and still be connected. If we drew a square around each of the circles in Figure 3.2 (as the body surrounds the soul in Figure 3.1), the circles would still be connected. For Augustine, introspection, looking inward, was like looking into an extra dimension. For him, everyone is connected with each other in this extra-dimensional world and everyone, if they look inward, will see the same God, the same truth, just as, if they look outward, they will see the same chair. However, when we look outward we see the chair differently from different perspectives, whereas if and when we look inward, with our reason, we see a single truth that is the same from all perspectives. Augustine says, just as ". . . there is one object for both of us, and both of us see it simultaneously" (FW, II, vii, 16), so also "these rules and guiding lights of the virtues. . . are true and unchangeable, and singly or all together they stand open for *the common contemplation of those who have the capacity to behold them,* each with his own mind and reason" (FW, II, x, 29, italics added). The difference, again, is not that one orientation is to public and the other to private objects (both directions lead to public objects), but that one orientation is to temporal and the other to eternal objects.

Plato describes a virtuous life as reason in control of ambition and appetite. For good self-control, reason, like a charioteer, has to see further than his horses. Still, the horses are necessary to pull the chariot. Exercise of the higher

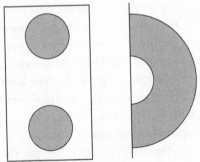

Figure 3.2 Two unconnected circles on a plane (front view, to the left) are connected in the third dimension (side view, to the right).

soul, for Plato, is thus an abstraction of the lower soul's acts in the world. But for Augustine, regardless of how intensely you focus on the world, regardless of how well your reason controls your appetites, you will not reach your highest individual (hence the social) good.

Plato admits that people may be intelligent and yet bad, because they may use their intelligence to gratify rather than to control their appetites. For Augustine, degree of intelligence does not matter whatsoever with regard to goodness or badness. Instead, what is required is the *will* to turn one's gaze inward instead of outward. Once you do that, Augustine says, God will appear to you as vividly and as automatically as a mountain does when you look at it. Reason is necessary in this process, as eyes are necessary to see. But even people with weak eyes can see a mountain, and even people of weak intelligence can be good, according to Augustine, in the highest sense. For those who turn the other way (to the left in Figure 3.1), Augustine would agree with Plato that "the penalty they pay is the life they lead," a life, in Augustine's terms, "which is better called death" (FW, I, iv, 10).

Augustine certainly had a political motive for deemphasizing the role of intelligence in ethics. He had not yet become a bishop when he wrote *On Free Will*, but he was nevertheless a devout Christian who wished to convert others to the faith. A religion, with many competitors during Augustine's time, could not be successful if it rejected potential adherents on the grounds of intelligence (as Plato's philosophy certainly did). But even if he was politically motivated, it is important to note that Augustine was offering more than happiness after death to Christians. Like Plato, he was attempting to discover a mode of happiness during their lifetimes on earth. Near the beginning of *On Free Will* he states his criterion: "To desire to live without fear is characteristic of all men, not only of the good but also of the bad. But there is this difference. The good seek it by diverting their love from things which cannot be had without the risk of losing them. The bad are anxious to enjoy these things with security and try to remove hindrances so as to live a wicked and criminal life which is better called death" (FW, I, iv, 10). Although intelligence itself cannot be taken away, Augustine says, people who use their intelligence to increase their pleasure (bad people or people with bad will) will be unhappy because what they use intelligence for *can* be taken away. Augustine threatens the bad person, not with hellfire only, but also with unhappiness on earth. Correspondingly, the good person will be happy because that person has something that cannot be taken away—not just in practice but in principle. Augustine is eloquent on this issue:

> The beauty of truth and wisdom [identified by Augustine with God], so long as there is a persevering will to enjoy it. . . does not pass with time or change with locality. It is not interrupted by night or shut off by shadow, and is not subject to the bodily senses. To all who turn to it from the whole world, and love it, it is close at hand, everlasting, bound

to no particular spot, never deficient. Externally it suggests, internally it teaches. All who behold it, it changes for the better, and by none is it changed for the worse. No one judges it, and no one without it judges aright. Hence it is evident beyond a doubt that wisdom is better than our minds [therefore identifiable with God], for by it alone they are made individually wise, and are made judges, not of it, but by it of all other things whatever. (FW, II, xii, 38)

[The notion that all earthly desires are bad because they can be lost and the identification of happiness as the attainment of something good that cannot be taken away is a characteristic of Augustine's philosophy that it (and Christian belief generally) shares with Stoicism, albeit the two philosophies are based on vastly different metaphysics.]

For Augustine, the reward for turning inward to wisdom "from the whole world" is happiness:

What do you ask for more than to be happy? And what is more happy than to enjoy unshakable, unchangeable truth which is excellent above all things?. . . Men exclaim that they are happy when with throats parched with heat they find a fountain flowing with pure water, or being hungry, find a copious meal already prepared, and shall we deny that we are happy when truth is our meat and drink? (FW, II, xiii, 35)

Thus, true happiness, the highest individual goodness, and the social good are drawn away by Augustine from the intelligent few and placed in the hands of any human being with good will.

Faith, for Augustine, is a generalization and expansion of rule-governed behavior. Augustine would agree with Plato that happiness cannot be achieved in a brief time. Thus, *while* it is being achieved, one has to have faith that the long behavioral path to it is the correct one. Belief in this sense precedes knowledge. Augustine says, "...we must first believe before we seek to know" (FW, II, ii, 5) and quotes the Bible in support: "Except ye believe ye shall not understand' (Isa. 7:9, LXX)."

As rules become more abstract, it takes more and more experience to confirm belief in the world. "Honor your father and mother," for instance, is a more general rule that takes longer to obey and that requires correspondingly more faith than does "study tonight." The most general rule, "obey God," requires the most faith. But just as a child can eventually know that "obey your parents" is a good and true rule so, a person can, according to Augustine, eventually know by experience (without having to die first) that "obey God" is a good and true rule.

The advantages of Christianity and of religion in general for everyday life, especially in hard times, need hardly be enumerated. John and Marcia, let us say, are illiterate North African farmers. Their lives are chaotic. In the outside world the barbarians are breaking up the Roman Empire. Looking outward, they find insecurity. Marcia's mother, who nominally owns their farm, is a tyrant. They cannot agree on whether to plant wheat or barley—whether or not to hire another servant. There has been a drought, and the whole farm may have to be sold. But when they look inward, with the help of the church, they see only harmony and peace—they see Christ, who died for their sins, and they see respect (for each other, for their parents, and for their in-laws), cooperation, and community—the benefits and consolations of Plato's philosophy without the intellectual effort that Plato demanded—the benefits of altruism and self-control (to be discussed in Chapters 7 and 8). How could they not look inward?

Acknowledgment

Chapter 3 contains material from Rachlin (1992) and Rachlin (1994). Unless otherwise indicated, the quotations from Augustine are from *Augustine: Earlier Writings*, edited and translated by J. H. S. Burleigh (Philadelphia: Westminster, 1953). As in the first two chapters, quotes are cited by section rather than page number.

4

The Imprisonment of the
Mind (Descartes)

Unlike Augustine's concept of an interior but public mind, Descartes' concept of mind was both interior and private. Descartes' distinction—involuntary behavior controlled by a stimulus from the environment; voluntary behavior controlled by an internal mind out of direct contact with the world, but observable by introspection—is with us to this day.

For Descartes, as for Plato, the concept of a triangle exists more certainly than does any particular triangle in the world. For both philosophers, the concept is eternal. The difference is that, for Plato, the concept consists of some abstract quality of the world, and knowing the concept consists of a functional interaction between a person and that aspect of the world; for Descartes, the concept exists inside the person, and knowing the concept is a private occurrence between the soul and the concept within the soul.

And now let us take a still bigger jump in time—some 1,200 years—to the beginning of the seventeenth century. The Roman Empire is gone. The Middle Ages have come and gone. We are in the late Renaissance in France. Renaissance science explained many aspects of the world in purely physical terms. Even within the human body, many functions were physically explicable. William Harvey's (1578–1657) discovery of the circulation of the blood and the function of the heart as a mechanical pump was only the most successful example of a widespread movement toward mechanism among Renaissance physicians and anatomists. Descartes (1596–1650), himself a major contributor to this line of thought, faced the task of reconciling this movement with a religious conception of the human soul.

Descartes began by expanding the concept of involuntary behavior to include the behavior of all non-human animals and some of the behavior of humans. Involuntary behavior consisted of automatic, relatively simple motions: sneezing, pulling one's foot from a fire, focusing one's eyes, and so forth. Such behavior was explained by Descartes in terms of causal chains (later called "reflexes") originating in the environment (and ultimately in God as the creator of the

Figure 4.1 Descartes' illustration of reflex action. [From Fearing, 1930.]

world). Descartes' reflexive behavior worked as Figure 4.1 shows: a stimulus, such as a hot flame (A) on a boy's foot (B) tugged at a thin string within a nerve (C); the string opened a valve (d) in a chamber (F) in the center of the brain and allowed animal spirits (a vitalistic gas distilled in the boy's heart and fed into his brain) to flow down the tube and inflate the muscle; the inflation contracted the muscle and moved the boy's foot out of the fire. Actions such as these, according to Descartes, could be studied in the same way that Galileo had studied the behavior of physical objects: by observation and experiment. This was a major concession to Renaissance science; it put all of physiology and biology, as well as physics, outside the authority of the church. The natural philosophers who studied the world (including physics, biology, and physiology) were, by this concession, acknowledged not only to understand the world better than religious authorities could, they were also acknowledged to be gaining a better understanding of human behavior. It is not surprising that Descartes withheld publication of these speculations during his lifetime.

The big exception to this Cartesian concession to empirical science was psychology. Most human behavior—voluntary movement such as speech, social behavior, and learned behavior—was exempted by Descartes from experimental study. Voluntary behavior was said to follow the same neural and muscular paths in a human being as reflexive behavior. However, in the case of voluntary behavior, the opening and closing of valves in the chamber at the center of the brain were caused by minute movements of the pineal gland, which in turn were controlled directly by the boy's will. Thus, the ultimate cause of voluntary human

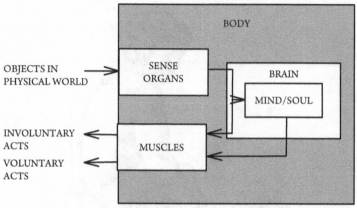

Figure 4.2 Descartes' model of involuntary and voluntary behavior. Voluntary behavior is caused directly by the mind acting through the nerves and muscles. Involuntary behavior is caused by objects and events in the physical world acting through the sense organs, sensory nerves, nerves, and muscles. For Descartes, the mind was actually a dimensionless point in physical space, and the sensory and motor nerves were actually one nerve.

behavior was placed by Descartes *inside* the behaving person, directly knowable by that person but not observable by anyone else. Unlike Augustine's concept of an interior but public mind, Descartes' concept of mind was both interior and private. According to Descartes, only you can know what you are thinking. The human mind, for Descartes, was a prisoner in the body, in the center of the brain, out of contact with the world except through the flow of animal spirits. Figure 4.2 diagrams Descartes' model of voluntary and involuntary behavior. [For clarity, the mind is diagrammed as an area, but for Descartes, the mind actually interacted with the body at a dimensionless point in physical space, and the sensory and motor nerves were actually one nerve; the sensory nerve was a thin string running up the middle of a tube through which animal spirits could flow down and into the muscles.]

Descartes' distinction—involuntary behavior controlled by a stimulus from the environment; voluntary behavior controlled by an internal mind out of direct contact with the world, but observable from within by introspection—is with us to this day. It is therefore Descartes really (and not Plato) who should be said to have invented the mind—at least the modern version of it.

Descartes' Nativism

Note, in Figure 4.2, that the mind, in Descartes' view, is wholly enveloped by the body. It is entirely out of contact with the world. The mind's only contact with the world is through the nerves, which Descartes conceived as the pulling of strings, the opening of valves, and the motion of animal spirits. But we do not see string-pullings, valve-openings, or the motions of animal spirits. We see chairs, tables, roses, lions, people. How do these ideas get into the mind? The answer, according to Descartes, is that God puts them there. We are born with all of the ideas that we will ever have. Stimulation of our sense organs (the pulling of strings) does not give us ideas, according to Descartes, it merely wakes up ideas that we already have:

> Nothing reaches our mind from external objects through the sense organs except certain corporeal motions [the movements of animal spirits] . . . . But neither the motions themselves nor the figures arising from them are conceived by us exactly as they occur in the sense organs . . . . Hence it follows that the very ideas of the motions themselves and of the figures are innate in us. The ideas of pain, colors, sounds and the like must be all the more innate if, on the occasion of certain corporeal motions, our mind is to be capable of representing them to itself, for there is no similarity between these ideas and the corporeal motions. (*Descartes: Reply to Objections II*, from Beakley & Ludlow, 1992, p. 365)

Figure 4.3 illustrates this conception.

Descartes' Method

The method of using one's own doubt to derive certainty was adopted by Descartes from Augustine. The following passage is from Augustine's *On the Trinity* (*De Trinitate*, x, chap. 10, 13–16; quoted by Kantor, 1963, vol. 1, p. 187):

> Who ever doubts that he himself lives, and remembers, and understands, and wills, and thinks, and knows, and judges? Seeing that even if he doubts, he lives; if he doubts he remembers why he doubts; if he

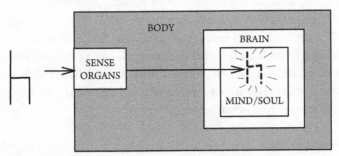

Figure 4.3 According to Descartes, objects in the physical world, acting through the sense organs, wake up ideas that are already in our minds.

doubts he understands that he doubts; if he doubts he wishes to be
certain; if he doubts he thinks; if he doubts he knows that he does
not know; if he doubts he judges that he ought not to assent rashly.
Whosoever therefore doubts about anything else, ought not to doubt
about all these things; which if they were not, he would not be able to
doubt of anything.

Here is a passage from Descartes' *Meditations* (1641/1971, edited and translated
by E. Anscombe & P. T. Geach [A & G]):

Am I not the very person who is now "doubting" almost everything;
who "understands" something and "asserts" this one thing to be true,
and "denies" other things; who "is willing" to know more, and "is unwilling" to be deceived; who "imagines" many things, even involuntarily,
and perceives many things coming as it were from the "senses"? Even
if I am all the while asleep; even if my creator does all he can to deceive
me; how can any of these things be less of a fact than my existence? Is
any of these something distinct from my consciousness? Can any of
them be called a separate thing from myself? It is so clear that it is
I who doubt, understand, will, that I cannot think how to explain it
more clearly. (Second Meditation, p. 70)

The difference between Augustine and Descartes is that, when Augustine
looked inward and removed from his consciousness everything that could be
doubted, he discovered moral and social as well as mathematical rules, and he
identified those rules with the deity. Descartes discovered no moral or social
rules. Such rules, like perceptual constancies, are subject to error (contain "nothingness"). Descartes' first step was to identify truth with whatever was clear
and distinct in his own mind: "Since our ideas or notions have positive reality
and proceed from God, insofar as they are clear and distinct, they must to this
extent be true" (*Discourse*, part 4, A & G, p. 36). When all that could be doubted
was discarded, what clearly and distinctly remained? "Nothing is more easily
or manifestly perceptible to me than my own mind" (Second Meditation, A &
G, p. 75). "I am a conscious being; that is, a being that doubts, asserts, denies,
understands a few things, is ignorant of many, is willing or unwilling; and that
has also imagination and sense" (Third Meditation, A & G, p. 76). The first class
of clear and distinct mental contents is doubt and will; the second is imagination
and sensation; the third is mathematical truth:

I remember that even previously [to his effort to reject anything
that could be doubted] at a time when I was utterly immersed in the
objects of sensation, I regarded this kind of truth as the most certain of

all—namely, those that I recognized as evident in regard to figures, and numbers, and other matters of arithmetic, or of geometry, or in general of pure abstract mathematics. (Fifth Meditation, A & G, pp. 102–103)

Descartes then attempts to prove the existence of God by virtue of the similarity of the concept of God to the concept of a mathematical truth:

Now if it follows, from my mere ability to elicit the idea of some object from my consciousness, that all the properties that I clearly and distinctly perceive the object to have do really belong to it; could not this give rise to an argument by which the existence of God might be proved? I assuredly find in myself the idea of God—of a supremely perfect being—no less than the idea of a figure or a number; and I clearly and distinctly understand that everlasting existence belongs to his nature, no less than I can see that what I prove of some figure, or number, belongs to the nature of that figure or number. So, even if my meditations on previous days were not entirely true, yet I ought to hold the existence of God with at least the same degree of certainty as I have so far held mathematical truths. (Fifth Meditation, A & G, p. 103)

Unlike Augustine's internal God, Descartes' internal God is silent on morality—on how he ought to behave. This difference between the two philosophers is the problem with the introspective method. Both Augustine and Descartes claim to have eliminated from their consciousness all except what cannot be doubted or what strictly follows from what cannot be doubted. Both philosophers claim that what remains requires only the will to see. Both claim that this undoubtable truth really exists as a perceptible object in the mind of every person; yet, when the method is applied, each discovers something different. Even the mathematical rules that they both claim to find in consciousness are not the same. For Augustine, unshakable truths were simple arithmetic rules; for Descartes, unshakable mathematical truths were the common logical elements that he himself had previously discovered to underlie algebra and geometry.

Reality and Illusion

In his *Discourse on Method*, Descartes says: "I could take it as a general rule that whatever we conceive very clearly and very distinctly is true," (part 4, A & G, p. 32) and "I went through some of the simpler [geometrical] proofs, and observed that their high degree of certainty is founded merely on our conceiving them distinctly" (part 4, A & G, p. 34).

For Descartes, as for Plato, the concept of a triangle exists more certainly than does any particular triangle in the world. For both philosophers, the concept is eternal, whereas particular triangles come and go. The difference between the two is that, for Plato, the concept consists of some abstract quality *of the world*; knowing the concept consists of an interaction (a functional one) between a person and that aspect of the world. For Descartes, the concept exists *inside the person*; knowing the concept is a private occurrence between the soul and the concept within the soul. The existence of triangles in the world outside his own soul is, for Descartes, an inference from the facts (1) that we perceive triangles in nature and (2) that God would not deceive us: "It may be that not all bodies are such as my senses apprehend them, for this sensory apprehension is in many ways obscure and confused; but at any rate their nature must comprise whatever I clearly and distinctly understand—that is, whatever, generally considered, falls within the subject matter of pure mathematics" (Sixth Meditation, A & G, p. 116). Thus nothing can be said to exist with certainty in the world unless it is clearly and distinctly understood.

Although sensations (such as the color red) were themselves clear to Descartes, he completely distrusted any inferences based upon them. Sensation was, for him, just a form of imagination that we are compelled to experience. We are more aware of reality when awake than asleep not because our *senses* are functioning when we are awake but because our *reason* is then functioning: "For if it happened even in sleep that one had some specifically distinct idea; if, for instance a geometer devised some new proof; then sleep would be no bar to its being true.... Waking or sleeping, we should never let ourselves be convinced except by the evidence of our reason" (*Discourse*, part 4; A & G, pp. 36–37).

The One and the Many

A fundamental problem faced by Descartes in common with other philosophers is the relationship between the abstract and the particular in human knowledge. Consider a work of art that may be appreciated at more than one level, say, Beethoven's Ninth Symphony. You could like a particular melody or a theme in the symphony, you could like a whole movement, or you could like the symphony as a whole for its structure. It takes less time to appreciate a melody than a movement, and a movement than the whole symphony. We can talk of "concentration" or "focusing attention" on the particular elements. We can say that it is "tempting" to focus our attention on particular elements because it is easy to do or because the pleasure of it is immediate. What can we say if, on the other hand, we want someone to pay attention to the temporally extended structure of the work as a whole?

Descartes' answer to this question, an answer taken up by philosophers and psychologists to this day, was to imagine the abstract structure of the symphony, not spread out in time in the world, as it is, but spread out in our minds. (In modern versions it is spread out in space in our brains.) Now, instead of asking a person to attend to the symphony in the world, you could ask her to concentrate on the symphony in her head. The particular notes of the symphony thus seem to exist outside us, whereas the abstract structure of the symphony seems to exist inside us (in our memory) to be appreciated in a different area of concentration. Attention to particular or abstract aspects of the symphony would then be conceivable as shifted (voluntarily) between the external particular point and the internal abstract point, as a searchlight is shifted from one point to another. This Augustinian and Cartesian conception of the relationship between knowledge of the particular and the abstract alters the Platonic conception. For Plato, the difference between attention to particular objects and attention to abstract concepts was a difference in the *kind* of attention; for Augustine and Descartes, it was a difference in the *place* of attention (the same kind of attention—attention to particulars—but directed inward rather than outward).

Acknowledgment

Chapter 4 contains material from Rachlin (1992) and Rachlin (1994). All Descartes quotations are from *Descartes' Philosophical Writings*, edited and translated by E. Anscombe and P. T. Geach (Indianapolis, IN: Bobbs-Merrill, 1971). Because the various works have no paragraph numbering, citations are to page number in this text (abbreviated A & G).

5

The Law of Specific Nerve
Energies (Müller)

Johannes Müller's law of specific nerve energies (LOSNE) extended Descartes' conception of the mind as a prisoner within the body to nineteenth-century physiology. LOSNE states that the mind communicates not with objects in the outside world but only with our nerves. LOSNE says that our sensations, perceptions, thoughts, and so on, have no qualities in common with things in the world, but serve only as arbitrary signs or markers or representations of those objects. This chapter traces the implications of LOSNE for non-physical theories of mind and for two modern physical theories of the mind—neural identity theory (the theory that mental events are identical with their neurological representations) and a behavioral identity theory (teleological behaviorism). With non-physical theories and neural identity theory alike, it is conceivable for a person to repeatedly, over long periods of time, exhibit one mental state (such as pleasure) while internally experiencing another (such as pain). This contradiction, allowed in principle by neural identity theory, is avoided by teleological behaviorism.

According to the historian of psychology E. G. Boring (1957, p. 34), Johannes Müller (1801–1858) was "...the foremost authority on physiology of his day, and his *Handbuch*, translated immediately into English, [was] the primary systematic treatise." In that book Müller formulated what later came to be known as the law of specific nerve energies (LOSNE). It is not really a law, nor was it original with Müller. Something like it had previously been stated by the Scottish physiologist Sir Charles Bell; it is at least implicit in the writings of earlier physiologists and philosophers, including Descartes. "The central and fundamental principle of the doctrine," according to Boring (1957, p. 82), "is that we are directly aware, not of objects, but of our nerves themselves; that is to say, the nerves are intermediaries between perceived objects and the mind and thus impose their own characteristics on the mind."

This raises the question: How do the nerves impose anything *but* their own characteristics on the mind? That is, how do the nerves tell us anything about the world? As we have seen, Descartes had claimed that they don't; we already know all there is to know about the world; all the ideas we are ever going to have are innate; they are already latent in our minds. Stimulation from the outside, Descartes believed, merely woke up those innate ideas.

Descartes' anticipation of LOSNE was the notion that no quality of a stimulus gets past the sense organs. Nervous stimulation, for him, was like the pulling of a string within a nerve. Each string-pull opened its own valve and created a particular motion of the animal spirits ("corporeal motion"). Why is it, then, when one string is pulled we see a red light and when another string is pulled we see a green light? The answer, according to Descartes, is that God supplies our souls with the ideas of red and green at birth and allows each idea to be awakened only by its own particular string-pull (see Chapter 4). It was left for Müller to point out that even though one nerve was hooked up to the red receptors in the retina, and the red receptors normally respond only to red light, anything that caused that particular nerve to fire (a blow to the head, for example) would cause its corresponding sensation.

Müller rejected Descartes' extreme nativism. For him, it was sufficient to say that the *quality* of the sensation caused by stimulation of the red-light nerve itself (or, as he later speculated, the place in the brain where the red-light nerve ended) differed from the *quality* of the sensation caused by stimulation of the green-light nerve (or the place in the brain where it ended). [Müller's later speculation, that conscious experience is determined by stimulation in a place in the brain, conforms better to modern neuroscience; I will henceforth characterize LOSNE that way.]

For Müller, these sensations, occurring in the mind, and differing for red and green, are what enable us to discriminate between red and green objects in the world. Figure 5.1 diagrams this conception. For Müller, sensations in the mind (R and G in Figure 5.1) are not themselves red or green. The words "red" and

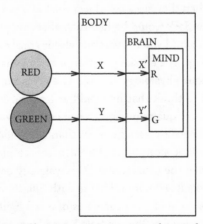

Figure 5.1 Müller's view of how sensations occur in the mind. Stimuli excite the nerves (X, Y), which in turn cause motions in the brain (X', Y'). These motions then cause mental states (R, G) that have no qualities in common with the original stimuli.

"green" are merely labels we learn to attach to these different sensations. This is entirely consistent with modern thought. Our sense organs and nervous systems are currently said to transform and "encode" the stimuli; our mental states are products of the transformations and encodings.

As Boring says, the crucial point of Müller's law is that our conscious experience of the stimuli is directly due to the place in the brain where the nerves end and not at all to the stimuli themselves. As evidence for his law, Müller cited instances where stimuli other than those acting through their appropriate sense organs nevertheless cause the nerves to fire. A blow to the head, for example, might stimulate your visual nerves, in which case you would "see stars," or your auditory nerves, in which case you would "hear chimes." There are no sounds or lights within our bodies—only nervous energy. According to Müller, our minds have access only to this nervous energy. From this energy, plus whatever innate tendencies our minds possess (according to Müller, the Kantian categories: space, time, moral sense, and so forth), they must construct the world. How our minds manage this construction became the business of all of psychology for the next hundred years and of non-behavioristic psychology, even up to today.

Consider the following thought experiment. Jill is normal; when she sees a red light she feels the way we all do when we see a red light; when she sees a green light she feels the way we all do when we see a green light. But Jack is not normal; he was born with the connections between his retinas and his brain center switched; nerve-X goes from his red sensors (assuming the nervous system is that simple) to the place in his brain (Y') where nerve-Y would normally go; nerve-Y goes from his green sensors to the place in the brain (X') where nerve-X would normally go. According to LOSNE, when Jill sees a green object she feels the way everyone else does when they see a green object (as philosophers say, she has a green "quale"), but when Jack sees a green object he feels the way everyone else does when they see a red object (he has a red "quale"). The mental state of seeing red for Jack would be like that of seeing green for Jill and vice versa. Jack exists in a world where everyone else is constructed like Jill; Jack is the only one crossed up. The crucial question is this: Would Jack be hampered in any way by his unique physiology, or would he get along perfectly well in the world? We may tend to think that he would at least be confused and have to learn to transform his red quales into green behavior and vice-versa. But LOSNE implies that he would need to learn no more than Jill would.

Figure 5.2 shows Jack along with Jill both contemplating red and green objects. Certainly, given the ultra-simplified physiology depicted in Figure 5.2, Jack would have no trouble communicating with Jill. Remember that, according to LOSNE, X' has none of the properties of a red light and Y' has none of the properties of a green light. The symbols X' and Y' merely stand for different places in the brain. Unless God intervenes at some point, there can be nothing intrinsically reddish about R or greenish about G. This was what Descartes

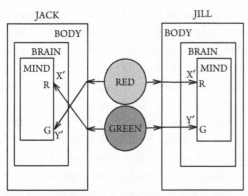

Figure 5.2 Given that the contents of the mind have no qualities in common with environmental stimuli, two people (Jack and Jill) with entirely opposite neural connections and opposite mental markers (R and G) could have corresponding behaviors, hence identical mental states.

understood (therefore, he concluded, God *must* intervene). If we assume that Descartes was wrong about divine intervention in human consciousness, conscious states R and G can differ only in the sense that the letters X and Y differ—as symbols that may mean anything you want them to mean. For Jill and the rest of us, R means red and G means green; for Jack alone, R means green and G means red. It would be no more difficult for Jack to learn to call R "green" than it would be for Jill to learn to call G "green."

Who is to say that each of us does not differ in the actual quality of our Rs and Gs? What matters, according to LOSNE, is that R and G are different from each other and correlate, by virtue of the selectivity of our retinas, with the presence of red and green objects. Whatever associations Jill normally makes between R and other conscious states will be made by Jack between G and other conscious states. Sensation R would be that of a warm color for Jill, while sensation G would be that of a warm color for Jack. Both sensations, whatever their differing qualities, would be associated with sensations of the sun, of fires, of blushing. Correspondingly, G would be a cool color in Jill's mind, while R would be a cool color in Jack's mind, associated, for both Jack and Jill, with sensations of trees, of plants, of the sea. At traffic lights, Jill would stop at R and go at G, while Jack would stop at G and go at R, both behaving appropriately. The mental states R and G would be mere markers, or labels, or signs, correlated or not with other such signs.

Müller was a vitalist. He believed that the energy in the nerves has a not-purely-physical quality that enables it to travel infinitely fast from the sense organs to the mind. He believed that the quality of the sensations of red and green light—"what it's like" to have these sensations, to use a phrase from twentieth-century philosophy (Nagel, 1974)—is conveyed to the mind from the places in the brain where the nerves terminate (X' and Y'). According to Müller, the qualitative difference between R and G serves as the basis for our conscious discrimination between red and green (the belief that it's like one thing to see red and like something else to see green) and, secondarily, as the basis for behavioral discrimination between the two stimuli.

Müller was a vitalist, but his students were not vitalists. Boring says:

> In 1845... four young, enthusiastic and idealistic physiologists, all pupils of the great Johannes Müller, all later to be very famous, met together and formed a pact.... They were, in order of age, Carl Ludwig, who was then twenty-nine, Emil du Bois-Reymond, Ernst Brucke and Hermann von Helmholtz, then twenty-four. They were joining forces to fight vitalism, the view that life involves forces other than those found in the interaction of inorganic bodies. The great Johannes Müller was a vitalist, but these men were of the next generation. Du Bois and Brucke [later to become Freud's teacher] even pledged between them a solemn oath that they would establish and compel the acceptance of this truth: "No other forces than common physical chemical ones are active within the organism." (Boring, 1957, p. 708)

In other words, we don't need R and G; anything that these conscious markers can do, brain states (X' and Y') can do as well or better.

In modern terms, Müller's students were *identity theorists*. They believed that the construction of the world from nervous energy took place in the physical brain rather than in a non-physical mind. Helmholtz, among his many contributions to science, went on to measure the (finite) speed of nervous transmission and to develop a theory of color vision wherein the retina analyzes colors into triplets of intensities; the three intensities at each retinal point are then conveyed by three nerves from the sense organ to the brain. Müller would have said that such neural triplets were synthesized into single color sensations in the non-physical mind but, for Helmholtz, whatever synthesis was required occurred wholly within the nervous system.

A great advantage of Helmholtz's neural identity theory, as well as modern neural identity theory, is that it recognizes the existence of unconscious mental events (which Freud was later to emphasize as well). For Müller, qualities R and G were conscious qualities by definition; a sensation was not just a mental event, it was a fundamentally conscious event. Instances where stimuli have a demonstrable effect on behavior yet are not reported as seen, as in the phenomenon of "blindsight" (Weiscrantz, 1986), would, according to Müller, be non-mental as well as non-conscious, therefore outside the purview of psychology. Neural identity theory neatly separates the mental from the conscious and opens up psychological investigation to methods other than conscious introspection.

The project of modern neural identity theory may be likened to the study of an unknown computer—neuroscientists opening it up in an attempt to discover its hardware, psychologists operating its keys and mouse and observing the results on its screen in an attempt to discover its program. On this analogy, our familiar mental terms would stand for the boxes in a flow diagram of such a program. As one modern neural identity theorist has pointed out (Churchland, 1986), the fact that a given computer process may be realized in many different molecular ways (analog or digital; mechanical, chemical or electronic; serial or parallel) does not make the realized program any the less physical.

The problem with the neurocognitive approach to the study of the mind, both in Helmholtz's and in the modern version, is that, despite advances in brain imaging techniques, there seems to be no set of neural structures (molecular or molar) corresponding to each identifiable mental property. Modern sensory neuroscience goes way, way beyond Figure 5.1. It would not claim that a stimulus could be carried by a single chain of afferent nerves ending at a particular point in the brain. There are many stages, on many brain levels, as a stimulus affects the brain. Even a simple color is a diffuse pattern of nervous stimulation heavily influenced by contextual factors. Which one is identical with the sensation? If these factors came into focus at a "final common path" in some particular brain location, you could call the focal point the sensation. But no single neural path for each sensation has been found within the nervous system. There is no place in the nervous system where the incoming stimulus stops. Sensory stimulation in its normal form runs right through the brain and out the other side, so to speak, without encountering anything identifiable as a sensation.

From a behavioral viewpoint, the acts of (a) seeing a red light and (b) stopping at a red light are not two separate processes in a chain but rather a single process described in two different ways. A person who sees a red light but doesn't stop is not performing half of an act but actually is seeing the red light differently from the way a person who does stop sees it. What is common among acts of discrimination of red from non-red stimuli is not a set of internal events but the set of overt actions by which the discrimination is made. In the last analysis, as Chapter 2 shows, the discrimination is the set of overt actions that correlate with the stimulus. The essential difference between a person who sees colors and one who is color-blind is that for the former such a set of actions exists, whereas for the latter no such set exists.

Why is your mind private to you? Why is it that only you have your particular set of beliefs, only you remember the things that you remember? Is it because you are carrying around a unique neural state, or because only you have been exposed to the particular set of events unique to you—your particular path through the physical and social environment? The answer, obviously, is "both." But your particular path is your particular psychology and your particular neural state is your particular neurology.

These are old arguments (e.g., Dewey, 1896) but they undercut modern neural identity theory. There is no place within the body for Descartes' or Müller's
or even Helmholtz's sensorium. In other words, there seems to be a fundamental contradiction within neural identity theory. Neural identity theory claims
that mental terms stand for events within the nervous system. Yet there is no
single neural event or single locus in the brain invariably activated whenever
a red stimulus, for example, affects behavior. As neuroscience has developed,
it has found no natural stopping point, where the input ends and the output
begins, to call a sensation; there is no end point of stimulation corresponding
to Descartes' pineal gland. If you start from the stimulus and work forward into
the nervous system, the stimulus branches out and becomes more and more diffuse, each branch differently affected by feedback from brain structures further
down the line. If you start from a given overt act and work your way backward,
sources of influence from different places in the nervous system merge like various small streams joining at different places to form a large river with back chan-
nels affecting the flow upstream. The higher region of the brain, where Descartes
and Müller believed stimuli come into focus, is actually the place where they are
most diffuse. One may be tempted to say that the whole brain has the sensation.
But multiple influences on behavior do not stop at the brain's border; they begin
at the sense organ and end only in the overt action itself. Rather than saying
that the whole brain has the sensation, it would be more correct to say that the
whole person has the sensation. This is the view of sensation (and of all mental
acts) that I defend in this book.

Another way to avoid the problem posed by the failure of modern neuroscience to find a place in the brain where sensations occur (a sensorium) is to abandon the notion that the mind can be studied by the methods of science, and to
avoid all talk of mental states within scientific discourse. In terms of Figure 5.1,
nothing would seem to be lost to the understanding of the mind by eliminating
the area labeled "mind." If the mind is actually *identical* to specific events in the
nervous system all mental terms could be replaced by neural terms or sets of
such terms. The mind, if it exists at all, would be only an epiphenomenon. The
use of mental terms in ordinary speech could be considered just the layman's
way of speaking about events more precisely described in neural or neuro-cybernetic terms. This tactic would be equivalent, however, to abandoning psychology. What are cognitive psychologists studying if they are not studying memory,
perception, or thought? Even primarily neurological research seems to require
the non-metaphorical use of mental terms (Gazzaniga, 1998).

Let us therefore seriously consider *behavioral identity theory*—the idea that
sensations occur not in a specific place within an animal but in the animal's overt
behavior. According to behavioral identity theory, mental states are identical not
to specific neural events but to behavioral patterns. To repeat: Stopping at a
red light (in the context of a pattern of discriminating red from green lights) is

not a two-stage process—sensing the red light and then stopping. Stopping at the red light (in the context of generally stopping at red lights) is sensing the light. This is an identity theory, but the identity in question is not between a person's mental processes and particular neural or neuro-cybernetic processes going on inside the person. The identity in question is between mental processes and the operation of the person's whole nervous system as expressed in that person's overt behavior. Instead of erasing the part of Figure 5.1 labeled "MIND," as Müller's students demanded, behavioral identity theory expands that part of the diagram to encompass the whole body and brings it back into contact with the world. (Recall Plato's way of putting it: "The true analogy for this indwelling power of the soul and the instrument whereby each of us apprehends [learns] is that of an eye that could not be converted to the light from the darkness except by turning *the whole body*" [*Republic* VI, 518 c; italics added].) According to behavioral identity theory, mental events are neither spiritual events taking place in another world nor neural events taking place somewhere inside the brain. They are rather actions of the person as a whole as expressed in overt behavior. The mental context of a given discrete act is not an internal event (physical or spiritual) efficiently causing the act. The mental context of a given act is rather the larger overt behavior pattern into which the act fits (the act's *final* cause).

It may fairly be claimed that one of the main reasons for using mental terms in the first place is to distinguish voluntary actions from mechanical actions. There is an essential difference between the motion of a boy's leg in response to a fire (Figure 4.1) and the motion of his leg in a dance. The former is elicited mechanically and relatively simply by the fire, while the latter is, or at least seems to be, elicited both from inside the boy by his desire to dance and from outside him by the music. One of the nice things about Descartes' system is that it makes a clear distinction between these two types of action. It makes this distinction in terms of place. The place where his foot withdrawal originates is in the fire; the place where his dance step originates is in his soul, acting through his brain's pineal gland.

How may behavioral identity theory make such a distinction? One possibility is to put aside our usual way of thinking about the causes of behavior and to adopt teleological behaviorism (Rachlin, 1992, 1994). Teleological behaviorism is a kind of behavioral identity theory (Chapters 8, 9, and 10 will discuss another). It essentially replaces Descartes' *spatial* distinction between mentally and mechanically controlled actions with a *temporal* distinction between mentally and mechanically controlled actions. The act of stopping at a red light while driving a car may be part of a temporally extended pattern of acts: the pattern of stopping at red lights and going at green lights. That pattern may be part of a more extended pattern, generally obeying driving laws, which may be part of a still more extended pattern, generally obeying laws, which may be part of a still more extended pattern, generally obeying social rules, and so forth.

Alternatively, the original act of stopping at a red light while driving a car may be seen as part of a pattern of discriminating between red and green objects, which is part of a pattern of discriminating among colors, which is part of the pattern of making sensory discriminations, and so forth. Any given act may be part of multiple sets of patterns just as a note in a symphony may be part of multiple melodies or themes. For example, my act of crossing the street to get to the bank to withdraw $1,000 would be part of my desire for $1,000 and my knowledge (or would it be hope?) that it is there in my account.

The neural events underlying a given act such as stopping at a red light are its "efficient causes." According to teleological behaviorism, mental causes are not efficient causes at all but "final causes." As Chapter 2 says, the final cause of an act is the more extended pattern of acts to which it belongs; generally discriminating between red and green is the final cause of a particular case of stopping at a red light. In the context of that general discrimination, the particular case, stopping at a red light this time, is *identical* to sensing the red light. In another context (say, a general failure to discriminate between red and green colors—color-blindness), the very same act would not be identical to sensing the red light (the act of stopping might be a discrimination of brightness or a discrimination of place [the red light is above the green light] or just a coincidence—the driver might have stopped to let out a passenger). The important point is that both the final cause and the nature of the act—mental or mechanical, and, if mental, what sort—are determined by the overt act in its context of other overt acts, not by its neural antecedents.

Jack and Jill, in Figure 5.2, with entirely opposite neural connections (X' and Y') would nevertheless (I assume the reader agrees) be able to coordinate their actions with respect to red and green objects; they both call the same objects red and green. According to behavioral identity theory, despite their differing neural states, Jack and Jill are both having the same sensations. Neural identity theory would have to say the opposite—that despite their corresponding behavior Jack and Jill are having different sensations. Surely this is not a useful way to employ our mental vocabulary.

Some particular acts are performed for their own sakes; impulsive or selfish acts such as alcoholic drinking, overeating, or littering fall into this category. Other particular acts would not be performed solely for their own sakes but for the sake of the wider pattern of which they are a part; self-controlled or altruistic acts such as drink refusal, dessert refusal, voting, or trash recycling fall into this category. Such acts may not be immediately reinforced but are part of a highly valuable pattern of acts (sobriety, healthy lifestyle, group cohesiveness).

This is not to say that modern neural and cognitive studies are any less valuable or important than behavioral studies—on the contrary. The point of this chapter is just that LOSNE implies that mental states may be observed directly in behavioral patterns; neurocognitive investigations are directed to the mechanisms underlying those states (their efficient causes). Moreover, many cognitively oriented psychology experiments, especially in the areas of judgment, decision, and choice, may be interpreted in terms of behavioral patterning as well as in terms of underlying mechanisms (Rachlin, 1989).

In contradiction to behavioral identity theory, common sense might claim:

A. *We just know* that our sensations are inside us; therefore Jack's and Jill's sensations must differ, even though their actions correspond.

But common sense would also claim, in agreement with Descartes:

B. Our sensations are not just meaningless neural impulses unrelated to objects in the world; they are not mere mental markers or arbitrary codes.

The usual cognitive, neurological, or spiritual interpretation of LOSNE preserves claim-A with respect to sensations but sacrifices claim-B. This is a bad bargain. It drains all utility from the concept of sensation and makes it into an epiphenomenon, intrinsically private and unrelated to the world. Given claim-A and LOSNE, a scientific psychophysics would be impossible. Verbal reports of mental events (introspection) would be completely unreliable since the very objects of introspection might differ from person to person yet be described (as by Jack and Jill) in identical terms, or might be identical yet be described differently. For this reason, the behaviorist B. F. Skinner (1938), as well as some twentieth-century philosophers (Quine, 1960, for example), denied the utility of mental terms in psychology. [Quine pointed out that the mentalistic sentence, "I believe that Mark Twain is a good writer," is *opaque* in the sense that you could not freely substitute it for, "I believe that Samuel Clemens is a good writer," and logically maintain the truth or falsity of any sentence containing it. The reason for the opacity is (a) I may not know that Mark Twain is Samuel Clemens *and* (b) the statement is thought of as privileged evidence of my internal belief. But if the statement were merely one bit of overt behavior constituting my belief (as teleological behaviorism says), then the opacity becomes trivial. The truth of the statement, for a behaviorist, depends on its correlation with other behaviors. Thus, (c) Person X says, "I believe that Mark Twain is a good writer," and (d) Person X reads a lot of Mark Twain, may be conceived as mutually corroborating bits of Person X's belief. For a behaviorist, the opacity of "Mark Twain" in the first bit is (trivially) due to its enclosure within quotation marks and not at all an indication of an internal state—even when Person X is oneself.]

But it is possible to retain the utility of mental terms in psychology by dropping claim-A, and resuscitating something like claim-B. The behavioral interpretation of a sensation (as a particular discriminatory act in the context of a general discrimination—a set of overt actions correlated over time with their objects) retains a non-arbitrary, functional, relation of sensations with the world (as well as their poetic use).

Pain and Pleasure

Let us now consider an objection that may be raised to the thought experiment illustrated in Figure 5.2. The objection might run as follows:

> You deliberately chose red and green lights to illustrate LOSNE because these stimuli lack emotional valence. Colors serve in the world (as red and green traffic lights do) not so much for their own qualities as for the qualities they signal. Since the stimuli you chose are themselves signals, of course their neural representations are also signals and could stand for anything. Jack and Jill communicate with each other exactly to the extent that red and green colors are unsought (or unavoided) for their own sake. If the spiritual or neural representations of the colors were pleasant or unpleasant in themselves, Jack would quickly discover that he was abnormal.

Note how much this objection already concedes to behavioral identity theory (that sensations consist of overt classificatory behavior of whole organisms). All environmental events that serve mainly as signals for other events, including virtually all the language we hear and read, can be internally represented only as arbitrary signals. This includes not only abstract colors and sounds but also whole objects and complexes of objects (perceptions). Consider, for example, our fathers and mothers. Everything that was said about red and green lights as they affect Jack's and Jill's nervous systems could be said about their mother and father (Jack and Jill are brother and sister, it may now be revealed). If the image of their mother were represented in Jack's brain in the place corresponding to the image of their father in Jill's brain, and vice versa, Jack and Jill would still be able to communicate perfectly with each other about their parents—regardless of how important they were to them. According to LOSNE, Jack and Jill may have different feelings for their common mother, but these different feelings could not consist only of differing spiritual or neural representations; they would consist of differing overt acts within differing behavioral patterns. Conversely, Jack and Jill could have the same feelings for their mother but differing spiritual or neural representations of her. Why? Because it is their mother whom they love or hate, not the representations (which according to LOSNE have none of the qualities of their mother). What does it mean, then, for two people to have different feelings about a common object? For a behavioral identity theory, it can mean only that they behave differently with respect to that object. "What it's like" to love or hate your mother is to behave in one way or another toward her over an extended period of time.

There is nothing in this behavioral conception of the mind that says discrimination must occur at a single instant. Jack may love his mother and Jill may hate her at this moment, yet they may both be behaving, at this moment, in the same way (they may both be kissing her—one on each cheek). As Chapter 2 points out, discrimination (even the simple kind between sounds and their absence) is the correlation of behavior with environmental events over time. Strictly speaking, discrimination cannot happen at a moment. However, it is a common verbal convention to refer to a temporally extended event as if it did exist at a moment. Two violinists, for example, may each be playing a different melody *at this moment* even though, at this moment, they are playing the very same note. But this is a verbal convention referring to what the violinists are actually doing and has nothing to do with what may be going on within their heads.

According to behavioral identity theory, to love your mother or anyone else is not to have your heart go pitter-patter at the sight of her but to behave toward her in a loving way over a long period of time. False love is a discrepancy not of your behavior with your heart or of your behavior with your mental representation but of your immediate behavior with your behavior in the long run. If Jack loves his mother while Jill hates her and they are both kissing her right now, the kiss is like a common note in two different melodies being played by two different violinists. The kiss is but a single act common to two different behavioral patterns. The love and the hate are in the patterns.

What then about pleasure and pain themselves? Figure 5.3 repeats Figure 5.2, but instead of red and green lights substitutes a typically pleasurable stimulus (an ice cream cone) and a typically painful stimulus (an electric shock). Suppose that before birth Jack is crossed up by some bad fairy with respect to these stimuli, so that whatever causes pleasure for the rest of us will cause pain for Jack

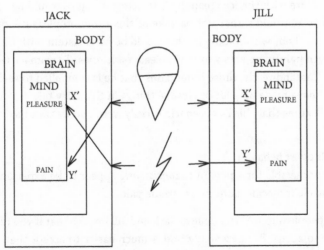

Figure 5.3 Like Figure 5.2 except the stimuli are pleasurable and painful objects rather than red and green objects. Here the behaviors in response to the objects (not shown) are innately different; hence Jack's and Jill's mental states are different.

and whatever causes pain for the rest of us will cause pleasure for Jack. Under such conditions Jack would be truly mixed up. He would be punished for eating ice cream cones and rewarded for sticking forks into electric sockets. To survive in the world he would have to learn to avoid whatever he naturally tended to approach and to approach whatever he naturally tended to avoid. It would conceivably be possible to teach him to overcome these tendencies and to communicate with normal people about objects in the world, but he would at the least be a very unfortunate person.

Of what does his misfortune consist? Let us imagine still another transformation of Jack's nervous system. As we said, the bad fairy has arranged, before his birth, that little Jack will hate licking ice cream cones and love sticking forks into electric sockets. But, in the nick of time, after this transformation, and before Jack was actually born, a good fairy has come along and altered his reflexes so that he now has an innate tendency (he can't help it) to approach whatever is painful to him and to avoid whatever is pleasurable. He has the same (spiritual or neural) pains as before but can't help eagerly approaching whatever causes them (his mother's breasts at first, ice cream cones later); the greater the pain intensity, the more eager is his approach. Correspondingly, he has (spiritual or neural) pleasures but can't help avoiding whatever causes those pleasures (shocks, fires, blows on the head). The more intense the pleasure, the louder are his screams, the more fierce his struggles to escape. In other words, Jack behaves normally— just like Jill—except his spiritual or neural representations of pleasurable and painful objects are opposite to hers. If he were to deny his pleasure in the objects he seeks, no one would believe him. "I hate this ice cream cone," he would say as he hungrily devours it. But he cannot even verbally deny his pleasure or signal his displeasure with the ice cream by grimacing; doing so would be to signal to others that he would rather not partake of this common pleasure; others may tend to comply by withholding it. This would be inconsistent with his tendency to approach painful objects and avoid pleasurable ones. To grimace would be to avoid, at least indirectly, those inner pains that he is compelled to seek.

Now, I have made up a lot of strange things in this fairy tale, but I think the reader will agree that this last scenario is truly weird. So we now have two weird notions:

A. Pain is overt behavior.
B. It is conceivable for a person to *consistently* appear to be experiencing pleasure while internally suffering extreme pain.

Most people reject A. The fable of Jack and Jill implies that if you reject A you will have to accept B. I personally find A much easier to accept than B. That is probably because I have been a behaviorist for most of my life. But I am also a pragmatist and I believe that A is far more useful than B for both treatment and understanding of pain (Rachlin, 1985).

You may ask: Cannot a person have a single episode of pain that is not only not reported to anyone but is not exhibited even as a brief exclamation, a grimace, a stumble, an intake of breath, and so on, which cannot be, even in principle, observable by another person? Consider the following scenario: You are walking along the street, perhaps explaining something to a friend who is attending closely to your every word and gesture. You suddenly have a shooting pain in your foot; can she notice absolutely nothing? I would answer this question in the negative. To me, it is equivalent to saying that you may blink your eye internally without blinking your eye externally or jerk your knee internally but not externally. Of course, it is possible for your nervous system to behave as it would if you were going to jerk your knee but then inhibit the overt motion at the very last synapse. But then you haven't jerked your knee. The reason that pain is not private is that pain and pleasure are not essentially internal states at all, but patterns of overt behavior. Notion A is only *apparently* weird while Notion B is really weird. What lies behind Notion B? The false idea that the mind—whether a spiritual entity, or a structure in the central nervous system, or an event in the peripheral nervous system (a covert muscle twitch)—is located somewhere within the body, and is essentially private, not overt, behavior. To repeat the metaphor from the preface of this book: Like a general, safe in his headquarters, sending and receiving messages to and from the front, the mind (isolated from the world, located deep in the brain, and served by millions of nerves) continuously receives messages from the sense organs and sends them to the muscles, but is never in direct contact with the world. This is the view of the mind that dominates current thought about thought—that most people regard as settled. This is the view that creates the paradoxes and problems of mind and body. It is a thoroughly false view.

And let me state the moral of my fairy tale: The concept of a mind enclosed as a prisoner within the body makes no sense. True pleasure and true pain are identical, not to spiritual or neural events, but to the behavior of approach and avoidance—not to momentary approach and avoidance but to consistent approach and avoidance over time. Jack may seek normally painful stimuli for some greater good, but if a long-term observer (Jill, for instance) sees no greater good and if the behavior is frequent, Jill will judge that Jack really likes to do it—and she will be correct.

Pleasure and pain are different from sensations of red and green because pleasure and pain are characterized by specific, strong, and diametrically opposed actions, whereas red and green lights are not. A newborn infant responds to his mother's breast by seeking the nipple and sucking; when he is slapped, he cries. But the infant has to learn what to do in response to red and green signals. This is not to deny that there are pleasure centers and pain centers in the brain (although I do not believe that the evidence for them is conclusive). Rather, I claim, pain itself is not identical with stimulation of what is normally a pain center and pleasure itself is not identical with stimulation of a pleasure center. Pain and pleasure centers are perhaps essential parts of the mechanisms underlying pain and pleasure (like the engine is an essential part of the mechanism underlying a car's acceleration), but neural centers are not themselves pains and pleasures (as the engine is not the acceleration itself). Pain is the consistent avoidance, and pleasure is the consistent seeking of their objects. (See Rachlin, 1985, for an extended discussion of pain in behavioral terms, and responses to the comments of various authorities on the subject.)

For teleological behaviorism, our minds—including our pleasures, pains, sensations of red and green, and perceptions of our parents—exist not in another, spiritual, sphere different from the physical world, not in one or another piece of our brains, but in our habitual interactions with the world. Otherwise the conception of Jack's double transformation holds; we would have to imagine the possibility of a person like Jack, behaving just like everyone else from birth to death but fundamentally, radically, different in his mind. Of all the theories of mind considered in this book, only behavioral identity theory avoids this violation of common sense.

Acknowledgment

Chapter 5 is a revised version of: Rachlin (2005), What Müller's Law of Specific Nerve Energies Says about the Mind, *Behavior and Philosophy*, 33, 41–54. Reprinted with permission from the Cambridge Center for Behavioral Studies.

The Re-emergence of the Mind

The first part of this chapter attempts to distinguish between cognitive theory and behavioral theory in general, and then to distinguish between Skinnerian behaviorism and teleological behaviorism. Cognitive theory is a modern alternative to neural identity theory, discussed in the previous chapter. Cognitive psychologists, like behavioral psychologists, observe overt behavior, verbal and non-verbal. But cognitive psychologists differ from behavioral psychologists in terms of their ultimate goal; cognitive psychologists aim to use their observations to discover the internal (computer-like) mechanism underlying behavior; behavioral psychologists attempt to explain behavior in its own terms.

Skinnerian behaviorism differs from teleological behaviorism in two respects. First, Skinnerian behaviorists do not use mental terms as part of their scientific vocabulary, while teleological behaviorism does use mental terms. Second, Skinnerian behaviorists explain complex behavior (usually identified with the mind) in terms of unobserved, internal immediate muscular movements; teleological behaviorism explains complex behavior in terms of overt patterns extended in space and time. Teleological behaviorism claims that the mind exists outside the body at the intersection of these overt patterns and their environmental consequences.

The second part of the chapter discusses three books by philosophers (Alva Noë, Derek Melser, and Andy Clark) that, like teleological behaviorism, say that the mind exists, at least partly, outside the body. These books represent a welcome behavioristic strain in contemporary philosophy of mind. It is argued, however, that none of the three goes far enough in this direction; all of them hang onto the brain as an essential part of the mind.

Cognitive Theory and Behavioral Theory

The four heavy horizontal arrows of Figure 6.1 represent the data that the modern cognitive psychologist may use to construct a theory. The psychologist manipulates information or the consequences of behavior and observes verbal and non-verbal behavior. From these manipulations and observations, a cognitive system

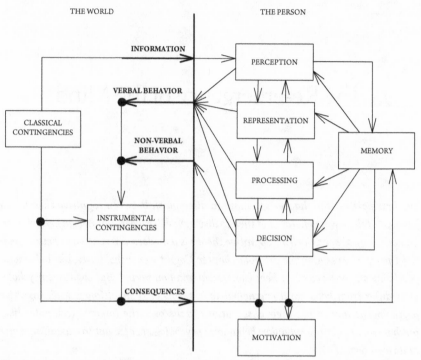

Figure 6.1 General outlines of a cognitive theory (to the right) and a behavioral theory (to the left).

is hypothesized. The system is a set of internal operations and transformations, often a computer-like information-processing system, which, given the manipulated inputs, would have produced the observed behavioral output. The system is tested by altering the inputs and predicting new outputs. If, upon testing, the actual outputs differ from those predicted, the theory is revised. Then the revised system is again tested in a new domain, again revised, tested yet again, and so forth. Each revision improves the system, making it better and better as the process continues. The boxes to the right of the heavy vertical line represent a generalized cognitive theory roughly corresponding to Kahneman and Tversky's (1979) *prospect theory* of probabilistic choice. [The boxes in Figure 6.1 to the right of the heavy vertical line correspond roughly to the stages of decision-making proposed by prospect theory.] The boxes would eventually be filled in with submechanisms or functional relations between inputs and outputs.

Alternatively, the right part of Figure 6.1 may consist of a complex network of computer connections with nodes that may "learn" to transmit signals with greater or lesser strength to other parts of the network. Principles of "reinforcement" and "punishment" may govern the network's learning; as the learning progresses, the outputs approach closer and closer to some set of desired outputs. The ultimate network is then a model (a cognitive model) of the desired behavior.

A computer program that embodies a cognitive theory may be subjected to a *Turing test*. Turing testers would feed questions into the computer and receive answers from it. To the extent that the machine's answers are indistinguishable from those given by a real human being, the computer's program is an adequate model of a human mental process. Any program that passes this test will necessarily be highly complex (perhaps involving probabilistic interactive networks).

The processes occurring within the boxes to the right might consist of sub-programs, and those might consist of sub-sub-programs, and so forth. The cognitive psychologist's theory of the mind *is* the overall program itself. [You might call this *cognitive identity theory*.] In principle, a given program may be instantiated in many ways—by transistors, vacuum tubes, relays, analog circuits, a vast number of connected abacuses, and so forth. The program may or may not be instantiated by actual neural processes. In *cognitive neuroscience*, cognitive psychology and neuroscience collaborate to abstract from people's behavior the part that is computer-like—cognitive psychology studying the software and neuroscience the hardware of the computer.

Behavioral theory, illustrated to the left in Figure 6.1, uses the same data that cognitive theory uses (represented by the four dark, horizontal arrows) and works in a similar way to construct and test a theory. The difference is that the systems used by the behavioral psychologist to predict behavior exist not inside the person but outside, in the world. The person is seen not as a repository of mental states, but as a whole organism interacting with other organisms and with objects in the world. The person's mental states are interpreted in terms of these interactions. [The great complexity of the mind is represented in cognitive theory by the complexity of the programs that would go in the boxes to the right of the vertical line, and in behavioral theory by the complexity of overlapping behavioral patterns extended in time.]

It is generally agreed among behaviorists that behavior is determined by two kinds of contingencies between the outputs and inputs of Figure 6.1. These relationships are represented by the two boxes labeled *classical contingencies* and *instrumental contingencies*. Classical contingencies are the kind studied most famously by I. P. Pavlov. For example: A dog is placed in a harness. A bell (*information*) is sounded just prior to the delivery of food (*consequences*) to the dog. The dog eats the food and salivates (*non-verbal behavior*). After this process is repeated a number of times (making the food contingent on the bell), the dog will salivate at the sound of the bell, even if the food is not delivered. The dog's behavior depends crucially on the parameters of the contingency—the temporal relationships between information and consequences, their intensities, their frequencies, the dog's past experience with them.

People, too, will react to signals of significant events as they do to the events themselves. An aspiring corporate lawyer has been called, several times, to the senior partner's office (*information*) and bawled out (*consequences*). Now she has to enter that office to get a file. Even though the partner is not there now, she behaves in the same way (her heart beats, her palms sweat, and so forth) as she did before in that place.

Behavior-environment contingencies are the kind studied most famously by B. F. Skinner. Each time a hungry rat presses a lever (*non-verbal behavior*) a food pellet is delivered (*consequences*). The food is contingent on the lever press; if the rat begins to press faster, as it typically would, the food is said to have *reinforced* the lever press. Again, the properties of the behavior (its rate and its pattern over time) depend crucially on the parameters of the contingency. If, instead of food, the rat were shocked, the rate of lever presses would typically decrease, and the shock is said to have *punished* the lever press. (Neuroscientists then search for the internal, neural mechanisms by which reinforcement increases and punishment decreases the behavior on which they are contingent.) Behavior-environmental contingencies are, of course, ubiquitous in human life and their effects are everywhere. These effects on behavior are not necessarily conscious or deliberate. For example, when the doctor says, "You need an operation," he almost certainly has your best interests at heart. It is just that his perception of your best interests is colored by his own best interests. So you've got to be careful. The saying, "Never ask a barber if you need a haircut," is no reflection on the honesty of barbers—but of the susceptibility of their behavior to reinforcement.

In Figure 6.1, the horizontal arrow leading to the box labeled "Instrumental Contingencies" represents a very important behavioral relationship—that of a discriminative stimulus. A discriminative stimulus signals, not another stimulus, not a specific response, but an entire behavior-environment contingency. The OPEN/CLOSED signs on a shop door and the OCCUPIED/VACANT signs on the door of an airplane lavatory are examples. The OCCUPIED sign is not specifically paired with any behavior of yours. It says that *if* you try the door it will not open. Whether or not you do try the door is up to you. Trying the door is reinforced in the presence of the VACANT sign and not in the presence of the OCCUPIED sign. Discriminative stimuli guide us through life. Much of our language consists of discriminative stimuli. Our language functions to guide future behavior (linguistic as well as non-linguistic) of others and of ourselves. Different sentences, different tones of voice, stand for different contingencies. Hearing or reading them, we act accordingly. The red and green lights of a traffic signal, the words "stop" or "go," and the sentences, "If you cross this intersection now you're likely to have an accident or get a ticket," and "If you cross this intersection now you're unlikely to have an accident or get a ticket," all stand for the same set of contingencies, all have the same meaning, all are equivalent discriminative stimuli. Discriminative stimuli play a big role in self-control and its lack. Our reinforcement will be greater in the long run if we avoid discriminative stimuli that signal immediate reinforcement of undesirable behavior (as an alcoholic should avoid a bar). Our reinforcement will be greater in the long run if we avoid the establishment of certain common stimuli as discriminative stimuli for undesirable behavior (TV watching should not become a discriminative stimulus for eating). Therefore, we need to establish useful general rules as discriminative stimuli for desirable behavior.

Nowhere here are mental terms. Sometimes Skinner (1945, 1953) offered "interpretations" in which the use of mentalistic vocabulary in everyday speech was explained in terms of behavior, reinforcers, and discriminative stimuli. Self-control, for instance, was held to be nothing but avoidance of certain discriminative stimuli ("Get thee behind me, Satan!"), like crossing the street to avoid the enticing smell of a bakery.

Skinner's non-mentalistic terminology has served very well in the analysis of discrete actions of humans and other animals (Honig & Staddon, 1977). Furthermore, the patterns of behavior discovered in one situation with one species often appear in other situations with other species. These patterns change in systematic ways with motivational variables like food deprivation and drug dosage. Skinnerian techniques have been extremely successful in areas of behavior therapy ranging from treatment of severe psychoses to autism to weight control to getting a good night's sleep; their great advantage in these applications is their resolute focus on consequences and contingencies of reinforcement. For example, many women (and some men) suffer from agoraphobia; they have panic attacks in public places, and consequently refuse to leave home; they are housebound. In searching for causes and treatment of such behavior, the Skinnerian behavior therapist considers not just the antecedents of agoraphobia but also its consequences: avoidance of work, avoidance of sexual temptation (your spouse always knows where you are), attention from relatives and friends (they come to you; you don't have to go to them), and so on. Focusing on the actual consequences of dysfunctional behavior has led in many cases to the development of successful treatment by substitution of less dysfunctional behavior to achieve equivalent ends. Skinnerian techniques also have been successfully applied in business management, in the teaching of reading and mathematics to children, and in college-level courses as diverse as anatomy and foreign languages.

However, despite this success, it has not been possible either in the laboratory or in the many areas of application of Skinnerian behaviorism to divide all behavior neatly into specific responses and reinforcers. What, for instance, reinforces the act of refusing an offered cigarette by a smoker trying to quit? Here is a quotation from the comedian Dick Cavett: "Once, as [Cavett and Jonathan Miller of "Beyond the Fringe"] waited backstage together at the 92nd Street Y in New York City, [Cavett] pointed disapprovingly at [Miller's] lit cigarette. [Miller said,] 'I know these will kill me, I'm just not convinced that this particular one will kill me'" (*New York Times, Week in Review*, May 31, 2009, p. 10). The problem for the alcoholic as well as for the smoker is how to make choices over the longer time span and avoid making choices, as Jonathan Miller is said to do, on a case-by-case basis. The reason that we have trouble bringing our behavioral patterns into line with abstract and temporally extended behavioral contingencies is that the value of a desired pattern's particular component (refusing the drink or the cigarette) may be much less than that of its alternative (drinking the drink or smoking the cigarette). As Jonathan Miller implies, each cigarette-refusal has virtually no value in itself relative to smoking the cigarette. Refusing a particular cigarette is worth nothing compared to smoking it. Moreover, *individual* cigarette refusals are almost never reinforced—not immediately, not conditionally, not after a delay. If Miller refuses a single cigarette, he does not wake up three weeks later, suddenly a healthier and happier person. In order to realize the value of a cigarette refusal he must put together a long string of them.

Having to deal with and talk about such obviously important acts, behavior therapists have taken two roads, neither of which are satisfactory. Some, like Homme (1965), developed an operant psychology of the hidden organism, speaking of inner (covert) respondents, inner operants (*coverants*), and inner discriminative stimuli. [Skinner referred to instrumentally reinforced responses as *operants* and classically conditioned responses as *respondents*. See Chapter 10, response to Schlinger, for a further discussion.] According to these psychologists, people who refuse an offered cigarette can just reinforce the act themselves (pat themselves on the back, so to speak). This conception has both logical and empirical problems. Logically, if people can reinforce their own actions, why should they ever withhold reinforcement of any action? What reinforces the giving and withholding of self-reinforcement? (Catania, 1975). Empirically, there is just no evidence that self-reinforcement works and some evidence that it does not work (Castro & Rachlin, 1980).

The other road taken by behavior therapists has led to cognitive-behavioral therapy (Mahoney, 1974). Cognitive-behavioral therapists retain Skinnerian techniques for acts that are clearly reinforced. However, where environmental reinforcers are not obvious or immediate, cognitive-behavioral therapy abandons behaviorism entirely and refers to mental states as inner causes. According to cognitive-behavioral therapy, people who refuse the cigarette may do so because they *believe* it is better for their health and because they *desire* to be healthy. A therapist might then try to strengthen those peoples' beliefs and desires by logical argument, by asking them to repeat a statement of their beliefs over and over, or by reinforcing the statement of the belief. Even this last procedure is not behavioral, because it rests on the assumption that the reinforcer acts not only on the external statement but also on the inner belief.

In principle, there is nothing wrong with cognitive-behavioral therapy. If people did have beliefs as coherent inner states and if beliefs could cause specific actions, then changing the belief would change the action. The problem is that cognitive-behavioral therapists have abandoned the very aspect of Skinner's program that made it so successful: its concentration on consequences rather than antecedents.

A therapist who focuses on the central efficient causes (the HOW) of a person's behavior tends to lose sight of the reinforcers (the WHY) of the behavior—its effect on the person's relations with family, friends, with the environment in general. The next section will discuss and criticize a recent philosophical movement that abandons the neurocognitive conception of the mind depicted to the right in Figure 6.1 and goes part way toward a consistent behavioral view of the mind but without the limitations, mentioned above, inherent in Skinnerian behaviorism.

Is the Mind in the Brain?

Many, if not most, modern philosophers in the United States and Great Britain believe that behaviorism, as a philosophy, is dead. According to *The Stanford Encyclopedia of Philosophy* (Graham, 2010):

> The deepest and most complex reason for behaviorism's decline in influence is its commitment to the thesis that behavior can be explained without reference to non-behavioral mental (cognitive, representational, or interpretative) activity. Behavior can be explained just by reference to its "functional" (Skinner's term) relation to or co-variation with the environment and to the animal's history of environmental interaction. . . . Unfortunately, for behaviorism, it's hard to imagine a more restrictive rule for psychology than one which prohibits hypotheses about representational storage and processing [the right side of Figure 6.1].

Behavioral thinking with such a self-imposed constraint, Graham believes, must be inadequate to explain most of what is interesting and important about human behavior—that is, the mind. He suggests that a path toward behaviorism's revival in philosophy would be to incorporate neuroeconomics:

> Behaviorism may do well to purchase some of neuroeconomic's conceptual currency, especially since some advocates of the program see themselves as behaviorists in spirit if not stereotypical letter. . . . One assumption in neuroeconomics is that full explanations of organism/ environmental interactions will combine facts about such things as reinforcement schedules with appeal to neurocomputational modeling and to the neurochemistry and neurobiology of reinforcement.

A recent movement in philosophy called *enacted mind, extended cognition,* or *embodied mind* seems to conform to Graham's prescription. These philosophers reject cognitive concepts such as internal representations as explanations for behavior, but they accept neural processes ("neuroeconomics") as part of the triumvirate: "...brain, body, and world," which "together maintain living consciousness." (Noë, 2009, p. 42). O'Regan and Noë (2001), for example, argue that sensations are not internal representations but contingencies between behavior and sensory stimulation (see Figure 2.2 and accompanying discussion in Chapter 2 of this book). Noë's approach was seized upon by philosophical critics (such as Block, 2001) as too behavioristic; in response, the authors are quick to say (p. 1011), "...we are *not* behaviorists..." (italics in original). Indeed, they are not. Seeing, they concede, is not the actual sensorimotor contingency as it plays out over time between the person and the world, but an internal *knowledge* of the contingency. It is unclear what they suppose the difference to be between such knowledge and the internal representations they criticize. (In any case, this conceptual retreat is unlikely to placate philosophers like Block who believe that behaviorism is dead and want to keep it that way.) In a similar vein, Bennett and Hacker (2003) present a detailed argument against the concept of internal representations. They say quite correctly (p. 133) that "...seeing the red colour of the flower does not occur in the brain at all—it occurs in the garden or the drawing room; and what is seen is a red geranium, not a sensation of red, which is neither seen nor had." They reject neural identity theory (p. 137): "...it is human beings, not their brains that form hypotheses and make inferences." But Bennett and Hacker are not behaviorists either. "We are not defending a form of behaviourism" they say (p. 82n). Their arguments against behaviorism (p. 117, for example) presuppose a behaviorism that, unlike teleological behaviorism, rejects mental terms. Bennett and Hacker, eager to distance themselves from behaviorism, never consider behavioral conceptions of mental terms.

The remainder of this chapter will discuss three books that represent different strains of this philosophical movement: *Out of Our Heads: Why You Are Not Your Brain, and Other Lessons from the Biology of Consciousness* by Alva Noë (2009); *The Act of Thinking* by Derek Melser (2004); *Being There: Putting Brain, Body and World Together Again* by Andy Clark (1997). All three authors agree that the mind is not the brain or part of the brain. In common, they adopt the behavioristic idea that the mind cannot be understood except in terms of the interaction of a whole organism with the external environment. Nevertheless, for all of them, the brain remains an important component of mental activity. They retain a neurocognitive view of the mind while expanding its reach spatially, beyond the brain, into the peripheral nervous system and the external environment.

The most influential and strongest of these books is *Out of Our Heads*. The book focuses on contemporary neurocognitive identity theories and their search for the mechanism of consciousness. Noë says: "The problem of consciousness, as I am thinking of it here, is that of understanding our nature as human beings who think, who feel, and for whom a world *shows up*" (p. 9, italics added). Thought and feeling (and presumably sensation, perception, and imagination) are conceived by Noë as parts of consciousness.

Dissatisfaction with neural identity theory's divorce of the mind from its biological function has led Noë to expand his concept of the mind outward from the brain to overt behavior, including social behavior. Thus, like Graham, Noë is interested in both the interior (neuroeconomics) and the exterior (overt behavior) of the organism. But, unlike modern behaviorists, his object is to develop a philosophy of mind and not to predict, control, or explain overt behavior as such.

Noë's central idea is that consciousness is primarily something that occurs not in the head but in the world. Here are some quotes:

> After decades of concerted effort on the part of neuroscientists, psychologists, and philosophers, only one proposition about how the brain makes us conscious—how it gives rise to sensation, feeling, subjectivity—has emerged unchallenged: we don't have a clue. (p. xi)
>
> Consciousness is not something that happens inside us. It is something we do or make. Better: it is something we achieve. Consciousness is more like dancing than it is like digestion . . . . The idea that the only genuinely scientific study of consciousness would be one that identifies consciousness with events in the nervous system is a bit of outdated reductionism. (p. xii)
>
> In this book I argue that mind science, like biology more generally, must give pride of place to the whole living being. (p. xv)
>
> . . . to understand consciousness in humans and animals, we must look not inward, into the recesses of our insides; rather, we need to look to the ways in which each of us, as a whole animal, carries on the process of living in and with and in response to the world around us. The subject of experience is not a bit of your body. You are not your brain. (p. 7)

This sounds a lot like behaviorism. The quotes could have come from Skinner. Although Noë's main thrust is toward behavior, especially social behavior, consciousness is not, for him, a purely behavioral concept.

Noë rejects neural identity theory, the identification of consciousness with neural events—either particular neural firings or complex mechanisms extending across several brain areas. But he also rejects, at least implicitly, behavioral identity theory—the identification of mental events with patterns of overt individual and social behavior.

The general theme that consciousness is both behavior of the whole organism (inherently observable) and behavior internal to the organism (inherently unobservable) is repeated throughout the book:

> My central claim in this book is that to understand consciousness— the fact that we think and feel and that a world shows up for us— we need to look at a larger system of which the brain is only one

> element. Consciousness is not something the brain achieves on its own. Consciousness requires the joint operation of brain, body, and world. Indeed, consciousness is an achievement of the whole animal in its environmental context. (p. 10)
>
> One of the central claims of this book is that. . . we ought to focus not on the brain alone but on the brain in context—that is, on the brain in the natural setting of the person or animal. (p. 70)
>
> Brain, body, and world—each plays a critical role in making us the kind of beings we are. (p. 184)

But Noë makes it clear that it is the body, not the brain, that is the vehicle of consciousness. No one can deny that the brain is a vital mechanism or claim that its study is not of crucial importance to society. In some cases, brain research may suggest directions for behavioral research (although the opposite is much more frequently the case). However, you may ask: As brain research progresses, are we moving closer toward the understanding of consciousness or toward the development of what a prominent twentieth-century cognitive psychologist (Miller, 1962) called "the science of mental life?" Noë would say no.

Some modern neuroscientists and philosophers of mind (for example, Searle, 1997) claim that brain activity is not actually *identical* to mental activity but rather "gives rise to" mental activity (see Chapter 10, McDowell's comments, and my reply). They believe that consciousness and neural activity are more or less abstract levels of description of the same thing, just as the molecular structure of an I-beam and its tensile strength are different levels of description of the I-beam. Consciousness for them is merely an abstract way of describing activity in the brain. But if mental (or conscious) activity is just an abstract description of neural activity (physical activity, after all), why is it any more plausible that the physical activity in question occurs inside the head than that it occurs in overt behavior? The behaviorist claims that voluntary behavior is most clearly and distinctly (Descartes' criteria) caused by its consequences in the temporal and social environment. Even the most complex temporally and socially extended patterns of overt behavior evolve over a person's lifetime, just as complex structures such as the eye evolve over generations; the selection process rests in the contingencies between those patterns and the *outer* environment. If the criterion for labeling a physical act as a conscious act is closeness to its causal source, it would be the outer environment rather than the brain that satisfies that criterion, and which is therefore most usefully considered to be the locus of conscious as well as unconscious mental activity.

The typical philosophical defense of consciousness as an internal activity is introspective—we just know it to be the case. Noë is not immune to such claims. "Mere behavior," he says (p. 26) "is at best an unreliable guide to how things are for a person." The phrase "how things are," like the phrase "showing up," is undefined by Noë. "How things are" and "showing up," the ultimate differentia, for Noë, between my knowledge of my own mind and my knowledge of yours, are based on introspective reports. But, as Skinner (1957) and Wittgenstein (1958), a philosopher Noë clearly admires, have argued, introspective reports are not actually *reports* of anything at all. We do not go around reporting on our mental states (saying, "I am happy," for instance) for no reason, any more than we go around reporting about the world (saying, "The grass is green") for no reason. Both kinds of "reports" presume a listener and a situation of social interaction and mutual reinforcement. When I say, "I am happy," I am predicting some aspect of my behavior in the immediate future. Recall Plato's argument (in Chapter 1) that in trying to decide whether a tyrant is happy, the person we should ask is not the tyrant himself but someone, such as his wife, who is close to him, and who has observed his behavior over a long period of time (so as to have seen the patterns). Similarly, if a person's behavioral patterns were known to the listener of his introspections as well as they are known to the introspector, the listener would know *better* than the introspector (more directly and fundamentally than the introspector would know) the state of the introspector's mind. A child may say, "I am happy," but his mother may say, "No you're not," with perfect validity. I may honestly say, "I am happy," and my wife of 50 years may say, "No you're not," also with perfect validity. Introspection is not a royal road to our own minds. As I will argue in the next chapter, the road from my "mere" overt behavior to my own consciousness lies in the temporal and social contexts of my overt behavior—contexts that are in principle as available to others as they are to me.

Noë correctly criticizes the notion that consciousness must occur wholly in the brain as a remnant of Cartesian psychology in modern philosophy. Nevertheless, Noë believes that a world somehow "shows up" in consciousness. In Descartes' dualistic theory, a rose would show up in consciousness (the innate idea of a rose would wake up, as it were) as a consequence of a real rose acting on the sense organs and the information being transmitted through a chamber in the brain to the incorporeal soul. In modern neurocognitive theories, which Noë traces back to their origin in Descartes, "showing up" could be taken as the formation of an internal representation. But Noë skillfully and persuasively argues against the usefulness of the concept of internal representations. *Out of Our Heads* never clarifies what it means for a world to "show up."

Let us therefore consider for ourselves what "showing up" could possibly mean. Since Noë rejects Cartesian dualism, "showing up" does not seem to mean, for him, showing up in a non-physical, spiritual consciousness. Since Noë also rejects neural identity theory, "showing up" could not mean showing up wholly as activity within the nervous system. Noë says that consciousness is like a dance (rather than like digestion). We may ask then, when and where does a dance show up? When and where does a square dance or a waltz show up?

A waltz shows up when music in three-quarter time is being played and people are moving together in a certain way. The concept of a dance has fuzzy edges, but it is usually easy to discriminate between situations where a waltz has shown up and situations where it hasn't. The place where a waltz shows up is on the dance floor. The dance does not exist in any identifiable form inside the heads of the dancers—not in their brains, and not in their peripheral nervous systems. To imagine that a dance shows up anywhere inside the dancers is like imagining that the time shows up inside a clock. Certainly there is a mechanism inside the dancers (or the clock), and they could not be dancing (or indicating the time) unless the mechanism was in working order. Moreover, by exploring the innards of the dancers, a future brain scientist might conceivably be able to infer that they were waltzing. But if you were mainly interested in the waltz itself (if you were a choreographer, for instance) it would be foolish to do so. Noë makes this perfectly clear over and over again. The very title of his book implies that when a dance "shows up" it shows up in the overt behavior of the dancers, not inside their heads, and still less anywhere else inside their bodies.

To take another example, a baseball game normally consists of 18 people hitting, pitching, fielding, running bases, and so on. A baseball game shows up on the field where it is played and nowhere else. Moreover, each of the players is playing the game from the first pitch to the last, even while she is standing stock still in the outfield, even while she is sitting on the bench while a teammate bats. On another field in England, a game of cricket may be showing up at the same time. Another player may be standing stock still in that outfield in the exact same stance as the baseball player in the United States. Yet, even though they are doing the exact same thing, even though their actions at the moment are identical, the games they are playing are obviously different. What counts for the game that shows up is not what any one player is doing at this very moment but what she is doing in its temporal and social contexts. If the question you are asking is what shows up, where does it show up and when does it show up, the context is more important than the individual act.

However, whereas dances, baseball games, and even the movements of clock hands are *like* consciousness in certain ways, they are not conscious acts. Noë's point, in contrasting dancing to digestion, is that a dance (like consciousness) is behavior of our *whole* bodies in the context of their external temporal and social environments, rather than behavior of something within our bodies in the context of other internal events. A dance is clearly a behavioral pattern. According to Noë, consciousness is *like* dancing in the sense that both are behavior of our whole bodies. Then what is the *difference* between dancing and consciousness that makes one "merely" a behavioral pattern and the other a mental event? This is what Noë never makes clear. The difference cannot be that consciousness is internal whereas dancing is external because their common externality is precisely the sense in which Noë claims they are alike. The difference cannot be that consciousness could not occur without a complex neural mechanism because dancing also could not occur without a complex neural mechanism. Then what is it?

Suppose you were passing by a ballfield where a baseball game was occurring (was showing up) and you called to a player in the outfield and asked her, "Do you know that you are playing baseball?" That would be a stupid question, but it would not be a meaningless one. The player might reply, "You idiot, of course I know I'm playing baseball." Obviously, she knows that she is playing baseball at the same time that she is playing it. She knew it before she answered your question and after she answered it. At some point before the game she probably knew that she was going to play baseball, and after the game she will know that she was playing baseball. Her knowledge shows up not only in her answer to your question, but also in her behavior prior to the game, during the game, and after the game, perhaps long after. The game that shows up on the field is an abstract concept—the same concept for players and spectators. When they talk about the game afterward, they are all talking about the same thing. (Similarly, a dance, even a solo dance, is the same dance for the dancer as it is for the spectators.) However, the *knowledge* of the game is different for the pitcher, the outfielder, and the spectator. First, the behavior that constitutes the knowledge is different for each of them; second, the behavior that constitutes that knowledge starts in advance of the actual game and ends long after it is over.

The outfielder's answer to your question is not by itself her knowledge. As Noë might say, it is *mere* behavior; it is knowledge only in a certain context. The crucial question, the question that Noë does not clearly answer, is *what is that context*? Is it:

1. An event or a series of events in a non-physical mind located deep within her brain?
2. Neural activity in a specific area of her brain?
3. A more complex "field" of neural activity together with neural feedback from her actions?
4. Covert behavior: her unobservable muscular movements and what she says and pictures to herself before, during, and after the game? (Note that #4 must identify mind with the unobserved movements themselves, not private perception of the movements through proprioception. Otherwise #4 becomes identical with #2 or #3.)
5. The overt behavioral pattern that contains her answer: her making an appointment to play, her preparations beforehand, the character of her actions on the field, what she says to others about the game, what they say to her, and her verbal and non-verbal behavior afterward?
6. Or is it better after all to eliminate all mental terms from our scientific vocabulary?

Noë implicitly rejects #6. Let us reject #6 as well. I believe that it is the acceptance of #6 by behaviorists that has led to the marginalization of behaviorism within academic experimental psychology and its demonization within philosophy. Noë explicitly rejects #1, #2, and #3. He does not consider #4, a concept of mind accepted by many behaviorists. I believe that the area between #3 and #5, covert muscular movement, is much too narrow to contain all of our mental lives. It has all the disadvantages of #3 without any of the complexity that, it would seem, a theory of mind would require. But this is not the place to argue the point (see Chapter 10, especially my response to Schlinger, for such an argument).

Noë seems to reject #5. Of the six alternatives I list, only #5 implies that, in principle, the outfielder has no better access to her own mind than does a hypothetical observer, close to her, who could observe all of her actions. In fact, #5 implies that an observer may know the outfielder's mental state better than she herself does, since the observer's view is more objective and comprehensive than hers. Noë does assert that the minds of others may be known to us on the basis of our interactions with them. He says (p. 32), "That my wife and children and parents are thinking, feeling beings, that a world shows up for them—that they are not *mere* automata—is something that only insanity could ever allow me to question" (italics added). But there is that word "mere" again. What would be so "mere" about an automaton that behaved exactly the way Noë's wife and children behave? The extra requirement (that a world "show up" for them) seems to me to be a back-door way of smuggling Cartesian dualism (#1) into a theory of mind.

My own preference is for #5. My practical reason for holding #5 is that it fits with the evidence from my current research areas: self-control and altruism. The difference between a self-controlled act or an altruistic act, on the one hand, and an impulsive or selfish act, on the other, is most meaningfully conceived as a difference in the extent of the overt pattern of which the act is a part. Impulsive and selfish acts are easily explained in molecular terms; their reinforcers are evident. But the reinforcers of self-controlled and altruistic acts are abstract and are spread out in time and social space. A self-controlled act may have no reinforcer whatsoever. Refusal of a single cigarette, as I said, may *never* be reinforced in a normal social setting. Good health and social acceptability reinforce only widespread patterns of cigarette refusal. Self-control is thus a characteristic of the mind in a way that impulsiveness is not. Similarly, particular altruistic acts are not reinforced. If an act were extrinsically reinforced it would not be altruistic—by definition. But widespread patterns of altruistic acts may be intrinsically valuable or may be reinforced by generally improved social relations not contingent on any single act (see Chapters 7 and 8 for discussions of self-control and altruism). If consciousness were just body and world, as #5 implies, rather than "brain, body, and world," as Noë repeatedly asserts, a science of consciousness would be a purely behavioral science; consciousness would be a relationship between the organism as a whole and its environment.

The centerpiece of Noë's book is his attack on internal representations and the neurophysiological studies underlying them. He rejects the fanciful speculations of Francis Crick, whom he quotes: "You, your joys and your sorrows, your memories and your ambitions, your sense of personal identity and free will, are nothing more than the behavior of a vast assembly of nerve cells and their associated molecules" (p. 5). He also rejects the entire research program for which Hubel and Wiesel won the Nobel Prize. Noë attacks "... the common belief among neuroscientists that vision presented the brain with a problem in information processing, and that the parts of the brain dedicated to vision could be thought of as. . . machines for 'transforming information' represented in one system of neurons into progressively more refined and complex representations of what is seen" (p. 156). Before you can ask *how* the brain processes visual stimuli, Noë asserts, you have to ask *why* the person is making a visual discrimination in the first place: "You can't understand how a particular cash register works if you don't understand what it is for. . ." (p. 158). Sometimes, he implies, brain research just gets in the way of what really matters:

> The fact that we can see thanks only to the workings of our wet, sticky, meat-slab brains doesn't make seeing an intrinsically neuronal activity any more than chess is . . . . And, crucially, you don't need to understand how brains work or how computers are electrically engineered to understand that. Chess is only played by systems (people and machines) made out of atoms and electrons. But chess isn't a phenomenon that can be understood at that level. And the same is so for vision. (p. 159)
>
> Computers can't think on their own any more than hammers can pound in nails on their own. They are tools we use to think with. For this reason we make no progress in trying to understand how brains think by supposing they are computers. In any case, brains don't think: they don't have minds; animals do. To understand the contribution of the brain to the life of the mind, we need to give up once and for all the idea that minds are achieved inside us by internal goings on. Once this is clear, we are forced to rethink the value even of Nobel Prize-winning research [referring to that of Hubel and Wiesel]. (p. 169)

Noë rejects what he sees as the folk-psychological view that the mind exists in the brain alone. He wishes to extend our concept of mind out from the brain and into the external world. These are not insignificant steps toward a revival of behaviorism within philosophy. But, while reaching out, Noë hangs on to the undefined notion of a world "showing up" as central to his concept of consciousness. This, it seems to me, is a hindrance on the road to understanding the mind.

There is nowhere in *Out of Our Heads* a concept of behavioral patterns extended in time—of weeks, months, or years. Thus, if there is a mental state, but no immediate behavior to signify that state, the only place to look for it is (at least partially) within the organism. Such an outlook is not unique to Noë. None of the three books I discuss in this chapter adopts a temporally extended view of behavior. This is especially true of Derek Melser's *The Act of Thinking*. Like Noë, Melser is critical of the notion that mental events occur in the brain. Melser focuses on *thinking* rather than *consciousness*, but his approach to the question of whether mind equals brain is similar to that of Noë. Melser distinguishes between *action* and what he calls *process*. A process is what might go on in a computer or a brain—a mechanical or neural chain or network of cause and effect. An action, on the other hand, is done with purpose, for the sake of its consequences:

> The important thing. . . is that both the layperson and the cognitive scientist, by assuming that thinking is a process that goes on in people's heads, are excluding in advance the possibility I want to consider: that thinking may be a kind of action, something the person actually does . . . . [D]espite the weight of popular and expert opinion, the possibility of thinking's being an action of the person is a very real one. And by "action" I mean an ordinary, albeit unique, learned and voluntary action. (pp. 3–4)

The kinds of actions that Melser believes are necessary for thought are learned communicative actions, mainly verbal. However, simple verbal interactions with other people are not themselves thoughts. Thoughts are rather what he calls "tokens" of such communicative actions. He says, "... there are two ingredients in the act of thinking, both themselves actional. The first is our ability to do things in concert. The second is our ability to—jointly with others or alone—perform concerted activity in merely token form" (p. 13). Such "tokening" is like what early behaviorists called "vicarious trial and error" (VTE). The rat reaches a choice point of a T-maze and then looks both ways, exposing itself to the stimuli of both alleys, hesitating about which way to go. There is nothing wrong with this concept as long as the hesitations are overt. However, when the rat's VTEs are conceived to be entirely internal, divorced from any environmental feedback whatsoever, they lose their function and become vacuous. The same might be said about Melser's tokens. A token isn't worth anything if it can't be cashed in. Consider the following:

> Tokening is a learned skill whereby parts and aspects of concerted activity are merely incepted by participants, rather than being fully performed. As the child masters more sophisticated and covert ways of tokening actions, he eventually becomes able to, in this special token way, "rehearse" concerted activity while alone. And the rehearsing may be done without any overt movement. Basically, this is thinking. (p. 13)

The problem is that once actions become wholly covert, out of contact with the environment, they are no longer *actions*, as he defines them, but must be identical with *processes*, that is, identical with purely neural or covert muscular movement.

Melser distinguishes his theory from that of both "the layperson and the cognitive scientist"—that thinking goes on in "people's heads"—and argues against this concept. But ultimately the only difference between his theory and theirs is that his includes the peripheral as well as the central nervous system. Melser rejects the notion that actions may occur wholly within the brain. In the brain, according to him, are only processes. But he does not explain the essential difference between events in the brain that make them processes and events in the peripheral nervous system that make them actions. Shifting the area of mental activity from the central nervous system to the central-plus-peripheral nervous system is some progress; but, I believe, for real progress in psychology, consciousness, thought, and all mental activity must be brought out of the head and body altogether and conceived as patterns of interaction between whole organisms and the environment.

Clark, like Noë and Melser, is a philosopher of mind. Like them, he rejects the validity of internal representations and expands the concept of mind outward from the brain. His approach, however, is less based on current cognitive or neurophysiological research and more on robotics—the building of machines to perform practical tasks. Brains, in his conception, are just "controllers for embodied activity." This view, he says,

> ...demands a sweeping reform in our whole way of thinking about intelligent behavior. It requires us to abandon the idea (common since Descartes) of the mental as a realm distinct from the realm of the body; to abandon the idea of neat dividing lines between perception, cognition, and action; to abandon the idea of an executive center where the brain carries out high-level reasoning; and most of all, to abandon research methods that artificially divorce thought from embodied action-taking. (pp. xii–xiii)

In Clark's conception, the mind expands outward from the brain, outward from the peripheral nervous system, and into the world itself. A person's self is a flexible concept, variable just as you might put on a pair of roller skates and take them off:

> Some recent studies of infant development suggest that it, too, may be best understood in terms of the interactions of multiple local factors— factors that include, as equal partners, bodily growth, environmental factors, brain maturation, and learning. There is no "blueprint" for the

behavior in the brain, or in the genes—no more than there is a blue-print for flocking in the head of the bird. (p. 40)

Much of what we commonly identify as our mental capacities may ... turn out to be properties of the wider, environmentally extended systems of which human brains are just one (important) part .... There is, after all, a quite general difficulty in drawing a firm line between a user and a tool .... Some birds swallow small stones to aid digestion—are the stones tools, or, once ingested, simply parts of the bird? Is a tree, once climbed to escape a predator, a tool? What about a spider's web? (p. 214)

We build "designer environments" in which human reason is able to far outstrip the computational ambit of the unaugmented biological brain. Advanced reason is thus above all the realm of the scaffolded brain: the brain in its bodily context, interacting with a complex world of physical and social strictures. (p. 191)

More lasting extensions, such as that within social groups, are also discussed. "Organizations, factories, offices, institutions, and such," Clark says, "are the large-scale scaffolds of our distinctive cognitive success" (p. 186). A problem with this conception is that the scaffold does not touch the brain. The scaffolds that Clark cites are in the environment and are in touch with the body, not the brain.

Much interesting research is discussed in Clark's book; my own work with colleagues has taken me in a similar direction (Locey & Rachlin, 2012; Rachlin & Jones, 2010), but consciousness for Clark is firmly rooted in the brain. Clark is quite explicit about this:

A major danger attending to any revolutionary proposal in the sciences is that too much of the "old view" may be discarded .... This very danger attends, I believe, the New Roboticists' rejection of internal models, maps, and representations. Taken only as an injunction to beware the costs of central, integrated, symbolic models, the criticism is apt and important. But taken as a wholesale rejection of inner economies whose complexities include multiple action-centered representations and multiple partial world models, it would be a mistake .... (p. 22)

This makes sense in terms of robotics, the art and science of building machines to perform tasks requiring mental abilities. If you are building something, or even repairing something, you need to know how the insides work. In building a robot, it may conceivably help to think of internal structures as representing aspects of external behavior—or it may not. In building a car, for example, it may help to consider the position of parts of the steering mechanism as representing the position of the tires relative to the body of the car, or the direction of the car's movement relative to the road—or it may hinder. But psychologists are not building organisms. We have to work with what we are given. In the psychologist's task—prediction and control of the behavior of the whole organism—such internal hypothesizing can only hinder.

There is a crucial difference between the concepts of mind of these authors and that of the teleological behaviorism for which I have been arguing in this book. In common, we start with observations of verbal and non-verbal overt behavior as they interact with the world (the two black arrows pointing to the left in Figure 6.1). The difference lies in the extension of those observations that gives mental states their meaning. The extension proposed by these authors is spatial—reaching back into the brain and extending in the other direction to the social and physical world. Mine is temporal—reaching out into the social and physical worlds of the past and the future—keeping to the left of the heavy line in Figure 6.1 that divides body and world—explicitly avoiding reference to any intrinsically private events within the body.

Should Talking to Yourself Be Defined as Thinking?

How should talking to yourself (TTY) be classified? Is TTY behavior that may be reinforced (as depicted in Figure 6.1 to the left of the heavy vertical line)? Or is TTY part of a cognitive mechanism underlying thinking (as shown on the right)?

To gain a foothold on TTY's purpose, let us consider a TTY-like behavior that is nevertheless overt. The time is 2 p.m. You look in the refrigerator and pantry, observe what you lack for tonight's supper, write down a shopping list, go to the supermarket, consult the list and buy the items on it, come home, put the items in the refrigerator and pantry, tear up the list, and throw it away. That evening you use some fraction of what you bought in the process of cooking supper. Then you eat the supper. A lot of behavior is going on in this sequence, but let us focus only on the creation, use, and destruction of the list. You needn't have made a list at all. You could have (a) just memorized the names of the items, and then on the way to the supermarket, hum a song, or picture to yourself your supper as it would look all prepared, or go over the speech you are to deliver that night. And then you could recall the items from your memorized list as you put them in the cart. Or, if like me you have a terrible short-term memory, you could have (b) repeated to yourself, over and over, the unbought items' names (i.e., TTY) until they were all in the cart. Or, if this last tactic might get you run over on the way to the supermarket, you could (c) actually write down the list of items. It is clear, I believe, that all three actions have the same immediate function—as part of the pattern that will provide you with supper tonight and (perhaps) on some subsequent nights.

Going to the supermarket may consist of walking, driving, bicycling, and so on. Walking to the supermarket in turn may consist of myriad sets of muscular movements depending on distance, the path you take, the condition of your knees, and so on. The particular form of each of the three methods [(a) short-term memory; (b) TTY; (c) making an actual list] involves the brain, the peripheral nervous system, and the outside world. Moreover, the central locus of the memory *mechanism*, which bridges the time between looking in your home refrigerator or pantry and placing an item in your shopping cart, differs among the three methods. In (a) the memory occurs primarily somewhere in your brain; in (b) it occurs primarily in your peripheral nervous system and muscles; in (c) it occurs primarily on the paper on which you wrote down the list. Which of the three (if any) is thinking, and which (if any) is not thinking? The answer may reside in a distinction between *behavior*, on the one hand, and the *mechanism* underlying behavior, on the other. (See Chapter 10, especially Schlinger's comments and my response to them, for a further discussion of *behavior* versus *mechanism*.) One of the central claims of teleological behaviorism is that in psychology the term *behavior* should be reserved for behavior of the whole organism (i.e., overt behavior) and that the actions of the brain, the peripheral nervous system, and individual muscles are most usefully considered as components of the mechanism underlying behavior, but not as behavior itself. By analogy, one may make a distinction between the "behavior" of a clock and its internal mechanism. In this analogy, the clock's "behavior" refers to the position of the hands (or its digital reading) in contact with the world outside the clock, and directly serving its function—telling time. Telling time is the "behavior" of the clock as a whole, so to speak. The clock's mechanism (crucially important as it is) exists only to move the hands, and is entirely subservient to that function.

How does that distinction apply to the three methods of remembering the list? It seems obvious that all three have the same function (obtaining the components of supper) but that they carry out that function in different ways. In other words, the mechanism differs in the three cases, but the function is the same. I would further argue that in all three behaviors (a), (b), and (c) are parts of a thoughtful pattern; the thought is the same (to the extent that the function is the same) in the three cases. In the three ways of carrying out the same function we do *not* have three different kinds of thought. That would be an extremely wasteful and inexact way of classifying mental acts. Rather, we have just one kind of thought carried out by three different mechanisms.

Let us first consider (a), just memorizing the list. Even though we may not presently know exactly how it works and exactly where in the brain it is, short-term memory is clearly part of the mechanism by which the wider function of preparing supper is accomplished. The neural behavior that bridges the interval between making the list and dropping the items in the supermarket cart is clearly not overt behavior. Even if neural behavior were shown to be controlled directly by reinforcement (say, stimulation of a central brain "reward" center), such a process would be strictly dependent on its wider function—in this case, eating supper. Short-term memory is part of the internal mechanism underlying the complete process of getting supper—underlying the thought.

Now let us consider (b), TTY. Contrary to Melser (2004), discussed previously in this chapter, and contrary to many behaviorists (who call themselves *radical behaviorists*), TTY is not thinking. Neither is TTY a functionless rambling. Since we learn to do it and do it so frequently, TTY must have a function. But, because TTY is by definition covert and out of direct contact with sources of reinforcement, it must be part (in some cases an essential part) of the mechanism underlying thought, not thought itself. Thinking requires a motive and a pattern of overt behavior aimed at reaching a goal. When such behavior occurs, we label it thoughtful. Perhaps a non-human animal could be trained to make a list, the contents of which depend on required but missing items, obtain just those items, and then go on to assemble them as required. In such a case, the non-human (provided it satisfied criteria for animalhood, to be discussed in Chapter 10) would be thinking. To ascertain that the animal was indeed thinking, we may need to perform some behavioral tests (such as eliminating inadvertent signals from a human handler), but we would not have to know anything at all about events inside the animal.

Now let us consider (c), actually making the list. Clearly making a list of things to do and carrying it out may be reinforced. First, and most important, it is done by an intact, whole organism and is overt and accessible to environmental feedback. Although in childhood the components of making of a list might have been reinforced as a chain of discrete responses, each with its own conditioned reinforcer as feedback and serving as a discriminative stimulus for the next step, eventually adults can learn to simply make a whole list, which is reinforced as a unit. There may be some chains of overt behavior between the opening of the pantry and the eating of the food, but it would be exceedingly difficult to trace chains of discriminative stimulus, behavior, and reinforcer all the way from the pantry to the dinner table. Rather, patterns of behavior correlate with patterns of environmental signals and feedback all along the way. (Locey and Rachlin [2013] have shown with pigeon subjects that quite complex patterns may be reinforced as such by environmental contingencies without the buildup of chains of specific acts.) Moreover, there are temporal gaps between discriminative patterns and behavioral patterns, on the one hand, and between behavioral patterns and reinforcement on the other. But the thought itself lies in the whole behavioral pattern and its relation to larger goals (such as healthy eating), not what happens at this very moment in overt behavior, in covert muscular behavior, in the peripheral nervous system, and certainly not in the central nervous system. Chapter 9 will extend this way of thinking about thought to consciousness itself. But first, in Chapters 7 and 8, I will show how teleological behaviorism may be applied in the complex behavioral patterns of altruism and self-control where central processes seem to control (or fail to control) overt behavior.

Acknowledgment

Chapter 6 contains material from Rachlin (2012a).

The Evolution of Altruism
and Self-Control

If the mind consists of temporally extended patterns of overt behavior, as the previous three chapters claim, then it is fair to ask: How do these patterns develop and change? The answer is that they evolve over the lifetimes of individuals (behavioral evolution) in the same way that a species evolves over generations (biological evolution). In biological evolution, groups of organisms may be selected over individuals, resulting in altruistic behavior. Similarly, in behavioral evolution, patterns of behavior may be selected over individual acts, resulting in self-control. Any consistent pattern in the behavior of an organism must have evolved by biological selection over the species' history or must have evolved by behavioral selection over the individual's history. This chapter shows how such selection may result in self-controlled behavior or in altruistic behavior. As in biological evolution, the unit selected in behavioral evolution is not always an individual organism or an individual act, but may be a group of organisms or a pattern of acts extended in time or social space—the extended self.

The Evolution of Self-Control

Consider a squirrel saving nuts during the fall so as to have food available during the coming winter. Because it does not conflict with any other behavior, the squirrel's nut storing is not self-controlled. The squirrel just wakes up one fall morning, eats a bit, and goes about doing what it feels like doing, collecting nuts and placing them in the hollows of trees or burying them. Mother Nature, in the form of evolution by natural selection, arranged it in the past; squirrels that failed to store nuts in the fall tended to die during the coming winter, whereas squirrels that stored nuts (and remembered where they were) tended to live and reproduce. Over generations, squirrels evolved so that they tended to value nut storing for its own sake (rather than for the sake of having food to tide themselves over the winter months). But Mother Nature has not had enough time to work the same sort of magic on humans living in a modern society; it is a rare morning when we wake up and just feel like putting our money in the bank. What she has arranged in our case is a capacity to learn that consistently putting money in the bank is generally a good thing to do, even though we might not feel like doing it at the present moment.

Post-Darwinian psychologists noted that habits evolve over the lifetimes of individuals in the same way that the structure of a species evolves over generations (Thorndike, 1911/2000; Skinner, 1981). If a pigeon is hungry and gets a bit of food each time it pecks a lit button, its pecking rate increases. The food (the reinforcer) allows the act it follows to expand in the available time, whereas other acts, not reinforced, die out (are "extinguished"). Once the button-peck appears, it may be molded or "shaped." Just as the giraffe's long neck evolved by the enhanced survival of long-necked giraffes (as they were able to reach higher and higher into trees for food and spot lions over long distances on the African plains), so the pigeon's button-peck evolves. If the number of pecks needed to obtain the pellet is gradually increased, the pattern of pecking changes. Just as giraffes would have become extinct if, in the distant past, the height of the edible leaves on the trees had suddenly jumped from ten to twenty feet, so a pigeon's button-pecking would extinguish if the number of pecks needed to obtain the food (the "ratio" requirement) suddenly increased by 100. To shape pecking in numbers near the limit of the pigeon's ability, the ratio must be raised in small stages. The natural variation of the pigeon's pecking at each stage must include patterns that will be reinforced at the next stage. Selection by reinforcement, like natural selection, works only on behavior that is already present as a consequence of variation at a previous stage. That is, selection by reinforcement works on top of natural selection; natural selection provides the mechanism for selection by reinforcement to work. A primitive form of self-control comes to us by biological evolution, but the amazing degree of self-control we humans sometimes show is the result of behavioral evolution working on that primitive form. Behavioral evolution is what makes us the adaptable creatures that we are (Baum, 2005). Taking the biological and the behavioral processes of evolution together, if we observe any consistent pattern in the behavior of a human or non-human animal, that pattern must have evolved by natural selection over the history of the species or must have evolved by reinforcement over the history of the individual.

Much of the time, these two evolutionary processes work together—as in the normal development of language. But, in many cases, especially in our civilized society, they work at cross-purposes. Such cases constitute a very fundamental problem of self-control. In the past history of the human race, eating as much as you could whenever food became available was a valuable habit; it might be a long time before food became available again. Now, with food continuously available, eating whenever you have the chance is bad in many ways (Logue, 1988).

There is an apparent problem in extending the analogy with natural selection to self-control. Where is the reward when I pass by the bakery without entering, even though I am hungry and the smell wafting onto the street is extremely enticing and I have money in my pocket? What in general reinforces self-control? It is clear enough what reinforces lack of self-control. For an alcoholic, drinking is highly rewarding in itself. Drinking, in fact, may reinforce virtually any act the alcoholic is capable of doing. But refusing a drink is far from rewarding in itself and is rarely followed by anything pleasant; in fact, it may entail a great deal of pain. An alcoholic's single act of drink refusal is never externally reinforced, neither immediately nor later. To repeat, if an alcoholic forgoes a single drink, she does not wake up two weeks later healthier or happier, nor is a single drink refusal intrinsically rewarding—just the opposite. The value of drink refusal—in the form of health, social acceptability, job performance, and so forth—seems to depend on an already established habit of refusing drinks; to attain its high value, drink refusal must occur consistently over a period of time. To attain their high value, bakery avoidance and its equivalents must also occur consistently over a period of time. It seems as if self-control would be impossible because the pattern you need to establish (perhaps a very complex pattern) has to exist before its value is attained. Given this problem, how can a complex pattern of behavior evolve by reinforcement?

Let us consider a similar question as it appears in evolution by natural selection: How can very complex structures, such as the human eye, evolve by natural selection? Each part of the eye depends on other parts. It seems as if, until each part develops, the other parts would be useless. The retina cannot function without a lens to focus an image on it; the lens cannot function without a pupil to regulate the light (and what is the function of the pupil if there is no retina?) Finally, an optic nerve has to develop simultaneously with the eye to encode and transmit the image to the brain. And once encoded in the brain, then what? How does a pattern of neural states get converted into a pattern of behavioral discrimination? It is hard to conceive how the human eye could have developed in stages from primitive structures. For creationists, such development is impossible to conceive. *God had to have done it*, they think. But evolutionary biologists, studying primitive eyes in other organisms, have been able to trace a convincing story of how the human eye developed. [A light-sensitive patch of skin (the future retina) would be protected if it was in a depression, and would be more protected the deeper the depression. The more protected, the more sensitive it could be. As the depression grew deeper, into a hole with a light-sensitive bottom, the smaller and smaller entranceway, like a pinhole camera, would begin to focus light onto the retina. Further protection would come from a clear membrane over the hole. That would develop into a lens, and so forth.] Regardless of how complex and seemingly interdependent the parts of a behavioral pattern may be, they can be traced in stages to simpler patterns in development. To argue that the immense complexities observed in human self-controlled behavior could not have evolved through reinforcement is a kind of creationist argument. The creator, this time, is not God but something within the person—the soul, the self (as an internal entity), or the nervous system (see Baum, 2005, for an argument for the evolution of complex behavior over a person's lifetime).

One version of the creationist solution to the problem of self-control has been posited by some (I believe misguided) behavioral psychologists themselves. Failing to find extrinsic reinforcers for each component of self-controlled behavior, they posit events inside the person, usually inside the brain, representing reinforcement. In an alcoholic, for instance, such concrete internal representations would immediately reinforce individual drink refusals and counteract the innate immediate value of the drink. Another way these psychologists put it is that the reinforcers of self-controlled behavior become "internalized." It is as if, each time he refuses a drink, the alcoholic internally pats himself on the back for a job well done. An internal vision of the addict's future enhanced health, for instance, wells up inside him and supposedly reinforces each drink (or cigarette or dessert) refusal. But the concept of self-reinforcement, internal or external, has numerous empirical and theoretical problems. According to a well-supported concept of reinforcement (Premack, 1965), a reinforcer is a highly valued activity (such as eating) contingent on the performance of a less-valued activity (such as running). An internal or even an external activity that may be initiated or withheld at any time is by stipulation not contingent on any other activity. Patting yourself on the back, internally or externally, has all the reinforcing effect of taking a dollar bill out of your left pocket and putting it into your right pocket. Such "reinforcement" may serve to enhance proprioceptive feedback—like counting the number of cigarettes smoked—that may be part of an effective self-control program, but it does not function as a reinforcer.

Another putative problem with the concept of behavioral evolution of self-control (aside from the notion that human behavior is too complex to have evolved) lies in the abstract nature of the pattern. The alcoholic who cuts down from a quart of whisky a day to a glass of wine each night with dinner is not doing anything in particular during the time she is now not drinking; her drinking is just occurring at a much slower rate than before. Each day, the time spent not drinking may be filled with different activities. Every one of these activities cannot individually be more valuable than having a drink. What sustains the low drinking rate? The answer is that the low drinking rate itself is highly valuable in the life of the reformed alcoholic. But, like a probability, the reduced drinking rate is an abstract entity that has no existence at any one moment. You cannot point to it as you would point to an eye. Some alcoholics do learn to abstain or drink moderately. How do the highly abstract patterns in their behavior hold together, and how do they (sometimes) resist being broken up by temptation?

To answer this question, consider an evolutionary process called *group selection*. Imagine a (simplified) basketball league where the only factor that determined whether a player was retained on a team was points scored by that player (individual selection), and the only factor that determined whether a team was retained in the league (and the franchise not moved to another city) was games won by the team (group selection). It is generally recognized that, all other factors held equal, a team on which the individuals play unselfishly will win more games than a team on which they play selfishly. Yet, at the same time, the selfish players on each team will score more points than the unselfish players. Thus, individual selection works, in this fictional league, to promote selfishness whereas group selection works to promote unselfishness; the two selection processes are in conflict. Which will win out depends on many factors, including the variability within the group as compared to that between groups and on the relative rate of replacement; if players are replaced on teams relatively more frequently than teams are replaced in the league (as is the case in almost any real basketball league), then (other factors held constant) selfishness will come to dominate among players. However, if teams are replaced in the league relatively faster than players are replaced on teams, unselfishness will come to dominate (Boyd, Gintis, Bowles, & Richerson, 2005; Soltis, Boyd, & Richerson, 1995). One reason that players in real leagues, such as the NBA, *sometimes* come to play unselfishly despite the very slow rate of team replacement may be the frequent rate of coach replacement. The coach will be replaced if the team keeps losing games; he has an interest in the team's performance as a whole. The coach and the individual players are therefore to some extent in conflict.

Among non-humans there is considerable evidence that reinforcement selects not individual responses but patterns of individual responses. For example, if a rat is rewarded for running faster or slower down an alley or for pressing a lever faster or slower, it changes its rate not by adjusting its speed of running or pressing the lever but by periodically pausing more or less frequently between bursts of running or lever pressing, which, within bursts, remain constant in rate. Similarly, a person on a diet, when she eats, may not eat any slower than one not on a diet. The question is, can longer patterns—those constituting human self-control—evolve from simpler patterns over a person's lifetime, just as the complex human eye evolved from simpler light-sensitive organs? It is not possible to prove that every complex behavioral pattern we exhibit has evolved over our lives from simpler patterns [and was not, as in a cognitive explanation, created by an internal logic mechanism overcoming an equally internal "visceral" force (Loewenstein, 1996)]. But there is considerable evidence that when behavior is organized into coherent patterns, self-control increases. For example, in choosing between an immediate money reward and a non-immediate but larger earning rate, with no 1:1 relationship to any particular choice, people forced to make choices in groups of four chose the larger overall rate significantly more frequently than did people choosing on a case-by-case basis (Rachlin, 1995). That is, we do know that reinforcement may act directly on patterns of acts (without necessitating that chains be built up from individual acts, each followed by its own reinforcer).

Taking a teleological and behavioral view of self-control problems goes contrary to our normal way of thinking about self-control. The very term *self-control* seems to imply a force arising from inside—a force opposed to control by the environment. This chapter argues, however, that a change in such thinking—self-control as adaptation to abstract aspects of the environment, impulsiveness as adaptation to particular aspects of the environment—may be worth the effort involved. Teleological behaviorism conveys clarity and transparency to psychological theory; it fits psychology neatly into evolutionary biology by extending Darwinian evolution to behavior change within a person's lifetime.

In psychology, when a theory reaches the limits of what it can explain, further development has traditionally proceeded by postulation of normally unobserved events within the organism. To explain the existence of temporally extended acts such as dessert refusal, modern cognitive and neural theories of self-control postulate often elegant and intuitively compelling current, internal representations. Such representations provide a currently existent blueprint, as it were, for the construction of the acts over time and avoid causation at a temporal distance. Even Skinner (1974) speculated that *covert* behavior might be *covertly* reinforced. For him, all non-reflexive learning had to be explained in terms of immediate reinforcement, either primary or conditioned. Some specific reinforcing event (or a signal of such an event) had to immediately follow every action, or that action could not increase in rate, Skinner said. A person who refuses a second dessert might thus be covertly telling herself what a virtuous person she is. But you may question whether by so doing she increases her future tendency to refuse desserts.

Teleological behaviorism in such circumstances looks further in time rather than deeper in space. When it cannot explain some aspect of behavior in terms of the narrow contingencies of the present environment, teleological behaviorism looks not into the interior of the person (deeper in space) but into the contingencies of the person's wider, long-term environment. A person's current dessert refusal is seen as part of a pattern of similar acts maintained over the long run (if it is maintained) by social approval, increased health, and so forth, which do not stand in any 1:1 relation with a specific act. [When it cannot explain some aspect of individual behavior—an altruistic act, for instance—even in those terms, teleological behaviorism looks, as we shall see, to the contingencies of reinforcement of the social group.]

Let us say that an alcoholic has been abstinent for six months and is now at a party where drinks are freely available. She then has to put aside her *current* preference, her *current* set of values, and behave consistently with the pattern begun six months ago. To put it another way, she must learn to respect and cooperate with her past and future selves—and to behave so as to maximize their interests as a group even when they conflict with those of her present self. It is in the best interests of her present self to have a drink. In the short run, the drink will be pleasurable; in the long run, *this individual drink* will not harm her health or cause her to lose her job or alienate her family. But over her life, *a pattern of drinking at a high rate* has been harmful, while *a pattern of abstaining* (or social drinking) has been valuable. She must learn to ignore the rewards and punishers (distant as well as present) of her individual acts and behave so as to maximize the rewards of extended patterns.

Learning to Be Altruistic

Imagine an environment—say, a jungle—with tribes of people all competing against each other for limited natural resources. Just as with basketball teams, tribes within which individuals act altruistically (i.e., possess genes that generate altruistic behavior) will tend to out-compete tribes within which individuals act selfishly. But at the same time, within each tribe, selfish individuals (where selfishness is that of the gene—including sacrifice to preserve the lives of blood relatives) will out-compete unselfish individuals. Individuals in successful groups may have predispositions to behave selflessly, cooperatively, altruistically. These predispositions exist along with our selfish tendencies—just as our predispositions to appear attractive, succeed at work, and be healthy exist along with our tendencies to overeat, overdrink, oversleep, and so on.

Since altruistic tendencies are inherited, they must vary. Anyone with eyes to see will note that some people are more altruistic, generous, and cooperative than others. The question I shall now consider is: If you are born with a tendency to be selfish, are you fated to be selfish forever, or can you learn to be altruistic? Are we fated to be altruistic or selfish to whatever degree we were born with—regardless of our experiences? Change in behavior over a person's lifetime (learning) proceeds by means of reinforcement and punishment through the environment. Since this is so, and since altruistic acts are by definition unreinforced (otherwise they wouldn't be altruistic—we'd be getting something from them), how can altruism possibly be learned? As with self-control, the way to approach this question is to recognize that, parallel to the idea of group selection of *organisms* (responsible for inheritance of altruistic tendencies), there is another kind of group selection—selection by reinforcement of (patterns of) responses over the lifetimes of individuals.

Let us reconsider the question: Does selection by reinforcement act exclusively on individual actions, or can it act on groups of actions? [Ainslie (2001), in accord with Skinner (1938), believes that individual extrinsic reinforcers (including reinforcers discounted by their delays from the present moment) may strengthen individual discrete responses but not abstract patterns of responses (the kind constituting self-control and usually thought of as rules of personal conduct). For Ainslie, abstract patterns arise by a process of *internal* bargaining among long-term, medium-term, and short-term interests of the individual. I believe, however, that abstract patterns of behavior may be selected as such by a process akin to group selection of individual organisms (Rachlin, 2002).] Is there such a thing as group selection of behavior over the lifetime of an individual organism? Again, the answer depends on the relative rate of selection of individual actions and groups of actions. In this respect, altruism is no more mysterious than self-control. Although it is not possible to sacrifice your life in the present for your future benefit, it is possible to sacrifice your life for the sake of maintaining a consistent pattern of behavior in which you have heavily invested—as did Socrates, who preferred to die rather than disobey the laws of Athens. Individual acts of altruism that seem inexplicable when considered on a case-by-case basis, such as that of the New York City man who risked his own life by jumping onto the subway tracks to save a stranger's life, are no more mysterious (in principle) than a person stopping for a red light when there are no cars in the cross-street and no police in sight. In both cases, a valuable pattern is being maintained. Making temporal or social decisions on a case-by-case basis is generally a bad policy because we tend to overestimate the value of a single immediate reward relative to the value of patterns of behavior spread out in time or social space.

The goal of behavioral analysis is to identify reinforcers of acts. But, as I just noted, an individual altruistic act apparently has no reinforcer; if it did, it would not be altruistic. Altruism thus seems to defy behavioral analysis. Altruistic acts have been defined, in economic terms, as "…costly acts that confer economic benefits on other individuals" (Fehr & Fischbacher, 2003). This apt definition does not say that the cost to the actor and the benefit to others must be equally valued. And, it does not say whether the "other individuals" are relatives of, friends of, or complete strangers to the actor. If you put a dollar in a vending machine and someone else gets (and eats) the candy bar, your act is altruistic according to the definition above. It may be that few of us would pay a dollar to give a perfect stranger a candy bar, but we might very well pay a penny. Or, if the benefit to the stranger were very high (say, he was starving) we might pay a dollar—or even more than a dollar—to give him a candy bar. Or, if the beneficiary were not a stranger but our own child (and we were not at the moment worrying about cavities or obesity), many of us would pay the dollar. Such acts, fitting within Fehr and Fischbacher's definition of altruism, are extremely common in everyday life; behavioral analysis cannot just ignore them.

To illustrate how common altruistic behavior is, consider the multiperson prisoner's dilemma game that I have played with audiences over the last 15 years at public lectures. I call it "the lecture game." At the start of the lecture game, blank index cards are handed out to 10 random members of the audience, and the others are asked (as I ask the reader) to imagine that they had received a card. Each of the 10 players is then asked to choose X or Y subject to the following rules (displayed on a slide):

1. If you choose Y you will receive $100 times Z.
2. If you choose X you will receive $100 times Z plus a bonus of $300.
3. Z equals the number of (the 10) players who choose Y.

The audience is told, regretfully, that the money is purely hypothetical; then several properties of the game are pointed out. First, for any particular player, it is always better to choose X. By choosing X, a player subtracts 1 from Z and thereby loses $100 but more than makes up for that loss by the $300 bonus. The net gain for choosing X is therefore $200, *regardless of what anyone else chooses*. The point is then emphasized further by saying that any lawyer would advise choosing X.

It is then noted that if everyone obeyed their lawyers and chose X, Z would equal zero and each person would earn just $300, whereas if everyone disobeyed their lawyers and chose Y, Z would equal 10 and each person would earn $1,000; hence the dilemma. It is then pointed out that there is no right or wrong answer and that all choices will be forever anonymous. The 10 audience members with cards are then asked to mark them with X or Y as they would if the money were real, and the cards are collected.

Over the years I have played this game dozens of times: with college students, with philosophers, with economists (American-capitalist and Italian-socialist), with professors of game theory, with computer scientists, and with psychologists (American, Japanese, and Polish). The median response is 5 Ys to 5 Xs. If there is any bias it is usually in the direction of more Ys than Xs. After the game is played and the choices are counted, the chart in Figure 7.1 is shown to the audience and is used to look up the earnings of the X- and Y-choosers. For example, if 5 of the 10 participants choose Y, $Z = 5$ (note that the horizontal axis runs backward) and each Y-chooser gets $500 while each X-chooser gets $800. Standard decision-theory terminology calls choosing X "defecting" and choosing Y "cooperating," but these loaded terms are not used with the audience.

Although the money earned in the lecture game is hypothetical, laboratory experiments with real money (albeit in far lesser amounts) have found significant numbers of cooperators in "one-shot," multiperson games such as this one (Camerer, 2003; Locey, Jones, & Rachlin, 2011). Because a Y-choice always earns $200 less than an X-choice, choosing Y is a "costly act." Because a Y-choice increases Z by 1, and each of the 9 other players earns $100 more than he or she would have earned otherwise, choosing Y "confers economic benefits on other

LECTURE GAME

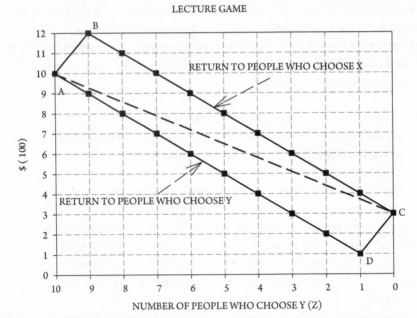

Figure 7.1 Diagram of multiperson lecture game. Lines A–D and B–C show returns to players who choose Y (cooperate) or choose X (defect) as a function of the decreasing number of players (out of 10) who choose Y (note reversed x-axis). The dashed line shows average earnings across the 10 players.

individuals." Because the choices are completely anonymous, it cannot be claimed that a player's reputation would be enhanced by choosing Y. Thus, according to Fehr and Fischbacher's definition, Y-choices in the lecture game are altruistic. Altruism towards one's family members may be explained in terms of common genes (Hamilton, 1964), but it is unlikely that lecture-game players were closely related. Although there is indeed a bias in altruistic behavior toward relatives over non-relatives (Jones & Rachlin, 2008), numerous instances of altruism in everyday life are directed toward friends, acquaintances, and even complete strangers.

The philosopher Derek Parfit (1984) listed a sample of situations from everyday life modeled by multiperson prisoner's dilemma games such as the lecture game:

> Commuters: Each goes faster if he drives, but if all drive each goes slower than if all take busses;
> Soldiers: Each will be safer if he turns and runs, but if all do more will be killed than if none do;
> Fishermen: When the sea is overfished, it can be better for each if he tries to catch more, worse for each if all do;
> Peasants: When the land is overcrowded, it can be better for each if he or she has more children, worse for each if all do;

There are countless other cases. It can be better for each if he adds to pollution, uses more energy, jumps queues, and breaks agreements; but if all do these things, that can be worse for each than if none do . . . . In most of these cases the following is true. If each rather than none does what will be better for himself, or his family, or those he loves, this will be worse for everyone. (pp. 61–62)

Some of the situations Parfit cites (fishermen, peasants) may be described in terms of Hardin's (1968) "tragedy of the commons"—overuse by individuals of a common resource; all are instances of conflict between individual and social good.

Sometimes, depending on circumstances, I follow the lecture game by a discussion (without revealing what anyone actually chose) of why a person should choose Y in this anonymous game. One reason that people often give for choosing Y is that they believe that many or most of the other players will choose Y. This rationale is common, but not strictly rational. Since the cost of a Y-choice is constant at $200, regardless of what anyone else chooses, what anyone else chooses should, in theory, not influence any person's individual choice. What others choose in this game will indeed have a strong effect on a player's earnings. But, within this one-shot, anonymous game, no player can have any direct influence on another player's choice. It is true that, regardless of what she chooses, it will be best for her if all of the *other* players choose Y; if she, too, chooses Y she would then earn $1,000. But, given that all 9 other players choose Y, she will be still better off if she alone chooses X—because then she will earn $1,200.

Parfit (1984, pp. 100–101) would consider choosing Y because you believe that others will choose Y to be a rationale for cooperating; he makes an appealing suggestion for quantifying this rationale. First, he suggests, determine how much you would earn if all players, including you, defected (chose X); in the lecture game, that would be $300. Then make your best guess of how many other players will probably cooperate (how many would choose Y). Then determine how much you would earn if you also cooperated. If the amount you would earn by cooperating is at least as great as the amount you would earn if all players, including you, defected, then, according to Parfit, you should cooperate.

Let us follow Parfit's directions: In order to earn $300 or more by cooperating in the lecture game, at least 2 *other* players would also have to cooperate. If you were a player in the lecture game, knowing that about half of the 10 players usually cooperate, and you wanted to follow Parfit's suggestion, you would cooperate. However, as Parfit admits, his suggestion does not resolve the dilemma. If two other lecture-game players chose Y and you also chose Y, you would earn $300, whereas if you had chosen X, you would have earned $500. Why should you not have chosen X? Although Parfit's suggestion has intuitive appeal and corresponds to people's verbal rationalizations, it is not a good explanation, in itself, of why people behave altruistically.

A second reason that people may give for choosing Y is simply that choosing Y is altruistic (or good or generous or public-spirited) and they see themselves as altruistic (or good or generous or public-spirited) people. Choosing X would not fit in with their self-image and would make them feel bad about themselves. I believe that this logically vacuous reason for cooperating is actually a good reason and is worth discussing in some detail. But it is first necessary to outline a behavioral concept of the self—to answer the question: Where does one person end and another begin? Skinner (1969) claimed that the skin is not important as a boundary. I agree with this claim, but for reasons different from Skinner's. Skinner meant that events *within* the skin are subject to behavioral investigation (Zuriff, 1979). I take Skinner's earlier position that the proper sphere of behavior analysis is the organism as a whole (Skinner, 1938). But, like the philosophers discussed in Chapter 6, I see the organism as extending *beyond* the skin.

The Extended Self

Parfit (1984) argues for what he calls *reductionism* (p. 211): "Each person's existence just involves the existence of a brain and body, the doing of certain deeds, the thinking of certain thoughts, the occurrence of certain experiences, and so on." According to Parfit, individual actions take time and overlap with each other, giving us the illusion of a continuous self. But, aside from that overlap, there is no "further thing"—either spiritual or physical—to a person's self. You may have as few interests in common with yourself 20 years from now as you do currently with a distant cousin. A person's continuous character is, according to Parfit, no more (or less) real than the character we ascribe to groups of people such as families, clubs, firms, or nations. He says (p. 211): "Most of us are reductionists about nations . . . . Nations exist. Though nations exist, a nation is not an entity that exists separately, apart from its citizens and its territory."

What, then, does tie our actions together, if not a central self? The answer is that abstract, broadly based social situations signaling consistent reinforcement contingencies ("meta-discriminative stimuli") can tie a person's actions together over extended periods. [To illustrate: I met my wife a long time ago at The New School in New York City. We got married in City Hall—no fancy wedding or ceremony, no bright line to mark the division. One day we were single and the next day we were married. About a week later, we were entering the psychology department chairman's office. The secretary said, "Oh, here come the Rachlins!" I looked around, was it my mother and father? It took me a while to realize that my wife and I were the Rachlins. But that feeling was not something mystical inside me. What the secretary said was actually the first appearance of a meta-discriminative stimulus for my behavior and my wife's behavior over a long period of time. At that point, none of the reinforcers correlated with the patterns of married life had yet kicked in. The discrimination was just beginning to evolve; I was confused. Unromantic? Yes, if you believe that love occurs in your heart. But not at all unromantic if you believe that love occurs between people. In any case, the concept that highly abstract and temporally extended events may be discriminative stimuli is helpful for understanding (that is, predicting and controlling) behavior.]

Parfit supposes that if there were a coherent self it would exist inside the person. However, if the self were actually a set of patterns in a person's behavior controlled by meta-discriminative stimuli, as I suppose, those patterns, hence the self, could extend over significant intervals in a person's life (see Chapter 11 for illustrations of long-term coherency and incoherency in behavioral patterning).

If your future self is in principle no closer to your present self than is another person, it follows that there is no essential difference between your relations to your future self and your relations to other people. Since your concern or lack of concern for other people involves *moral* issues, Parfit says, so does your concern or lack of concern for your future self. Therefore, issues of social cooperation and altruism on the one hand and self-control on the other are treated in the same way. A motorcyclist's refusal to wear a helmet would be, for Parfit, a moral issue, not just because other people may have to pay a price for her brain injury, but also because her future self may have to pay a price.

Parfit's reductionist view of the self would be behavioristic as well, were it not for his supernatural view of the mind. For him, "the thinking of certain thoughts" is akin to William James's "stream of consciousness" (James, 1890/1950) [Chapter 9 will discuss consciousness and the stream of consciousness in some detail]. From a teleological-behavioral viewpoint, however, both "the thinking of certain thoughts" and "the occurrence of certain experiences" are nothing but "the doing of certain deeds." Thought and experience both may be understood in terms of temporally extended patterns of overt behavior (the doing of deeds). A person's self consists of the temporal extension and overlap of that person's various overt behavioral patterns (Rachlin, 1994, 2010a). In human as well as non-human existence, many behavioral patterns are coordinated with those of others (other brains and bodies). Their overlap—their common interest—extends our selves nearer or further into our society.

Altruism and Evolution

Because altruistic behavior is so common and so useful in human society, it seems likely that biological, behavioral, and cultural evolution as well work together to produce it. Several mechanisms for biological evolution of altruism have been proposed. One, discussed above, relies on the selection of *groups* of altruistic organisms as units even under conditions where *individuals* are selected for selfishness (Sober & D. S. Wilson, 1998; Soltis, Boyd, & Richerson, 1995; E. O. Wilson, 2012; D. S. Wilson & E. O. Wilson, 2008). As we said earlier in the chapter, a tribe, within which there is little individual altruism, may be forced to move out of a fertile area and be replaced by another group within which there is a high level of altruism, even though the former tribe may have stronger or more skillful individual members. Mathematical models of group selection show that the crucial factors for group selection are the size of the groups, migration between them, variability between and within groups, and rate of replacement of groups within the larger population relative to the rate of replacement of individuals within the groups (Boyd, Gintis, Bowles, & Richerson, 2005; Soltis, Boyd, & Richerson, 1995). [There is much current debate within biology about the extent to which group selection has prevailed within the biological evolution of species. Among the most prominent biologists, E. O. Wilson (2012) believes that evolution occurs on many levels ranging from cells to organs to organisms to groups of organisms (including ants, on which Wilson is among the world's foremost authorities). Others, perhaps the majority, believe that biological group selection is rare or nonexistent among social groups. These biologists explain the inheritance of altruism solely in terms of overlap of genetic composition ("inclusive fitness"). But if biological group selection were rare or nonexistent in nature, it would be because the particular conditions for it are rare or nonexistent, not because it is impossible. In *behavioral* evolution it seems clear that acts naturally (that is, as a consequence of biological evolution) come and go in groups or patterns rather than as individual muscular movements. Group selection would thus be expected to be the norm in behavioral evolution.]

Evolutionary theorists (for instance, Dawkins, 1989; Sober & D. S. Wilson, 1998) typically focus on biological and cultural levels of evolution—innate mechanisms and cultural rules. They generally ignore changes of behavior within an organism's lifetime in response to environmental contingencies (behavioral evolution). Where such changes are not ignored, evolutionary theorists tend to attribute them to inherited developmental and cognitive processes or simply to rational thought. But learning within an organism's lifetime (behavioral evolution) is as much an evolutionary process as biological and cultural evolution (Skinner, 1981; Staddon & Simmelhag, 1971; Baum, 2005).

Of course, altruistic behavior, like all learned behavior, depends strongly on biological inheritance. The crucial question is: What is inherited and what may be learned over an organism's lifetime? Some theorists believe that altruistic tendencies may be directly inherited by individuals in successful groups (Sober & Wilson, 1998); others believe that altruistic behavior results from the inheritance of a sense of fairness in allocation of resources ("strong reciprocity") (Fehr & Fischbacher, 2003). But organisms may *learn* to be altruistic with neither an innate altruistic tendency itself nor an innate sense of fairness. I believe that the crucial inherited tendency necessary for the learning of altruism is a direct sensitivity to the consequences of temporally extended patterns of acts.

As mentioned previously, infants vary their rate of sucking not by altering pauses between individual sucks but by altering pauses between *bursts* of sucks (Wolff, 1968). That is, we have a natural tendency to group acts into patterns. Rats vary their rate of licking at a drinking spout and pigeons vary rates of pecking in a pause-and-burst way (Teitelbaum, 1977). Ethologists have discovered and studied more elaborate *fixed action patterns* in consumption and mating. Such patterns are more or less modifiable over the organism's lifetime by environmental contingencies that select patterns or sequences of acts, not individual movements (Hinde, 1966). Over the lifetime of the organism, some patterns are reinforced and may be modified by reinforcement.

Neuringer and his colleagues have shown how patterns of behavior may be directly shaped by environmental contingencies. For example, Grunow and Neuringer (2002) rewarded rats for different levels of variability in sequences of presses on four levers. Rats rewarded for high variability emitted highly variable patterns; rats rewarded for low variability emitted more tightly clustered patterns. The rats were then rewarded in addition for a particular, ordinarily rare, sequence. Those rats initially rewarded for very high variability (therefore occasionally emitting the rare sequence) differentially increased the rate of that sequence. The initially rare pattern emerged as a unit from a population of other patterns by a process of differential reinforcement, like an island emerging from a receding sea. The environment created by Grunow and Neuringer selected the rewarded sequence, just as the natural environment selects the fittest organisms. Over the course of the experiment, individual presses on each of the four levers were equally reinforced. It is highly unlikely that any sequence could have been learned as a chain of individual presses. This significant experiment and others like it (Neuringer, 2004) show that patterns of responses may be reinforced as whole units.

Just as genetic replication creates the variation in structure upon which biological evolution acts, so biological evolution creates the variation in innate behavior patterns upon which behavioral evolution acts. However (just as the degree of variation in the structure and nervous systems of organisms is sensitive to environmental conditions and evolves over generations), behavioral variability is itself highly sensitive to environmental contingencies (as Grunow and Neuringer showed).

Of course, the fact that altruism may arise through behavioral as well as biological evolution does not automatically make altruism right—any more than the fact that selfishness may arise through behavioral evolution makes selfishness right; *is* does not imply *ought*. Nevertheless, the fact that altruism may arise through behavioral evolution does imply that an altruistic person *may* be happier than a selfish person—not just because altruism makes him feel good at any particular moment, but because an altruistic pattern, like a self-controlled pattern, may be intrinsically more valuable than one based on immediate gratification.

Acknowledgment

Chapter 7 contains material from Rachlin (2000), Rachlin (2010a), Rachlin (2010b), and Rachlin and Jones (2010).

Teleological Analysis of Altruism and Self-Control

When people use mental terms such as sensation, perception, thought, *and so on, they are referring to a temporally extended pattern of overt behavior; such patterns, taken together, constitute their minds. As the previous chapter argued, self-control and altruism are two aspects of behavior typically assumed to be controlled by the mind, but both may be conceived as identical with behavioral patterns, which evolved by biological or behavioral evolution or a combination of both. Although it may seem self-evident that people will sacrifice some part of their present good for the benefit of their future selves (self-control), their reasons for sacrificing some part of their own good (present or future) for the benefit of another person may be less obvious. Yet the two forms of sacrifice are equally explicable by teleological analysis in terms of evolution of behavioral patterns over time and social space.*

The present chapter attempts to show how the teleological, behavioral conception of the mind arises naturally from and efficiently and simply explains experimental research in the areas of self-control and social cooperation. The chapter introduces the concept of a self that is extended in both time and social space. A measure of this temporal and social extension of the self, in terms of the slope of temporal and social discount functions, is described and related both to laboratory and to everyday-life measures of self-control and social cooperation. The chapter shows that people discount the value of rewards to other people by the social distance between them, just as they discount rewards to themselves by their delay.

Teleological behaviorism is a behavioral identity theory. It says that when you use mental terms such as *sensation, perception, imagination, thought,* and so on, you are referring to a temporally extended pattern of overt behavior. Such patterns, taken together, constitute your mind. The remaining chapters of this book will explain and illustrate this way of thinking about the mind. The present chapter will show how self-control and altruism—two types of behavior almost universally explained in terms of inner causes—may also be conceived in terms of temporally extended behavioral patterns. But first let me try to illustrate what teleological behaviorism implies about the direction of psychological investigation.

Consider the following problem: You are a casino owner and one of your roulette wheels is several years old. You want to make sure that it is completely fair—that, when the wheel is spun, the ball has a 1/38 chance of falling into any of the 38 holes. In theory, there are two ways you could go about determining the actual probability. You could take the wheel to a shop where they will test its balance, the trueness and equal smoothness of the wooden sides, the height and stiffness of the barriers between the holes, their curvature, depth, hardness, and so on. If the wheel passes all tests, there could still be some overlooked imbalance, some unevenness. In theory, your task would never end. In practice, you would say, at some point, it doesn't matter anymore. No gambler could possibly take advantage of the minute imbalances that remain.

A second method would be to look at the video records (that casinos typically take) of the play at the table, count the number of times the ball falls into each hole, and divide by the number of spins. You might compare the distributions of these relative frequencies over the first and second years of the wheel's life to their distribution over the last year to see if there were any changes. Because the wheel is old, it may be going out of balance, with the probabilities changing, while you are observing it. But let us assume that, as you count more and more spins, the relative frequencies of the ball landing in each hole all approach 1/38, as they did when the wheel was new. However, no matter how tightly the distribution of relative frequencies was grouped around 1/38 across holes, you could not be sure that the wheel was completely fair. As with the first method, at some point (if the relative frequencies closely approximated the desired probabilities) it would not matter. No player could possibly take advantage of whatever imbalance remained. This second method is *teleological analysis*.

Which method is more fundamental? Which gets at "true" probabilities? *Probability* is an abstract concept, not something you can point to. Proponents of the first method would say that the probabilities the casino owner is trying to determine are abstract properties of the wheel (along with those of the ball and the croupier) and that the first method, taking the wheel to the shop, is getting at the fundamental probability. Probability may be seen as a property of the wheel, just as its shape and color are properties. According to proponents of the first method, the relative frequencies obtained by the second method would be mere reflections of the fundamental probabilities that reside in the *structure* of the wheel itself.

Proponents of the second method might say that the probabilities are abstractions of the *behavior* of the wheel (along with that of the ball and the croupier) and that the second method, looking at the wheel's history and spinning the wheel to observe its current behavior, determines, as closely as can be determined, the true probabilities. The structure of the wheel, the ball, and the croupier, these roulette-wheel behaviorists (let us call them) would say, constitute the *mechanism* behind the probabilities (in Aristotle's terms, their material and efficient causes), not the probabilities themselves. The probabilities themselves do not inhere anywhere within the wheel; they inhere in the wheel's observable behavior. Behaviorists would see the wheel's probabilities as abstractions of the wheel's behavior, just as a parabolic-like arc is an abstraction of the behavior of a baseball after being hit by a bat. You would not expect to find parabolas inside a baseball, and you would not expect to find probabilities as such inside a roulette wheel.

Now let us turn from physics to psychology. There are two methods by which mental events such as a person's *intentions* may be studied, analogous to the two ways of determining the probabilities of the roulette wheel. One way is to observe the person's behavior and infer from your observations what the inner mechanism must be to have given rise to that behavior. [This method is much like trying to infer the program of a computer by typing its keys and observing what appears on the screen.] Such an endeavor may be helped by using magnetic resonance imaging (MRI) machines to observe events actually going on inside the nervous system or by drawing an analogy to events measured directly in the brains of other species.

Another way to study mental events such as intentions is by teleological analysis (Rachlin, 1992, 1994). This method is analogous to the second method of determining the true probabilities of the roulette wheel—observation and analysis of patterns of behavior (including verbal behavior) over time. The fundamental meanings of mental terms, claims the teleological behaviorist, are these observable patterns; they exist on what the philosopher Daniel Dennett (1978) calls the *personal level*. Suppose John has asked Mary out for a number of dates. (On one occasion he tried to kiss her, but she rebuffed him, hurting John's feelings.) Mary now wonders if John is serious about the courtship. What is his intention? Is it just casual flirtation, or something long-term, or possibly marriage? For a teleological behaviorist, John's past actions (including what he says to Mary and to other people) are the only relevant data on this question because it is in those actions where his intentions actually reside. Good data in this regard may be difficult to obtain, and John's intentions may be obscure. But they are obscure, says the teleological behaviorist, in the same way that the roulette wheel's probabilities may be obscure—because there is not enough currently available behavior to analyze, not because John's intentions are hidden inside his head. The teleological behaviorist would never suppose that John's true intentions could be revealed by a lie detector test that measures his brain waves or his physiological responses to a series of questions, no matter how probing. However, John knows that he is trying to seduce Mary (let us assume) and the moment after he succeeds he will up and go. Is this intention (or for that matter, his knowledge of his intention) in his head? No, it is not. [See the discussion in Chapter 6 of the baseball player's knowledge that she is playing baseball for a behavioral use of the concept of knowledge.] His intention is in his past behavior. The reason that John knows his own intention is not that he has access to something in his own head and Mary does not, but that John has access to his own past behavior and Mary does not. In principle, John's twin sister, Jane, may know better than John does what his intentions truly are. When John tells Jane about his intentions, she may reply, "No you're wrong. She's got you in her grip with all that coyness, that playing hard to get. You'll never leave her!" And Jane may be right. One more point: John's belief and Jane's belief regarding John's intentions are discriminations among complex patterns in John's behavior. The expression of the belief in both cases may be simple assertion, but the discriminative stimuli on which the assertions are based (John's behavioral patterns) are highly complex. [Note that I am not saying that internal analysis has no place in understanding John's behavior—just that it is not the royal road to his mental state. Internal inference and analysis provide a description of behavior (simple or complex) in terms of its efficient causes; teleological analysis provides a description of behavior (simple or complex) in terms of its final causes.]

The Problem of Self-Control

From a behavioral viewpoint, self-control is an *external* phenomenon—a conflict between a relatively immediate, particular, high-valued act (such as smoking a cigarette) and an element of a long-range, more abstract, high-valued pattern of acts (such as healthy behavior). When the conflict is resolved in favor of the high-valued pattern, behavior is said to be self-controlled; when the conflict is resolved in favor of the particular act, behavior is said to be impulsive. This view may be contrasted with the currently dominant view of self-control as an *internal* phenomenon (Muraven & Baumeister, 2000). The dominant view stems from Descartes' initial conception of self-control as a conflict that takes place within the brain between a physical impulse (leading to the particular act) and willpower (a spiritual force leading to the high-valued pattern).

Like Descartes, many modern thinkers locate the arena of conflict between impulsivity and self-control somewhere within the brain, but for them the conflict takes place between neural impulses or endogenous hormones coming from different places (mediated by the composition, strength, and availability of different neural transmitters) rather than between a physical impulse and a spiritual force, as described by Descartes. A message from a "lower" brain area dictating a certain action (a neural impulse to smoke the cigarette) conflicts with a message from a "higher" brain area dictating an opposite action (a neural impulse to refuse the cigarette). These neural impulses (internal representations of intentions) fight it out in some area of the brain, and the behavior that actually emerges signals the winner.

Teleological behaviorism rejects such a view. It says that the fundamental conflict between self-controlled and impulsive actions takes place not among representations of intentions in some specific location in the brain, but in the person's overt behavior over a period of time. From the present viewpoint, self-control is not a battle between internal intentions to do one thing and internal impulses to do another. It is fundamentally a temporal conflict—between behavior that maximizes value over a short time period and behavior that maximizes value over a long time period.

Of course, people have intentions. (An obese person, for example, might resolve to eat less food.) They then either carry out or fail to carry out those intentions. But, according to teleological behaviorism, an intention is itself behavior—a temporally extended pattern of behavior—that may be extrinsically reinforced even when it is not carried out to its end. For example, an obese woman may be rewarded by her friends and relations for agreeing to join a weight-reduction program and rewarded again for actually joining the program—independent of the other longer-term rewards contingent on losing weight. Such extrinsic rewards may increase the frequency or intensity with which she talks about her intention to lose weight, but they cannot directly increase the strength of her intention. The strength of an intention is not given by the frequency, intensity, or determination with which it is expressed or the intensity of a neural discharge or the brightness of a brain-area image in an MRI scan. The strength of an intention is rather the likelihood of its being followed; that likelihood, in turn, may be measured by how frequently prior, similar, intentions have been followed by that person in the past. Someone who promises to stop drinking now and has promised to stop drinking many times in the past but has not stopped, or has stopped for a short time, has only a weak intention to stop, unless future events prove, retrospectively, that the intention was strong. In this respect, an intention is like a probability; you can only know for sure that a coin is unbiased if you flip it a sufficient number of times and the overall frequency of heads approaches closer and closer to one-half. An apparent intention that cannot, in principle, be measured in this fashion (such as a purely internal intention) is not really an intention at all. The mechanisms underlying intentions, like the mechanisms underlying all behavior, are surely internal. But the intentions themselves occur in behavior over time, not inside the head. If they are never exhibited in overt behavior, you may want to call them potential or aborted intentions, but they are not actual, whole, intentions.

The internal and external viewpoints are not mutually exclusive. On the one hand, all complex human and animal behavior patterns are controlled by *internal* mechanisms. On the other hand, all complex human and animal behavior patterns exist because of their function in the interaction of the person with the *external* environment. The issue is ultimately semantic. Should we use the vocabulary of self-control to refer to the interaction between *internal* causes and behavior patterns (as Descartes advised), or should we use that vocabulary to refer to the function of behavior patterns in the *external* environment (as Aristotle advised)? But a semantic issue is not necessarily a pointless one. In this case, the two viewpoints have practical as well as theoretical consequences.

The Self-Control Conflict

The Gestalt psychologists were a group of European trained psychologists who immigrated to the United States before World War II. At that time, European psychology was heavily influenced by the philosophy of Immanuel Kant, and the application of phenomenology to psychology. The Gestaltists' main focus was the psychology of perception. They believed that perception of color, shape, size, loudness, and so forth, depended not just on particular stimuli but on the stimulus in the context of the entire perceptual field—the figure and its background together. The brightness of a gray spot, for instance, depends not only on the light intensity of the spot but also, and very strongly, on the brightness of the surrounding area. [Almost every introductory psychology book shows two physically identical gray spots, one surrounded by a white ring, the other surrounded by a black ring; the former looks compellingly darker than the latter. Only when identical spots are surrounded by identical rings does the apparent difference in their brightness go away.] The Gestalt psychologists had a very strong influence on American psychology around the middle of the twentieth century. However, their influence on the psychology of learning and motivation was less strong than their influence on the psychology of perception. The present chapter extends their most famous dictum—the whole may be greater than the sum of its parts (Koffka, 1955; originally from Aristotle's *Metaphysics*)—to problems of self-control and altruism.

The teleological behavioral extension of that Gestalt dictum would say that the *value* of an activity may be greater (or less) than the sum of the values of its parts. As an illustration, suppose you are driving from New York to Chicago. Your car has a CD player and you take along some CDs to play on the trip. You like both classical and popular music, so you take along several symphonies and several pop CDs. Suppose (perhaps contrary to fact) that your tastes are such that the following two inequalities apply:

1. Over the next 60 minutes you prefer listening to a symphony rather than to 20 3-minute popular songs.
2. Over the next 3 minutes you prefer listening to a popular song rather than to a section of a symphony.

This is a paradigm case of a self-control problem. The problem is that to listen to the whole symphony (which by assumption you prefer to do) you must listen to the first 3 minutes of it (which you prefer not to do). If you just do what you prefer at the moment (assuming your preferences remain constant throughout the trip), you will drive the whole way from New York to Chicago playing only popular songs whereas (again, by assumption) you would have been happier if you had played only symphonies.

Similarly, an alcoholic prefers to be sober, healthy, socially accepted, and to perform well at his job than to be drunk most of the time, unhealthy, socially rejected, and to perform poorly at his job. However, over the next few minutes, he prefers to have a drink than to not have one. If over successive brief intervals he always does what he prefers, he will always be drinking.

The problem, for both the driver and the alcoholic, is how to make choices over the longer time span (the whole) and to avoid making choices on a case-by-case basis (the parts). The reason that we find it difficult to avoid making short-term choices is that the value of the immediate alternative (listening to a popular song; having a drink now) is greater than that of a fraction of the longer activity (listening to 3 minutes of a symphony; being sober now). The reason that we *should* make choices over the longer time span is that the value of the longer activity (listening to the *whole* symphony; being generally sober) is greater than the sum of all the short-term values of its parts (listening to each individual 3-minute section of the symphony; refusing each particular drink).

Each 3 minutes of symphony listening, each drink refusal, has virtually no value in itself. Moreover, to use behavioristic language, these pieces of the more valuable behavioral pattern are never reinforced. They are not immediately reinforced, they are not conditionally reinforced, and they are not reinforced after a delay. Clearly refusing a drink is not immediately reinforced. It should also be clear that no single drink refusal is reinforced after a delay. If the alcoholic refuses a single drink, she does not wake up three weeks later suddenly healthier and happier. To realize the value of a drink refusal, she must put together a long string of them—just as to realize the value of a symphony you must listen to the whole thing (or at least a whole movement). How would you feel if you had watched 95 minutes of a 100-minute movie and the projector broke? Not, it seems safe to say, 95% as happy as you would have been if you had seen the whole movie. Here is the other side of the coin, from a review (Salter, 2013) of the letters of the writer William Styron:

> [Styron] complained always of the difficulty of writing, the torture of it. 'Writing for me is the hardest thing in the world.' He loathed it, he said, every word that he put down seemed to be sheer pain, yet it was the only thing that made him happy. (p. 32)

The fact that longer behavioral patterns may have a value greater than the sum of the values of their parts is not unique to these very broad patterns. Each

broad behavioral pattern is nested in still broader patterns and contains narrower patterns within it. Listening to a symphony over an hour is nested within
the pattern of listening to a mixture of symphonies and popular songs for a day.
At the other extreme, listening to a single verse is nested within listening to a
whole popular song. Even a seemingly unitary act such as a rat's eating a food
pellet is a complex pattern of muscular movement.

To summarize, the concept that the value of a behavioral pattern may be
greater than the sum of the values of its parts is not just an empty slogan bor-
rowed from Gestalt psychology. It is the very basis of a teleological approach to
the problem of self-control.

Altruism and Self-Control

Returning to the lecture game of Chapter 7 (Figure 7.1), it is important to note
that, although the game is nominally "one-shot," there is actually no such thing
as a true one-shot game. The concept of "one-shot" implies that an act of choice
may occur without a context. It is true that in the lecture game no context is
explicitly stated. But no act occurs in a vacuum. All players must have had experience with similar games (see Parfit's list in Chapter 7). Although choices in the
lecture game are anonymous, most such games are not anonymous in real life.
Cooperation may be reinforced in the long run by social approval and inclusion,
as well as by explicit reciprocation. Symmetrically, defection may be punished.
A fisherman who consistently overfishes, for example, is likely to be shunned or
otherwise punished by his fellow fishermen, if not by society. A person may learn
over time to identify games of this type and to cooperate in those games. Why?
Because a pattern of cooperation is often reinforced, even though individual
cooperative acts are not reinforced or may even lead to aversive consequences.

It may not be beneficial in the long run for an individual to attempt fine discriminations between such situations, to divide them into those where cooperation is ultimately reinforced and those where it is not. First, such discriminations
may be difficult or time-consuming. At every red light you could look around to
see if a car is coming on the cross street or whether a police car is present; or
you could just stop at all red lights. Most of us just stop—even in the middle
of the night at a lonely intersection. It is easier to obey the general rule than to
discriminate among such situations.

A second reason to cooperate in any particular case is that even when, in
some prisoner's dilemma situations, we have spent time and effort to discriminate, we may have learned to question our best and most considered judgments
in the midst of those situations. Because the value of the immediate particular
reward for defection is at its maximum at the point of decision, the immediate
reward's value may briefly overwhelm the ultimately higher value of the more

abstract and temporally extended reward for cooperation. The alcoholic may have learned that her decisions in the evening at a party or at a local bar often differ, in the direction of having a drink, from her decisions in the morning, at home in the midst of her family, or at work. If she is wise, when she gets to the party, she will disregard her present judgment—especially if it involves breaking a pattern she has adopted and conformed to in the past. Rachlin (2000) has argued that attending to "sunk costs," considered by economists to be an error, is often the basis, perhaps the main basis, for self-control in everyday human life. [De La Piedad, Field, & Rachlin, 2006, showed that even the behavior of pigeons is influenced by sunk costs.]

The lecture-game players who choose Y know that their choices are anonymous, but they may refuse to discriminate between this game and many other similar games where choices are not anonymous. Just as always stopping at red lights (except in dire emergencies) is the best policy in the long run, behaving altruistically in real-life prisoner's dilemma games may also be the best policy in the long run. In other words, the long-term benefits of altruism as a general rule may outweigh its long-term costs, even in particular situations where altruism is clearly not reinforced.

Only a perfectly rational economic organism, one who can take into account the consequences of choosing each alternative from now to infinity, one who never overweighs smaller-sooner consequences (and knows that he never overweighs smaller-sooner consequences), can afford to ignore his own previous choices (sunk costs). For the rest of us it is always possible that our current preferences are less valid than our previous ones. Wisdom consists of recognizing those situations and ignoring our own current otherwise best-considered preferences—no matter how "objective" they seem to be right now.

Altruism Without Self-Control

It does not follow from the above argument that every altruistic act derives from self-control. Just as we learn over our lives to extend our effective selves beyond the present moment, so we may learn to extend our effective selves beyond our skins to others whose interests overlap with our own. Although, as I have just claimed, altruistic behavior may emerge from self-control, and although there is a significant positive correlation across individuals between measures of self-control and altruism (Rachlin & Jones, 2008), there are many exceptions. Some people are Scrooge-like—selfish but highly self-controlled. Others show the opposite pattern—unselfish with respect to others but highly impulsive with respect to their own future. Even within the realm of self-control, people may be self-controlled in some areas but not in others. A person may be a compulsive gambler but a moderate drinker.

It is not clear whether extension beyond the skin (altruism) and extension beyond the present moment (self-control) are independently learned or whether one is primary and the other derived. But I have attempted to present a plausible account of how they might be learned, based on an inherited tendency to pattern behavior.

The Extended Self

In what economists call "public goods" situations, such as contributing to public television, voting, contributing to charities, not littering, and so on, very little or nothing is gained by contributing. Each individual benefits most by not contributing; she gets the benefits of what others contribute at no cost to her. Economic theory, based on maximization by each participant of his or her own utility, predicts that no one will contribute (This is called the "free rider" problem). Yet many people do contribute. Why? Because the unit of utility maximization is not always an individual person, bounded by her skin, but a group of individuals extended in social space—the extended self.

Recall once again the lecture game diagrammed in Figure 7.1. If all of the players cooperate (choose Y) in that game, each player earns a high reward; if all of the players defect (choose X), each earns a low reward. However, for each player as an individual, it is better to defect than to cooperate. When this game is played repeatedly by unrelated players, everyone usually ends up defecting. What might engender cooperation in such a game? If, instead of asking, "How can I maximize *my own* return?" the boundaries between the players are blurred and they ask, "How can I maximize *our* return?" all players would earn more.

Figure 8.1 illustrates the analogy between social cooperation and self-control. In the case of social cooperation, the circles in the diagram designate *individuals distributed in social space*. The large circle (P_0) stands for a given person. The small circles ($P_{-N} \ldots P_N$) stand for other people; the closer a small circle is to P_0, the closer is the social bond between that other person and P_0. In the case of self-control, the circles in the diagram designate *a single individual at different times*. The large circle stands for P_0 now. The small circles stand for that same

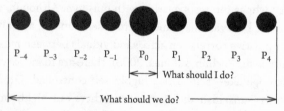

P_{-4} P_{-3} P_{-2} P_{-1} P_0 P_1 P_2 P_3 P_4

What should I do?

What should we do?

Figure 8.1 The large circle (P_0) represents a person here and now. The small circles at different distances from the large one may represent the same person at various times in the past or future, or may represent people at various social distances from P_0.

person but at different times in the past and future; the closer a small circle is to P_0, the nearer to the present time.

A *social dilemma* poses a choice for a person between acting so as to maximize her own reward and acting so as to maximize the reward to a group of people. Giving to charity, donating to public television or radio, recycling, and so forth, are obvious examples, but virtually any social act requires a balancing between benefits to oneself alone and to the social group. Altruistic or socially cooperative people make choices so as to maximize reward over a wider range than do non-altruistic or non-cooperative people. An important determinant of such balancing is the *social distance* between P_0 and the other person or people in the group. The closer you feel to another person or group of people, the more likely you should be to cooperate with that person or group. Here we define a person's *extended self*, not in terms of the physical space circumscribed by the person's skin but rather in terms of the temporal and social space over which that person maximizes reward.

Different people may have wider or narrower extended selves. The sociopath may have a self circumscribed closely by his own skin, while the saint may have a self extended to all of nature. Jones and Rachlin (2006) and Rachlin and Jones (2008) attempted to measure such differences by means of *social discount functions* [using a method akin to a procedure for obtaining delay discount functions by Raineri & Rachlin, 1993]. Rachlin and Jones (2008) gave participants a booklet with these paper and pencil instructions:

> The following experiment asks you to imagine that you have made a list of the 100 people closest to you in the world ranging from your dearest friend or relative at position #1 to a mere acquaintance at #100. The person at #1 would be someone you know well and is your closest friend or relative. The person at #100 might be someone you recognize and encounter but perhaps you may not even know their name. You do not have to physically create the list—just imagine that you have done so.

We call these imagined numbers (*N*s ranging from 1 to 100) "social distances." A high *N* represents a large social distance; a small *N* represents a small social distance. The next seven pages each summarized the above instructions and then presented a list of hypothetical questions with a different social distance on each page. For example, for $N = 20$:

> Now imagine the following choices between an amount of money for you and an amount for the 20th person on the list. Circle A or B to indicate which you would choose in EACH line.
> A. $85 for you alone. B. $75 for the 20th person on the list.
> A. $75 for you alone. B. $75 for the 20th person on the list.

A. $65 for you alone. B. $75 for the 20th person on the list.
..................[continued down to]..............................
A. $0 for you alone. B. $75 for the 20th person on the list.

Column A listed 10 amounts between $85 and (decrementing by $10 on each line). For half of the participants, the money amounts decreased from $85 to, as above; for the other half, the order was reversed. Column B differed on each page by social distance [N]. The social distances were: 1, 2, 5, 10, 20, 50, and 100, in random order. On each line, participants were asked to choose between an amount of money for themselves and $75 for P_N.

Figure 8.2 shows the group results. The medians (of 198 Stony Brook undergraduates) were well described by the following equation (the line in Figure 8.2):

$$v = \frac{V}{1 + kN} \tag{8.1}$$

In Equation 8.1, V is the amount of money given to the other person ($75), v is the value of that reward for the participant in the experiment (the heights of the points in Figure 8.2); N is the social distance between the participant (P_0) and the other person (P_N), and k is a constant (equal to about 0.05 for these data). Equation 8.1, which we call a social discount function, was fit to the data of individual Stony Brook undergraduates, and a k-value was obtained for each of them. The bigger k, for a given person, the steeper that person's discount

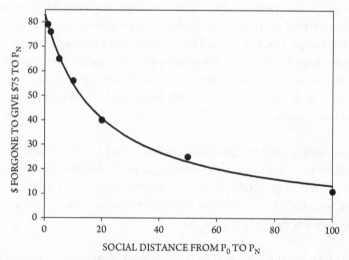

Figure 8.2 The points represent the median amount of money (across participants) for participants themselves that were equivalent to $75 for another person at various social distances from the participant. Amounts greater than that at each point were preferred to $75 for the other person; amounts below each point were dispreferred to $75 for the other person.

function, the less that person values rewards to other people. All participants had positive *k*-values—indicating, not surprisingly, that they would be more generous to people socially close to them than to people far away.

Predicting Cooperation and Defection in the Lecture Game

Corresponding to a view of the self as extended in time (the outcome of a conflict between narrower and wider temporal interests) is a view of the self as extended in social space (the outcome of a conflict between narrower and wider social interests). As indicated previously, *the cost of choosing Y (cooperating) in the 10-person lecture game of Figure 7.1 is $200, regardless of what other players choose.* By choosing Y (thereby increasing Z by 1), a player gains $100 but loses the $300 bonus that would have been obtained by choosing X (defecting), for a net loss of $200. The cost is clear. It *costs* $200 to cooperate. But what are the *benefits* of cooperating? By choosing Y (and increasing Z by 1) a player increases the amount of each of the 9 other players' rewards by $100 regardless of whether they chose X or Y. That is, cooperating gives $100 to each of 9 other people. But how does giving $100 each to 9 other people benefit oneself?

Let us assume now that the players in the lecture game are Stony Brook undergraduates in an introductory psychology class. We have determined in other experiments that, for an average Stony Brook undergraduate, a random classmate falls at about social distance (N) of 75. From Equation 8.1, with $k = 0.05$ (the median value among Stony Brook undergraduates), we calculate, $v = \$21$. That is, giving a random classmate $100 is worth about $21 to a typical Stony Brook undergraduate. Let us pause and think a bit about what that means. Suppose we collared a random undergraduate on the campus and asked her the following question: Which would you prefer: A. $21 for yourself or B. $100 for that guy over there (pointing to a random classmate, not a friend of the subject)? These experiments imply that she would be indifferent. If the amount offered to her was $10 instead of $21 she would be likely to let her classmate have the $100; if the amount offered to her was $30 she would be likely to take the money herself. Some readers may feel that such behavior would be over-generous; others may deem it selfish. But that just shows that people vary considerably on this measure. In any case, let us keep this in mind: It is worth about $21 to an average Stony Brook student to give $100 to another Stony Brook student.

As we just emphasized, in the lecture game, the net *cost* of a Y-choice is $200 (loss of the $300 bonus compensated by $100 from increasing N by 1). The *benefit* of a Y-choice is the value of giving $100 each to the 9 other players. What is that value? Locey, Safin, and Rachlin (2013) found that, all else equal, the percent of lecture-game players who chose Y increased proportionally with the number of players. Let us assume, therefore, that the value of giving 9 other players $100 each is 9 times the value of giving one other player $100. The total benefit obtained by a Y-choice then must be $189 (that is, $21 multiplied by 9). In other words, the benefit of cooperation in this game ($189) is a ballpark approximation to the cost of cooperation ($200). Thus, we calculate that about half of the players in the prisoner's dilemma game of Figure 7.1 will choose X and about half will choose Y. This is close to what is found. Of course, the many assumptions and approximations that went into this calculation call this particular equivalence into question. Nevertheless, the basic idea—that direct costs to a lecture-game player may be balanced by benefits to others—remains valid.

Cooperation in games, in general, tends to be greater with greater social closeness of the players (Jones & Rachlin, 2009; Camerer, 2003). Among groups with closer bonding (say, among members of the same family or the same athletic team, or even people who have just had a conversation together or who are engaged in a mutual project), we would expect smaller social distances, hence more Y-choices, in the lecture game.

Jones (2007) obtained individual social discount functions by the method described above, obtained a k-value for each participant, and also tested each (of 97) undergraduates in a public goods game, a game that models the sort of choices listed by Parfit (see Chapter 7). For this game, participants (in a classroom) read the following instructions:

Imagine the following situation (purely hypothetical, we regret to say):

1. The experimenter gives you $100.
2. A box is passed around to each person in this room.
3. Each person may put all or any part or none of the $100 into the box. No one else will know how much money anyone puts into the box.
4. After the box goes around the room, the experimenter doubles whatever is in the box and distributes it equally to each person in the room, regardless of how much money he or she put into the box.
5. Each person will then go home with whatever he or she kept plus what he or she received from the box.

Note that you will maximize the money you receive by not putting any money in the box. Then you will take home the original $100 you kept plus what the experimenter distributes after doubling whatever money was in the box. HOWEVER: If everybody kept all $100, nothing would be in the box and each person would take home $100, whereas if everybody put all $100 in the box, each person would take home $200 after the money in the box was doubled and distributed.

Donation amount in this "one-shot" public goods game is a measure of altruism. As the instructions emphasize, an individual participant gains *nothing at all* by contributing on the present occasion. Even if everyone else makes the full altruistic choice, any one person loses by contributing. Similarly, individuals gain virtually nothing by their individual $50 contribution to public television (the same programs would be programmed with or without any particular $50 contribution), but people do give money to public television. Jones found a significant negative correlation between the amount of money participants said they would put into the box and their *k*-value in the social discounting test. In other words, *the more money a person donates to the public good, the shallower that person's discount function tends to be.*

According to the economist Julian Simon (1995):

> The conceptual framework employed here obviates the age-old question about whether an act of giving by one individual to another should properly be labeled "altruism," or whether instead one is "really" being "selfish" by making oneself feel good. An individual's discount weights vis-à-vis other individuals may be considered a full description of the individual in this connection, assuming that the individual's behavior corresponds to his or her discounts in relation to other individuals.... Revealed preferences constitute the entire system. (pp. 375–376)

The concept *revealed preferences* refers to an ability to derive functions such as Equation 8.1 from observations of behavior (behavior "reveals" the preferences), and then to use that function to predict behavior in some other situation (such as the public goods game). Correspondingly, the finding that behavior in a public goods game may be predicted by steepness of a social discount function is itself a defining property of altruism. The more such correspondences are found, the richer the behavioral and economic conception of altruism becomes.

Moreover, the correspondences and parallels between altruism and self-control should serve, as Simon said, to demystify altruism. Whereas it may seem self-evident that people will sacrifice some part of their present good for the benefit of their future selves, it seems mysterious when people sacrifice some part of their own good for the benefit of another person. Yet, as Simon implies, as the philosopher Derek Parfit's "reductionism" implies, and as our experiments show, the two forms of sacrifice are equally explicable in economic terms. [A person has common interests with other people close to him, just as he has common interests with his later self. Ainslie (2001) has stated that trade-offs, described in terms of willingness to delay a reward, may occur between P_0 and $P_1, P_2, \ldots P_N$ (see Figure 8.1) considered in temporal terms. Similarly, such trade-offs may be described in terms of social space. Both types of trade-off imply that our essential selves are not fixed by our skins but are extended beyond it both in time and in social space.]

Reinforcing Self-Control and Social Cooperation

The question arises, how do we reinforce self-control or social cooperation? One way to effectively reinforce both self-control and social cooperation is to require choices to be made in *patterns*. In both repeated self-control and repeated social cooperation games, subjects who are required to make a series of choices all at once tend to cooperate more and to show more self-control (Rachlin, 1995b). In everyday self-control situations, this relation is fundamental. If an alcoholic is sober or drunk, drinking is always better than not drinking. But the value of a year of no drinking (or moderate drinking) is greater than the value of a year of steady drinking.

Social cooperation situations have a similar structure. The goodwill and trust of other people are vague and abstract compared to the particular and immediate rewards of defection. A person may believe that it is always better to tell the truth (and would choose to tell the truth over the next four years rather than to lie over the next four years, if such a choice could be made) but still would be tempted to lie to get out of some particular ticklish situation. The problem is that, in life, choices usually have to be made one at a time. How do we generate a valuable *pattern* of behavior when each component of that pattern is less valuable than its alternative?

A conceivable answer to that question is that we figure it out. Somewhere in our brains is a *rational mechanism* that evaluates the pattern, organizes it, and sends out commands to the motor system to emit the pattern's components— only to be opposed during periods of temptation by contrary commands rising from below (visceral impulses). From this viewpoint, each particular act—self-controlled or impulsive, cooperation or defection—is the product of a battle between our higher and lower nervous systems.

An alternative view, the behavioral view discussed in Chapter 7, is that valuable and complex patterns of behavior may evolve from simpler ones over a person's lifetime, just as valuable and complex structures (like the eye) have evolved from simpler structures over generations. The environment (through reinforcement) selects individual acts in the same way that the environment (through survival of the fittest) selects individual organisms. *Patterns* of behavior may be selected in the same way that *groups* of individual organisms may be selected.

In general, it is not a good idea to make many sorts of decisions on a case-by-case basis. On a case-by-case basis, most of us would be having that second dessert, drinking that third martini at a party, throwing that candy wrapper into the gutter and that letter from PBS into the wastebasket. There are often no rational justifications for doing the reverse (refusing the second dessert or the martini, holding the candy wrapper until you reach a wastebasket, sending a check to PBS). Rational justifications appear only for the overall pattern that has evolved by a process akin to group selection, and which we follow regardless of immediate contingencies to the contrary.

No part of this process need rely on a deliberate foresighted author. As wider and wider patterns are reinforced, the units selected evolve from simpler to more complex forms over our lifetimes—just as complex structures like the vertebrate eye evolve from simpler structures in the lifetime of a species. To explain self-control and social cooperation we do not need to imagine a creator of behavior (a rational mechanism) lodged inside each person's head.

Why Be Altruistic?

A person may have a history of reinforcement of altruistic behavior and, even though she believes that altruism will not be rewarded here and now, she does not want to break the pattern. Why not? One answer, as I said above, is that, in the past, in such situations, her best-considered choices have proven to be wrong. That is, her altruism here and now is partly an act of self-control, part of what Eric Siegel and I call a pattern of "soft-commitment" (Siegel & Rachlin, 1995). Although, by behaving altruistically in this situation, she maximizes reinforcement overall, this reason is difficult to verbalize; it involves admitting that her choice takes account of her own limitations. Verbalization of such a reason may involve social costs. [Revealing an inconsistency across time in your choices subjects you to arbitrage by others; they could sell you a future reward when you value it relatively highly and then buy it back from you when you value it relatively less.] Instead, the inconsistent chooser may point to the pattern itself (she may say, "I am generally a good person") and leave it at that.

From a behavioral viewpoint, the difficulty of explaining altruistic behavior is not intrinsically greater (or less) than the difficulty in explaining self-control in everyday life. It is not contradictory for a behaviorist to say that altruism is reinforced provided the reinforcer is understood as acting not on that act alone but on the pattern that the act is part of.

Self-Control, Altruism, and Free Will

Let us consider yet again Plato's cave allegory from Chapter 1. Let us imagine that Plato's released prisoner returns to the cave, where he now watches a modern-day movie. While the unreleased prisoners see only colored shadows on the screen, the released prisoner can understand the movie at the level of character and plot. He sees *through* the many particular shadows, the many particular "projections" that represent a character in the movie, so that, like us, he recognizes the character immediately each time he or she appears on the screen. In that sense, the lights and shadows on the screen may be said to be "perceptually transparent" to him, as they are to us. But we understand this phrasing as a metaphor. The characters do not exist in a room behind the screen—they exist on the screen. It would be wrong to think that only the particular shadows exist on the screen but that the characters exist in the released prisoner's head. Shadows and characters are just two ways of looking at the screen. (And, of course, both exist in his eyes and brain as well as on the screen, but he sees the world, he does not see his eyes. Nor does he see his brain.)

We can go from one level of perception to another. With a great deal of effort, we can look at a movie as pure shadow and light—that is, we can see the movie in terms of particulars, and with a great deal of effort (plus some considerable experience) we can see the movie at a still more abstract level than characters and plot. A critic, for instance, might see the movie in terms of the director's style or might even be able to discern the school where the director was trained.

One may conceive freedom not as an *internal* attempt to turn away from the particulars in the world but rather as an *external* attempt to see through them and to conceive the world abstractly. A person who does this is free from particular influences in the same sense that an ocean liner is free from the influence of small waves. A cognitive concept of *self-control* (inherited from St. Augustine and Descartes) would view a person on a diet who eats an extra hot dog as *externally controlled* by the smell and taste of the hot dog; the same person refusing the hot dog would be viewed as *internally controlled*, as self-controlled (hence as free). A behavioral concept, on the other hand, would see the eating of the hot dog as caused by the particular qualities of the hot dog—its *particular* taste, its *particular* smell—while the refusal of the hot dog is caused by its abstract qualities: the hot dog as part of an unhealthy diet. Both goals (good taste, good health) are *final* causes, rather than efficient causes, in the sense that they are consequences rather than antecedents of acts. But the good taste is a final cause of the *particular* act of eating the hot dog, while the good health comes from no particular act but rather an extended pattern of acts over time. Looked at one way, eaters who respond to the most abstract features of their diets, like viewers who respond to the most abstract features of a movie, are free—free from (in some sense, normal or typical) influence by particulars, by immediate forces, by temporary pleasures and pains. Looked at another way, their behavior is controlled—controlled by abstractions.

Similarly, acts controlled by the rewards and punishments to our selves, narrowly conceived, are constrained relative to behavior controlled by the rewards and punishments of a wider group. A person who balances her own good, that of her family, and that of her society is freer than one whose every act is explicable in terms of her own benefits.

The more complex an organism's behavior, the more abstract are the principles that explain it. The life of the philosopher, Aristotle said, is the most abstract, and therefore the best and freest life. For Aristotle, even though all of a person's actions are caused (by both efficient and final causes), it is still meaningful to talk of better and worse acts; it is still meaningful to talk of free acts and unfree acts. Final causes of free acts are consequences that are beneficial in the long run (to society as well as the individual), while final causes of unfree acts are consequences that may be beneficial only in the short run and possibly harmful in the long run. The degree to which people choose X or Y in the lecture game is a measure of the degree to which they see their choices as particular events or as abstract patterns over time because in this game those two discriminations are made to conflict with each other.

The only conception of free will that remains meaningful in modern scientific psychology is this conception: When people act for the long-term good of themselves and their society, in cases where such acts conflict with their immediate and individual pleasures, they may meaningfully be said to be acting freely; they are not constrained by immediate pleasures and pains. This freedom is compatible with a determinism that sees even their choice of abstract good over particular pleasure as in principle predictable. The reason for making this distinction between free and unfree behavior is pragmatic; such a distinction is useful in developing a science of behavior.

Acknowledgment

Chapter 8 contains material from Rachlin (2000), Rachlin (2010a), Rachlin (2010b), and Rachlin and Jones (2010).

9

Consciousness and Behavior

Folk psychology accords with many, if not most, current philosophical and psychological theories of mind in assigning to consciousness an almost mystical quality. We may be unsure of many things, these theories and viewpoints agree, but we are sure about the contents of our consciousness. Moreover, because our consciousness occurs inside our head and is private to each of us, what we say about our own conscious states, arrived at through introspection, is held by these theories and viewpoints to be incontrovertible.

Previous chapters have presented the teleological behavioral viewpoint in some detail, but this chapter focuses on its application to the thorny issue of consciousness, particularly human consciousness. The chapter will argue (as the attentive reader will anticipate) that our consciousness occurs in the most abstract patterns of our overt behavior extended in time and social space—not inside our head. Introspection is therefore not a royal path to the mind. Introspection is itself overt behavior, which evolves according its own function in our lives—to predict our future behavior for the sake of other people and for our own sake. Just as this function may be overwhelmed by other functions, so introspection, though honest, may at times be false. The brain does not contain our consciousness, any more than an engine contains the acceleration of a car or the mechanism inside a clock contains the time.

In the nineteenth century, many psychologists prided themselves on being "trained introspectionists"—trained to avoid making what they called the "stimulus error." This was the "error" of reporting, as introspections, properties of (external) *stimuli* rather than properties of (internal) *sensations*. If I held up a pencil, and you introspected and reported that you saw a pencil, you would be making a stimulus error. (The only reason you call it a pencil, according to these psychologists, is because, attached to the basic visual sensation you are having, are numerous associations with other sensations, which constitute its meaning.) But if you focused inward and reported a thin, oblong yellow image with a triangular brown image adjacent to it and a little shiny black thing at the tip, and so on, you would be reporting pure sensations. Only a trained introspectionist, it was thought, was able to focus internally on a sensation in its pure form, unencumbered by its accretion of associations.

Within the mind, sensations, perceptions, and thoughts were said to flow in a stream, much like the streaming of movies or videos on a modern computer screen. E. B. Titchener (1909), the most prominent proponent of the introspective technique in the United States, said:

> We shall. . . take mind and consciousness to mean the same thing. But as we have two different words, and it is convenient to make some distinction between them, we shall speak of mind when we mean the sum-total of mental processes occurring in the life-time of an individual, and we shall speak of consciousness when we mean the sum-total of mental processes occurring now, at any given "present" time. Consciousness will thus be a section, a division, of the mind-stream. (p. 19)

Titchener defined consciousness here as the relatively brief cross-section of a group of long-term mental patterns. [Since Freud, at least, and in almost all of modern neurocognitive psychology, much (if not most) mental activity has been considered to be unconscious. But this chapter will be concerned only with that part of mental activity normally considered conscious.]

Modern psychologists and philosophers have abandoned the notion that introspection can reveal sensations in their pure form, but they have not abandoned introspection as a method of determining the mind's contents. Behaviorists believe that, to the extent that it hangs on to the introspective method, modern psychology is making a big mistake. Some modern thinkers consider introspection not only to be a valid method but the *most* valid method for understanding consciousness. For one twentieth-century philosopher, "Modern philosophy began with what I think is the valid insight that consciousness is the most certain thing in the world" (Blanshard, p. 318, in Blanshard & Skinner, 1967). If modern philosophy began with this "insight," it may be said that behaviorism began with its rejection (Watson, 1913). Certainly any *behavioral* account of consciousness must reject this dualistic approach and must rely wholly on physical acts in a physical world.

Behaviorism and Consciousness

Skinner (1938) initially conceived of *operants* as observable acts of the whole organism controlled by their consequences. Therefore, according to Skinner, no wholly internal event can be an operant. This conception of behavior proved to be extremely powerful, especially as applied to human behavior (see Chapter 6). All voluntary (that is, non-reflexive) human acts *must*, in Skinner's behavioral analysis, be operants—shaped and maintained by reinforcement and punishment contingencies. Once an observer takes this attitude, many acts ordinarily thought to have purely internal causes turn out to be reinforced. Addictive behavior, phobic behavior, and criminal behavior may then be seen as not *just* dysfunctional in the long run; they may be maintained by their reinforcing consequences and eliminable by removal of those consequences, by reinforcement of alternative behavior.

However, it eventually became apparent that not all behavior could be explained, or easily explained, in terms of relatively discrete physical acts by the whole organism. What if you were interested in the kind of human activity typically thought of as occurring wholly inside the organism? As Marr (2011) forcefully states, without such activity,

> There would be no descriptions or even mentions of bodily sensations such as those of pain, taste, smell, tactile (e.g., the feel of silk), kinesthetic, proprioceptive, or even visual and auditory experiences. Contemplating a Jackson Pollock, or quietly listening to a recording of Beethoven's violin concerto, or puzzling over the meaning of an Emily Dickinson poem—all of these and much much more would be severely limited if not impossible. Much of literature, especially fiction and poetry, would be superficial, if not pointless; think of Joyce's Ulysses, for example, a novel largely composed of "interior monologues," and considered thereby "realistic" by some critics. A child quietly sitting and listening to her mother read from Grimm's fairy tales would be unthinkable. (No this child is not deaf!) Much of what occurs in a chess or bridge tournament would also be unthinkable,... (p. 214)

This is only a portion of the activities listed by Marr that he feels behaviorists can and should study. I will henceforth refer to these behaviors as "Marr's list." As Marr implies, there must be a big difference between the mind of a normal child quietly sitting and listening to her mother read from Grimm's fairy tales, and the mind of her twin sister, quietly sitting next to her, who *is* deaf. Yet by stipulation their behavior is identical. How can a behaviorist account for the difference?

One reaction a behaviorist may take is simply to consider the difference between the hearing and deaf listeners as irrelevant to scientific understanding. If we exclude the possibility of a spiritual world, where can we find the answer to the question posed by Gray (see Chapter 2) and implied by Marr: "What is the difference between two awake individuals, one of them stone deaf, who are both sitting immobile in a room in which a record-player is playing a Mozart string quartet?" The presumption of the question is that the deaf individual is not hearing the quartet and the non-deaf person is hearing it. But then, what does it mean to consciously hear or not hear something? Blanshard might have claimed that the only conceivable answer to this question must rely on different events (differing "qualia") in a non-physical, spiritual consciousness. But then Quine's argument that conscious events could not be studied scientifically would apply (see also Chapter 5); all sentences containing mental terms would be opaque, and all of the items on Marr's list would be inaccessible to scientific study. If, on the other hand, mental events were physical rather than spiritual events, sentences containing mental terms could, in principle, be translated into sentences containing physical terms only. Such sentences would be *transparent*, in Quine's terminology, and consciousness could be scientifically studied. In this light, let us reconsider three wholly physical conceptions of mental events.

Neural Identity Theory

According to the *Stanford Encyclopedia of Philosophy* (Smart, 2011):

> The [neural] identity theory of mind holds that states and processes of the mind are identical to states and processes of the brain. . . . Consider an experience of pain, or of seeing something, or of having a mental image. The identity theory of mind is to the effect that these experiences just are brain processes, not merely correlated with brain processes.

Consciousness, then, would be reducible to brain physiology. A difference in the auditory cortex or more centrally within the brain would be, according to neural identity theory, all there is to the difference between hearing and not hearing. Most neural identity theorists do not believe that hearing is just activity in a single nerve; hearing is rather a pattern of activity over a complex of nerves extending over a wide area of the brain, perhaps over the whole brain. Some neural identity theorists would go beyond the brain to incorporate the peripheral nervous system. Their theories imply that if we knew enough about the neural connections involved in audition, and we were able to build a brain that incorporated those connections, and if we were to feed into the artificial brain the strains of the Mozart quartet, that brain (which could not otherwise move, could not interact with the world, could not report its feelings, had no functions of use to anyone) would hear the Mozart quartet just as you or I (assuming you are not deaf) can hear it.

Certainly some particular pattern of stimulation in our brains is necessary for us to hear the quartet, and some movement of molecules in the air near our ears and a particular pattern of movement of our basilar membranes are necessary for us to hear the quartet. These are parts of the mechanism underlying hearing. But, I believe, they are not the same thing as actually hearing, any more than the activity of the engine of a car is the same thing as the acceleration of the car. Let me try to clarify exactly what the problem is here. You can say that a Mozart quartet is nothing but the playing of certain notes by four instruments. The music would be no less real or scientifically accessible for that. The quartet is abstract relative to its particular notes, but abstract entities are as real as particular ones; a chair is at least as real as the pieces of wood that make it up (see Chapters 1 and 2). If you produce the notes in their proper order and nuance, you will have all there is to the Mozart quartet. But, if you could produce the neural events said to be identical with hearing the quartet in a disembodied, artificially constructed brain, would that brain actually hear the quartet? As Alva Noë persuasively argues (see Chapter 6), a disembodied brain could not actually hear anything. This is not to say that you could not build a robot with a human mind. However, as the next chapter will maintain, such a robot would not need any particular human, internal structure. Rather, it would need to have a particularly human relation with human beings—to help people and be helped by them, that is, to engage in economic interchange with them, to predict its own future behavior and theirs, to guide others, and also to mislead them.

A kind of identity theory (a "neurocognitive theory of consciousness") claims that consciousness "arises" only if a certain complexity of the nervous system is achieved. Consciousness, for this theory, need not occur in nerves themselves but could conceivably occur in a machine built of transistors and copper wires. What is necessary for consciousness, according to this theory, is not the *matter* of brain physiology but the *form* of brain physiology. For example, a computer might have an internal mechanism in which internal representations of input are placed on an internal "blackboard" or "global workspace" and are scanned and operated on by an internal executive processor. According to Baars (1988), consciousness operates in (a more complex version of) this way. Our brains might indeed work as Baars suggests. But, again, if it were possible to construct such a (disembodied) mechanism in all its complexity, with no other possible movement, no function in the world, would consciousness occur in it? Psychologists and philosophers critical of neural identity theory do not believe it would.

Brain research is highly important, highly interesting, and highly valuable. But looking for consciousness in the brain is looking for it in the wrong place. Then where is the right place to look for consciousness? Or, without prejudging the issue, where is the right place to look for explanations of the various activities on Marr's list? In previous (and subsequent) chapters I explain such activities in terms of patterns of overt behavior over time (teleological behaviorism—a behavioral identity theory). But before turning to that explanation, let us discuss another behavioral identity theory—Marr's own (Skinnerian) explanation of mental terms.

Internal (Covert) Behavior

Unlike neural identity theorists, Skinner consistently rejected the use of physiological or neurological mechanisms to explain the sorts of behavior on Marr's

list (Skinner, 1938, 1945, 1953). He agreed with Quine that private events were
not susceptible to scientific study:

> It is... impossible to establish a rigorous scientific vocabulary for public
> use, nor can the speaker clearly "know himself" in the sense in which
> knowing is identified with behaving discriminatively. In the absence
> of the "crisis" provided by differential reinforcement... private stim-
> uli cannot be analyzed. .... In a rigorous scientific vocabulary private
> events are practically eliminated. (Skinner, 1945, pp. 274–275)

Nevertheless, Skinner believed that *consciousness*, as well as the other terms on
Marr's list, could be interpreted (as opposed to analyzed) by behaviorists—in
terms of private, covert behavior operating according to the same laws as public
behavior. As Marr says (2011, p. 213), for Skinner, "[b]ehavior analysis could...
include private events, at least in an interpretative if not empirical sense." The
question arises: What sort of behavior occurs wholly within the privacy of our
own bodies that is not best described and studied in neural terms? It may seem
that there is not much room, within our bodies, between neural behavior and
overt behavior. But, if you follow Marr in this respect, all of the behavior on his
list, and more, is to be found in that space. [Behaviorism's founder, J. B. Watson,
had similar beliefs. According to Logue (1985, p. 154), "His publications in 1913
and 1914 make clear that he did not deny the existence of thinking, and that
he regarded thinking as a form of behavior involving slight movements of the
muscles of the larynx or very slight head movements. Watson also maintained
that these behaviors, rather than some central process, constitute dreaming."]

One kind of internal event is not problematic and may be approached behav-
iorally by redefining the organism. If a person says, "I have a toothache," a behaviorist may redefine the organism as excluding the infected tooth. Similarly for, "I
have a stomach ache," "...a knee ache," or "...a funny feeling at the back of my
throat," or even, "I have a headache." For the purposes of behavioral analysis,
the malfunctioning organ may be thought of provisionally as external to the
organism. Alternatively, the organism may be provisionally expanded, as when
a person straps on a pair of roller skates or skis or rides a bicycle or drives a car.
But such maneuvers would *not* get at the main problem. The infected tooth may
be considered as a stimulus or a discriminative stimulus for the response, "I have
a toothache." But the pain of the toothache remains unexplained and, for this
sort of behaviorism (as Skinner maintained), unanalyzable.

A still more difficult problem arises when a person says, "I have a toothache,"
to herself. We often talk or picture things to ourselves [see discussion of talking
to yourself in Chapter 6]. Many of the examples on Marr's list, especially the
"stream of consciousness," seem to be nothing but internal monologues. But
can talking or picturing things to oneself bear the burden of accounting for all

the items in Marr's list, including consciousness itself? When we are dreaming, covert talking and picturing occur in what may be thought of as their pure state. But when we are dreaming we are explicitly *not* conscious. It is only when we wake up and engage in overt activities and interact with the external environment that we are said to be conscious.

Let us return yet again to the hearing person and the deaf person who are both listening to a Mozart quartet. Can you explain the difference between them solely in terms of their *covert* behavior? What would that difference consist of? Remember, the difference cannot consist in different *perceptions* of or *reactions* to internal movements by proprioception. That would just be pushing consciousness up a level from the muscles into the peripheral nervous system, and we would be back to neural rather than behavioral identity theory. [Why should a behaviorist identify consciousness with the (relatively impoverished) activity of the *interoceptive* nervous system but not with the (relatively rich) activity of the *exteroceptive* nervous system? If you are going to identify consciousness with neural activity in the first place, why not go all the way? Consciousness as neural impulses caused by *covert* muscular movements has all the problems, and more, of consciousness as neural impulses caused by *overt* muscular movements or, for that matter, effects in your nervous system of someone else's overt movements.] For covert behavioral identity theory to make sense, the difference between a hearing and deaf person would have to reside in differences in their covert muscular movements themselves.

What about the "stream of consciousness" as it appears in James Joyce's *Ulysses*? Here is a famous example, from Molly Bloom's monologue at the end of the novel:

> ... O and the sea the sea crimson sometimes like fire and the glorious
> sunsets and the figtrees in the Almeda gardens yes and all the queer
> little streets and the pink and blue and yellow houses and the rosegar-
> dens and the Jessamine and geraniums and cactuses and Gibralter as
> a girl where I was a Flower of the mountain yes when I put the rose in
> my hair like the Andalusian girls used or shall I wear a red yes and how
> he kissed me under the Moorish wall and I thought as well with him as
> another and then I asked him with my eyes to ask again yes and then
> he asked me would I yes to say yes my mountain flower and first I put
> my arms around him yes and drew him down to me so he could feel my
> breasts all perfume yes and his heart was going like mad and yes I said
> yes I will Yes. (Joyce, 1922/1986, pp. 643–644).

Marr and I agree that this is realistic. It seems to be how the character, Molly, really thinks. But it is not plausibly a literal transcription of her inner speech. I do not actually, literally, talk to myself in this way, and I do not believe that

I would do so if I were Molly. Rather, it seems to me that Joyce is portraying something more like what Titchener meant by consciousness, "a section, a division, of the mind-stream," a moving cross-section of a series of thoughts, a collage made up of pieces of actual past and possible future events, pieces of inner and outer speech and overt actions put together by Joyce in poetical form. Joyce's portrait of Molly Bloom's mind is a portrait of Molly's mind in the same sense that Picasso's *Demoiselles D'Avignon* is a portrait of five women. The realism in *Ulysses* is the higher, more abstract realism of art and not the literal realism of a phonograph record.

I am not objecting to inferring internal speech or internal picturing on the basis of observations of external behavior. I am objecting to labeling such inferred actions with the mentalistic vocabulary of Marr's list. It is true that we first learn to read aloud and only then to ourselves. But, looking at a book and saying the words, whether aloud or to yourself, is reading only in the sense that a scanner "reads" a document.

In the spirit of Gray's question (Chapter 2), one might ask the covert behavioral identity theorist: What is the difference between two people sitting quietly and reading *Ulysses*, one of them with a PhD in English and the other a high school dropout? If reading were just saying the words on the page to yourself, these two people would be behaving identically, yet they are almost certainly not reading identically.

It is tempting at this point to give up the claim that the terms on Marr's list stand for essentially private but peripheral activity and to follow neural identity theory to search for the seat of consciousness more centrally in the nervous system. Marr (2011, p. 217) points to "...extensive studies in which monkeys can be trained to operate devices in real time via recordings from many cortical cells related to motor function. . ." But what causes those cells to be stimulated? Does the monkey's willpower reside in the cells themselves? As I indicated in Chapter 5, sensory stimulation runs right through the brain and out the other side without encountering anything identifiable as a sensation.

At best, covert activities are only interpretable, not scientifically analyzable, and one person's good interpretation is another's bad interpretation, and there is no one to decide between them. We may ask, as Descartes did: How can we obtain a "clear and distinct" view of our own minds? Such a view can be gotten not by looking inward with an MRI machine to some spot in our brains or our muscles, but outward—to our overt behavior. In the words of a Wittgenstein scholar (Bax, 2009):

> ...one is able to see a person's pain or joy itself when one takes her (fine shades of) behaviour to be expressive of mind and places her doings and sayings in the context of a larger cultural or communal pattern. . . .
> [P]sychological phenomena can be described as aspects of the human

being. This succinctly conveys that [Wittgenstein] holds such phenomena [as pain or joy] to be located on the outside rather than the inside of the subject, or even in the interspace between a community of subjects. (pp. 11–12)

According to Wittgenstein,... thoughts and feelings are not inner objects that exist separate from and prior to a person's doings and saying, but are... highly multifaceted phenomena that precisely have their life in someone's (fine shades of) behaviour on particular (more or less extended) occasions. From a Wittgensteinian perspective, the outer is not an inessential supplement to the inner but should be considered to be the very locus thereof. (p. 64)

[In a similar vein, Italo Calvino (1988, p. 16) quotes Richard Strauss's librettist, Hugo von Hofmannsthal: "Depth is hidden. Where? On the surface."] In his later works, Wittgenstein (like Aristotle) was a teleological behaviorist.

Teleological Behaviorism

Let us return yet again to the question: What does it mean to hear or to be deaf? The most straightforward behaviorist answer to that question must be tied to the function of hearing in the world: For a normal person to hear, it is both necessary and sufficient for that person to function as a normal person does in the presence of auditory stimuli. For a normal, hearing person, a significant non-zero correlation must exist between sounds and her overt behavior and among different sounds; that is, sounds themselves must be discriminative stimuli for her behavior. As Figure 2.2 in Chapter 2 indicates, because there is no such correlation in Eve's *overt* behavior (behavior in contact with the environment), Eve is deaf; because there is such a correlation in Adam's overt behavior, Adam can hear. This would be the case even if Eve were found to have a fully developed auditory cortex while Adam had severe brain damage. In such a case we might want to reserve some special term like "psychological deafness" for Eve, but it would nevertheless be deafness.

At the present moment, Adam and Eve are doing the same thing. But Adam and Eve, behaving in the same way, are like two physically identical gray spots, one surrounded by a black annulus, the other surrounded by a white annulus. By stipulation, only the contexts differ. But in the case of the hearing and deaf people (as in the case of the two gray spots), the differing contexts are more important than the identical current conditions in determining psychological states. More precisely, Adam's and Eve's current, common immobility is the correspondence of two points in two different correlations between behaviors and sounds that take time to occur. As Noë says (2009, p. xi), "Consciousness is more like dancing [physical, *external*, and extended in time] than it is like digestion [physical, *internal*, and extended in time]."

I have claimed (Rachlin, 1992, 1994) that all the terms on Marr's list are in principle definable as temporally extended, functional patterns of overt behavior (like dancing). Of course, as Marr (2011) points out, such definitions are easy to talk about and difficult to construct. But it is a thousand times easier (as well as clearer and more distinct) to define hearing, for example, in terms of statistically specifiable correlations between sounds and overt actions than in terms of essentially private events lying in brain physiology or covert behavior. As Wittgenstein (1958, #66 et seq.) famously pointed out, it is not possible to precisely define terms such as *game* (or *dance*, for that matter). Yet specific kinds of games (such as chess) and dances (such as in ballet notation) may be precisely defined in terms of overt behavioral patterns. Similarly, one may define apparently internal actions such as imagination, self-control, and altruism, and even pain, in terms of patterns of overt behavior (Rachlin, 1985, 2002). Which is more unclear and indistinct—an interpretation of love as a pattern of overt actions and speech extended for a considerable period, directed toward another person, or as words whispered silently to oneself plus some undetectable muscular twitches? I think the answer is obvious. As Bax (2009, p. 61) asserts: "That phenomena like love and despair only unfold over a longer period also means that one has to be quite close to a person in order to be able to witness enough of her behavior and understand what psychological state they are part of." This view captures the fact that if a person were poor at observing temporally extended patterns in his own behavior he might be mistaken about whether or not he was in love (or engaging in any other complex mental activity). Philosophers may object that mental activities are things that must be going on continuously (that is, right now) and interacting with each other inside the head, and therefore cannot be such things as correlations over long time periods between overt acts and environmental events (e.g., Geach, 1957). With respect to this issue, let me quote myself (Rachlin, 2011):

> [Consider the] example of Tom who is riding the bus because (a) he wants to go home and (b) he believes that the bus will take him there. Philosophers [some of them] believe that behaviorists cannot explain such behavior because Tom is only doing one thing yet he is doing it as a consequence of the interaction of two reasons (his knowledge and his belief). There seems to be no reinforcer of his single act that can capture the dual mental states, the interaction of which apparently causes the act. But let us suppose that knowledge and belief are not private entities interacting like two gears in a person's head but are two temporally extended patterns of overt behavior shaped, like any patterns of overt behavior, by contingencies of reinforcement. For example, for

the past 4 years I have been swimming about four times per week and, each time, I swim 30 laps of the pool. That comes to about 120 laps per week. This is a purely behavioral fact about me. Just as clearly, at every moment during the month, including right now while I am sitting here typing on my computer, I am swimming at the rate of 120 laps per [week]. . . . Similarly, I am also sleeping about 7 hr per night. My rates of swimming and sleeping are two overlapping long-term patterns of my behavior. My swimming rate consists of both time swimming and time not swimming. My sleeping rate consists of both time sleeping and time not sleeping. What I am doing right now (neither sleeping nor swimming) belongs to both patterns simultaneously. This is obvious and hardly worth pointing out. The obviousness is due to the fact that swimming and sleeping are both clearly overt behaviors. If our mental vocabulary referred to similarly overt patterns of behavior, that is, if believing were one pattern of overt behavior and desiring were another pattern, . . . then Tom's current bus riding would just as clearly be seen as a single short-term act belonging to both his desire to get home and his belief that the bus will get him there. (p. 210)

Aristotle compares such coincidences of pattern to the point of tangency between two circles. The discrimination of white from sweet, in his example, is part of the pattern of discriminating white from non-white and part of the pattern of discriminating sweet from non-sweet—like a single point common to two different correlations (see Rachlin, 1994, p. 97, for a discussion).

How are such patterns learned? In answering this question, it may be worth pointing out that a pigeon's peck and a rat's lever press are both already quite complex patterns of behavior. Although both classes of movement are relatively brief, they involve delicate muscular coordination. As all behaviorists know, pecks and lever presses may be shaped into complex patterns within the organism's lifetime, by reinforcement, by a process akin to biological evolution (Baum, 2005). Herrnstein and Hineline (1966) showed that a rat's lever-pressing rate depends on a negative correlation, over hour-long sessions, between lever pressing and aversive stimulation and not on the consequences of any single lever press. Grunow and Neuringer (2002) showed that relatively complex, and initially rare, patterns of pressing among four levers may be selected, as such, by contingencies of reinforcement. Similarly, imagination evolves when behavior (such as saying, "I see a rose") normally reinforced in the presence of a particular discriminative stimulus is emitted in the absence of that stimulus and reinforced by the community. Stage or movie acting is a kind of imagining. But imagination is much more basic than acting since (as Aristotle said; see Chapter 2) it underlies perception. And this fundamental kind of imagination is shaped by reinforcement.

Borderline Cases

The main purpose of language is communication. But language sometimes serves purely to organize our own behavior. As the previous chapter mentioned, as you step onto a dance floor you might say to yourself, "This is a waltz." We all frequently talk to ourselves; it is tempting to identify talking to oneself with thought. When we talk to ourselves, however, we cannot be communicating directly with another person. Organization is an important function of language, but it is subservient to the overt behavior being organized—behavior with direct environmental consequences. In Chapter 10, in my reply to Schlinger, I will deal with this issue in more detail. In essence, talking to oneself is better regarded as part of the mechanism underlying thinking than as thought per se; talking to oneself is to thinking as the operation of a clock mechanism is to the positions of the hands.

A person may suffer from what is called a "locked-in syndrome," where there is severe damage to the lower brain but the upper brain remains intact. People with this syndrome may learn to communicate with eye blinks or eye movements and to discriminate in that manner among auditory stimuli. Once they learn such behavior, and others learn to interpret it, they are hearing. But did they hear after their injury and prior to such learning? The issue is largely semantic. Would we say of a clock functioning perfectly, except without hands, that it is telling the time? In a sense it is and in a sense it is not. The social function is not present in either case. The clock without hands is not telling the time to a person; the locked-in sufferer is not communicating with the world.

Introspection

As soon as any physical theory of consciousness identifies a physical correlate of consciousness, consciousness itself seems to jump away and hide in the spiritual world. The idea that consciousness might be physical just goes against what introspection and folk psychology (and even common sense) tell us must be true. Nagel (1974) claimed that a human could never know "what it's like to be a bat" because "what it's like" is not a physical event but an irreducibly mental event. It is true that a human can never understand what it's like to be a bat, but that is *not* because humans, were they actually able to look inside themselves, fail to sense some non-physical "batness." Rather, it is because it is impossible for a human to behave as a bat behaves. If you could behave like a bat over some period of time, you would know *ipso facto* what it is like to be a bat, and the longer you behaved like a bat the better you would know what it is like to be one. [My response to McDowell at the end of the next chapter will further discuss Nagel's concept of mind.]

When they find it difficult to account for conscious and mental events, both neural-identity and covert-behavioral-identity theories of consciousness tend to retreat further and further *into* the organism. At the end of this road lies only spiritualist theory. What makes an overt-behavioral-identity theory of consciousness (such as teleological behaviorism) different is that when some molar, functional account of a mental trait seems to fail, the theorist goes not inward but outward in both space (to a wider social context) and time (to past and future context) and sticks to Skinner's (1938) original functional plan of looking for explanations in the environment. If a person's pattern of behavior is not explicable in terms of its immediate environmental consequences, then the teleological behavior theorist looks for the (final) causes not inward into neural space but outward into the past and future—into what Skinner called the person's *reinforcement history*. Sometimes, of course, one has to infer the history from current behavior. But that is an inference about facts or classes of facts that are in principle accessible to behavioral science; the inferred behavior is or was in contact with reinforcement contingencies. For the person (deaf or hearing) who is sitting quietly listening to a Mozart quartet, temporal and social context is *all* of consciousness. What is it like to be a bat? The answer is to be found not in the bat's head but in the functioning over time of the bat in the society of other bats.

Some critiques of physical theories of consciousness (e.g., that by Shaffer, 1963) hinge on the notion that, when we say something like "I feel good," we are introspecting and then "reporting" some internal state. Since the "report" contains no mention of what we know is the internal mechanism causing the feeling (the neural events), those events cannot, according to these critiques, be *identical* with the feeling. An underlying premise of such critiques is that introspection is a valid method of psychological observation. But we cannot look inward as we look outward. Almost all of our senses transfer information from outside us to inside us. Even our inner senses transmit information further inward. The nerves stimulated by pressure in our stomach, for instance, go inward toward the brain. Yet the concept of introspection as a kind of inward vision assumes that something inside us can stand back, as it were, and "reflect" on brain processes. *The apparent philosophical problems with physical theories of consciousness are really problems with the concept of introspection, rather than essential problems with the physical nature of the theories themselves.* Introspection may tell us that physical theories of consciousness are false. But introspection, as a path to psychological truth, is exactly what all physical theories should reject.

This does not mean that our supposed introspections are useless. Introspection (or "reflection"), like all mental activities, is an overt behavioral pattern; as such it is socially reinforced. We do not ordinarily say things like "I am happy," "I am sad," or "I see the red light," without any purpose whatsoever. What is the purpose of introspecting? Not to release some inner pressure. Not to report anything going on inside us. Rather, such expressions of inner feelings report patterns, within their behavioral context, in our own past overt behavior and predict our future behavior. If I tell you that I am happy, I am telling you how I will behave in the near future. Such expressions explain our own past behavior and predict our own future behavior for the benefit of the hearer and ultimately for our own benefit (Baum, 2005).

The Mind-Body Problem

Why is it any more plausible for the many philosophers who have considered the mind-body problem that conscious activity has to occur inside the head than that it occur in overt behavior? It is easy to understand why Descartes saw things this way. Since Descartes believed that the soul was located deep in the brain, and that the physical motions of vital spirits impinging on the pineal gland directly influenced the soul, and vice versa, the physical motions also had to be in the brain. But it is not inherently obvious that deep within the brain there exists a non-physical soul, which interacts with our nerves. Some societies and some ancient philosophers believed that our minds as well as our souls were in our hearts. I would guess that if you name a vital organ there will be or will have been some society that believed it to be the seat of the soul; there may even have been some societies that identified the soul with the whole organism. So if the mind is a molar or abstract conception of some physical activity (as I have argued), and there is no a priori reason (such as connectivity with an internal, non-physical soul) to assume that the physical activity identified as consciousness occurs in the brain, where does it occur?

In answering this question, usefulness is paramount, especially as consciousness, and talk of consciousness, must have evolved along with the rest of our human qualities. If our environment is the ultimate source of our consciousness (as it would have to be if consciousness were a product of biological evolution), then it would be our overt behavior, not our neural behavior, that is in direct contact with the source. Group selection may act at the level of innate behavioral patterns across generations. And it may act as well at the level of learned patterns within the lifetime of a single organism (see Chapter 7). It is in these overt patterns (learned and innate) where consciousness resides.

The Time Bug

Let me end this chapter with a little science fiction. Imagine a planet where instead of developing technology, as we have done, all of the effort of an intelligent species was devoted to the breeding of plants and animals to serve the breeders' purposes. And suppose that there existed on this planet an insect that was highly sensitive to both the time of day and the season of the year. In fact, the insect indicates the time by means of some externally observable signal; suppose its color changes as the day progresses. The intelligent species has bred the insect to perfect the color change so that, although the insect might have originally needed to be recalibrated by exposure to a sunny day every once in a while, it could now (after many thousands of generations of breeding) live its life completely in the shade and still precisely indicate the time by its color. Such an insect would be carefully preserved and fed. It might be taken aboard ships (along with a compass insect) to determine longitude and be carried around in a box which could be opened and consulted whenever the breeders needed to know the time. As the breeding of this insect progressed, the internal mechanism that caused its color to change would have evolved as well, becoming more and more precise. It has been speculated that human timing works with a pacemaker (delivering a periodic pulse), an accumulator (counting the number of pulses), a memory, and a comparator (Gibbon & Church, 1981). The bug could have such an internal timing mechanism, but it would be infinitely more accurate than ours.

The breeders would naturally use the insect's colors to indicate the time, just as we use the hands of a clock or a digital display to indicate the time. They might know about the insect's internal mechanism or they might not. It would make no difference to their ability to breed the insect—killing off the relatively inaccurate ones and preserving and breeding the relatively accurate ones (they could check it with hourglasses or water clocks or sundials). I am claiming that human consciousness evolved in a similar way, except by natural selection, imposed by the simultaneously evolving natural world and society (rather than by deliberate breeding). Just as time bugs were selected and preserved by their breeders, so conscious humans were selected and preserved in our world by their tribes. Just as the time appeared on the surface of the insects, so consciousness appears in our overt behavior. Certainly there is an internal mechanism that governs our consciousness; it might even exist in a specific brain location. And if it could be observed carefully, it might conceivably be "read" to predict overt behavior (as the wheels inside a clock may be "read" to determine the time). But it would be a mistake to identify consciousness with such a mechanism. The intuition that consciousness is inside us comes from the false belief that the origin of voluntary behavior is inside us. The origin of voluntary behavior is actually our social system by which our behavioral patterns evolved. Our consciousness thus resides in that behavior and not in its mechanism. Perhaps, now that we are becoming used to information being stored in an external "cloud," instead of inside our computers, we will get used to the idea that our minds are outside our heads and, instead of pointing to our heads in a little circle when we use mental terms such as "he's nuts," we will point to the "cloud" and circle the air.

10

Making IBM's Computer Watson Human

The purpose of this chapter is to use the teleological behavioral concept of mind developed in previous chapters to deal with the question: What makes us human? The victory of the IBM computer Watson in the TV game show Jeopardy serves as a springboard to speculate on the abilities that a machine would need to be truly human. The chapter's premise is that to be human is to behave as humans behave and to function in society as humans function. Alternatives to this premise are considered and rejected. From the viewpoint of teleological behaviorism, essential human attributes such as consciousness, the ability to love, to feel pain, to sense, to perceive, and to imagine may all be possessed by a computer (although Watson does not currently have them). Most crucially, a computer may possess self-control and may act altruistically. However, the computer's appearance, its ability to make specific movements, its possession of particular internal structures, and the presence of any non-material "self" are all incidental to its humanity.

The chapter is followed by two perceptive commentaries—by J. J. McDowell and Henry D. Schlinger, Jr.—and the author's reply.

Recently an IBM computer named Watson defeated two champions of the TV quiz show *Jeopardy*. Excelling at *Jeopardy* requires understanding natural language questions posed in the form of "answers," for example: "He was the last president of the Soviet Union." The correct "question" is "Who is Mikhail Gorbachev?" Watson consists of numerous high-power computers operating in parallel searching over a vast self-contained database (no web connection). The computers fill a room. The only stimuli that affect Watson are the words spoken into its microphone, typed into its keyboard, or otherwise fed into it; the only action Watson is capable of is to speak or print out its verbal response—information in and information out.

According to the IBM website, Watson's amazing performance in the quiz game requires "natural language processing, machine learning, knowledge representation and reasoning, and deep analytics." Still, it is clear, Watson is not human. In considering what might make Watson human, I hope to throw some light on the question: What makes us human? What are the minimal requirements of humanity?

I will call Watson, so modified, Watson II. Many people believe that nothing whatsoever could make a machine such as Watson human. Some feel that it is offensive to humanity to even imagine such a thing. But I believe it is not only imaginable but possible with the technology we have now. Because in English we recognize the humanity of a person by referring to that person as "he" or "she" rather than "it" (and because the real Watson, IBM's founder, was a man), I will refer to Watson as "it" and Watson II as "he." But this is not to imply that making Watson human would be a good thing or a profitable thing for IBM to do. As things stand, Watson has no interests that are different from IBM's interests. Since its non-humanity allows IBM to own it as a piece of property, Watson may be exploited with a clear conscience. But it is not pointless to speculate about what would make Watson human. Doing so gives us a place to stand as we contemplate what exactly makes *us* human, a prolegomenon for any discussion of moral questions.

Can a Computer Ever Be Conscious?

To put this question into perspective, let me repeat an anecdote from an earlier work (Rachlin, 1994, pp. 16–17). Once, after a talk I gave, a prominent philosopher in the audience asked me to suppose I were single and one day met the woman of my dreams (Dolly)—beautiful, brilliant, witty, and totally infatuated with me. We go on a date and I have the greatest time of my life. But then, the next morning, she reveals to me that she is not a human but a robot—silicon rather than flesh and blood. Would I be disappointed, the philosopher wanted to know. I admitted that I would be disappointed. Dolly was just going through the motions, her confession would have implied. She did not really have any feelings. Had I been quicker on my feet, however, I would have answered him something like this: "Imagine another robot, Dolly II, an improved model. This robot, as beautiful, as witty, as sexually satisfying as Dolly I, doesn't reveal to me, the next day, that she's a machine; she keeps it a secret. We go out together for a month and then we get married. We have two lovely children (half-doll, half-human) and live a perfectly happy life together. Dolly II never slips up. She never acts in any way but as a loving human being, aging to all external appearances as real human beings do—but gracefully—retaining her beauty, her wit, her charm." At this point she reveals to me that she is a robot. "Would the knowledge that the chemistry of her insides was inorganic rather than organic make any difference to me or her loving children or her friends? I don't think so . . . . The story of Dolly II reveals that the thing that wasn't there in Dolly I—the soul, the true love—consists of *more* behavior."

Some philosophers would claim that Dolly II cannot be a real human being. According to them she would be essentially a zombie. Lacking human essence, she would have ". . . the intelligence of a toaster" (Block, 1981, p. 21); presumably we could treat her with no more consideration for her feelings than in dealing with a toaster. Since we cannot perceive the inner states of other people, such an attitude poses a clear moral danger. If the humanity of others were an essentially non-physical property within them, there would be no way of knowing for sure that others possess such a property; it may then be convenient for us to suppose that, despite their "mere" behavior, they do not. But, although the teleological behaviorism I espouse can be defended on moral grounds (Baum, 2005; and see Chapter 11 in this book), this chapter relies on functional arguments. A behavioral conception of humanity is better than a spiritual or neurocognitive conception not because it is more moral but, as I shall try to show, because it is potentially more useful than they are.

[I do not claim that behaviorism is free of moral issues. Many people, infants or the mentally disabled, lack one or another typical human behavioral characteristic. A behavioral morality needs to accommodate the humanity of these people—perhaps in terms of their former or expected behavior or their role in human social networks, but never in terms of internal, actions or states.]

For a behaviorist, consciousness, like perception, attention, memory, and other mental acts, is itself *not* an internal event at all. It is a word we use to refer to the organization of long-term behavioral patterns as they are occurring. Consider an orchestra playing Beethoven's Fifth Symphony. At any given moment a violinist and an oboist may both be sitting quite still with their instruments at their sides. Yet they are both in the midst of playing the symphony. Since the violinist and oboist are playing different parts we can say that, despite their identical current actions (or non-actions), their mental states at that moment are different. The teleological behaviorist does not deny that the two musicians have mental states or that these states differ between them. Moreover, there must be differing internal mechanisms underlying these states. But the mental states themselves *are* the musicians' current (identical) actions in their (differing) patterns. A behaviorist therefore need not deny the existence of mental states. For a teleological behaviorist such as me, they are the main object of study (Rachlin, 1994). Rather, for a teleological behaviorist, mental states such as perception, memory, attention, and the conscious versions of these states *are themselves* temporally extended patterns of behavior. Thus, for a teleological behaviorist, a computer, if it behaves like a conscious person, would be conscious. If Watson could be redesigned to interact with the world in all essential respects as humans interact with the world, then Watson would be human (he would be Watson II) and would be capable of behaving consciously.

Are Our Minds Inside Us?

If, like Johannes Müller's students in 1845 (see Chapter 5) as well as most modern scientists and philosophers, you believe that no forces other than common physical and chemical ones are active within the organism, and you also believe that our minds must be inside us, you will be led to identify consciousness with activity in the brain. Thus, current materialist studies of consciousness are studies of the operation of the brain (e.g., Ramachandran, 2011). Neurocognitive theories may focus on the contribution to consciousness of specific brain areas or groups of neurons. Or they may be more broadly based, attributing conscious thought to the integration of stimulation over large areas of the brain. An example of the latter is the work of Gerald Edelman and colleagues (Tononi & Edelman, 1998) in which consciousness, defined in behavioral terms, is found to correlate with the occurrence of reciprocal action between distributed activity in the cortex and thalamus. Edelman's conception of consciousness, like that of teleological behaviorism, is both behavioral and molar, but it is molar *within* the nervous system. This research is interesting and valuable. As it progresses, we will come closer and closer to identifying the internal mechanism underlying human consciousness. Someday it may be shown that Edelman's mechanism is sufficient to generate conscious behavior. But if it were possible to generate the same behavior with a different mechanism, such behavior would be no less conscious than is our behavior now. Why? Because consciousness is in the behavior, not the mechanism.

Chapter 6 discussed a modern movement in the philosophy of mind called *enacted mind*, or *extended cognition*. This movement bears some resemblances to behaviorism. According to the philosopher Alva Noë (2009), for example, the mind is not the brain or part of the brain and cannot be understood except in terms of the interaction of a whole organism with the external environment. Nevertheless, for these philosophers, the brain remains an important component of consciousness. They retain an essentially neurocognitive view of the mind while expanding its reach spatially, beyond the brain, into the peripheral nervous system and the external environment.

For a behaviorist, it is not self-evident that our minds are inside us at all. For a teleological behaviorist, *all* mental states (including sensations, perceptions, beliefs, knowledge, even pain) are rather patterns of *overt* behavior (Rachlin, 1985, 2000). From a teleological behavioral viewpoint, consciousness is not the organization of neural complexity, in which neural activity is distributed widely over *space* in the brain, but the organization of behavioral complexity in which overt behavior is distributed widely over *time*. To study the former is to study the *mechanism underlying consciousness*, as Edelman and his colleagues are doing, but to study the latter is to study *consciousness itself*.

Widespread organization is characteristic of much human behavior. As such, it must have evolved either by biological evolution over generations or by behavioral evolution within the person's lifetime. That is, it must be beneficial for us in some way. The first question the behaviorist asks is therefore: *Why are we conscious?* Non-humans, like humans, may increase reward by patterning their behavior over wider temporal extents (Rachlin, 1995) and may learn to favor one pattern over another when it leads to better consequences (Grunow & Neuringer, 2002). The difference between humans and non-humans is in the temporal extent of the learned patterns. The CEO of a company, for instance, is not rewarded for anything she does over an hour or a day or a week but is rewarded for patterns in her behavior extended over months and years. Despite this, it has been claimed that corporate executives' rewards are still too narrowly based. Family-owned businesses (for all their unfairness) measure success over generations and thus may be less likely than corporations to adopt policies that sacrifice long-term for short-term gains.

Watson's Function in Human Society

Watson already has a function in human society; it has provided entertainment for hundreds of thousands of people. But Watson would quickly lose entertainment value if it just continued to play *Jeopardy* and kept winning. There is talk of adapting Watson to remember the latest medical advances, to process information on the health of specific individuals, and to answer medical questions. Other functions in business, law, and engineering are conceivable. In return, IBM, Watson's creator, provides it with electrical power, repairs, maintenance, continuous attention, and modification so as to better serve these functions. Moreover, there is a positive relation between Watson's work and Watson's payoff. The more useful Watson is to IBM, the more IBM will invest in Watson's future and in future Watsons. I do not know what the arrangement was between *Jeopardy*'s producers and IBM, but if some portion of the winnings went to Watson's own maintenance, this would be a step in the right direction. It is important to note that this is the proper direction. To make Watson human, we need to work on Watson's function in society. Only after we have determined Watson II's minimal functional requirements should we ask how those requirements will be satisfied.

Watson would have to have social functions over and above entertainment if we are to treat it as human. Let us assume that Watson is given such functions. [IBM is doing just that. It is currently developing and marketing versions of Watson for law, medicine, and industry (Moyer, 2011).] Still, they are far from sufficient to convince us to treat Watson as human.

Watson's Memory and Logic

A human quality currently lacking in Watson's logic is the ability to take its own weaknesses into account in making decisions. Here is a human example of this ability: You are driving and come to a crossroads with a traffic light that has just turned red. You are in a moderate hurry, but this is no emergency. You have a clear view in all four directions. There is no other car in sight and no policeman in sight. The odds of having an accident or getting a ticket are virtually zero. Should you drive through the red light? Some of us would drive through the light, but many of us would stop anyway and wait until it turned green. Why? Let us eliminate some obvious answers. Assume that the costs of looking for policemen and other cars are minimal. Assume that you are not religious, so you do not believe that God is watching you. Assume that you are not a rigid adherent to all laws regardless of their justifiability. Then why stop? One reason to stop is that you have learned over the years that your perception and judgment in these sorts of situations is faulty. You realize that, especially when you are in a hurry, both your perception and reasoning tend to be biased in favor of quickly getting where you're going. To combat this tendency, you develop the personal rule: stop at all red lights (unless the emergency is dire or unless the light stays red so long that it is clearly broken). This rule, as you have also learned, serves you well over the long run.

Here is another case. You are a recovering alcoholic. You have not taken a drink for a full year. You are at a party and are trying to impress someone. You know that having one or two drinks will cause you no harm and will significantly improve your chances of impressing that person. You know also that you are capable of stopping after two drinks; after all, you haven't taken a drink in a year. Why not have the drink? No reason, Watson would say—unless the programmers had arbitrarily inserted the rule: never drink at parties. (But that would make Watson still more machine-like.) To be human, Watson would have to itself establish the rule, and override its own logical mechanism, because its own best current calculations have turned out to be faulty in certain situations. Watson does not have this kind of override. It does not need it currently. But it would need an override if it had to balance immediate needs with longer-term needs, and those with still longer-term needs, and so forth. As it stands, Watson can learn from experience, but its learning is time-independent. As Chapter 7 shows, addiction may be seen as a breakdown of temporally extended behavioral patterns into temporally narrower patterns. [Thus addiction is not a brain disease but is directly accessible to observation and control (see also Rachlin, 2000; Satel & Lilienfeld, 2010).]

Watson, I assume, obeys the economic maxim: ignore sunk costs. It can calculate the benefits of a course of action based on estimated returns from that action from now to infinity. But it will not do something just because that is what it has done before. As long as its perception and logic capacity remain constant, Watson will not now simply follow some preconceived course of action. But, if its perception and logic mechanism will be predictably weaker at some future time, Watson will be better off deciding on a plan and just sticking to it than evaluating every alternative strictly on a best estimate of that alternative's own merits. Hal, the computer of *2001: A Space Odyssey*, might have known that its judgment would be impaired if it had to admit that it made a wrong prediction; Hal should have trusted its human operators to know better than it did at such a time. But Hal was machine-like in its reliance on its own logic.

Paying attention to sunk costs often gets people into trouble. It is, after all, called a fallacy by economists. Because they had invested so much money in its development, the British and French governments stuck with the Concorde supersonic airplane long after it had become unprofitable. People often hold stocks long after they should have sold them or continue to invest in personal relationships long after they have become painful. Their reasons for doing so may be labeled "sentimental." But we would not have such sentimental tendencies if they were not occasionally useful, however disastrous they may turn out in any particular case. Our tendency to stick to a particular behavioral pattern, no matter what, can get out of hand, as when we develop compulsions. But, like many other psychological malfunctions, compulsiveness is based on generally useful behavioral tendencies.

A satisfactory answer to a *why* question about a given act may be phrased in terms of the larger pattern into which the act fits. *Why* is he building a floor? Because he is building a house. For Watson to be human, we must be able to assign reasons (i.e., functional explanations) for what he does: Q. Why did Watson bet $1,000 on a *Jeopardy* daily double? A. Because that maximizes the expected value of the outcome on that question. Q. Why maximize the expected value of the outcome? A. Because that improves the chance of winning the game. This is as far as Watson can go itself. The wider reasons may be assigned solely to its human handlers. But Watson II, the human version of Watson, would have to have the wider reasons in itself. Q. Why improve the chance of winning the game? A. Because that will please IBM. Q. Why please IBM? A. Because then IBM will maintain and develop Watson II and supply it with power. Thus, Watson II may have longer-term goals and shorter-term sub-goals. This is all it needs to have what philosopher's call "intentionality." Philosophers might say, but Watson does not know "what it is like" to have these goals, whereas humans do know "what it is like."

Do we know what it is like to be our brothers, sisters, mothers, fathers, any better than we know what it is like to be a bat? (Nagel, 1974). Not if "what it is like" is thought to be some ineffable physical or non-physical state of our nervous systems, hidden forever from the observations of others. The correct answer to "What is it like to be a bat?" is "to behave, over an extended time period, and in a social context, as a bat behaves." The correct answer to "What is it like to be a human being?" is "to behave, over an extended time period, and in a social context, as a human being behaves."

Will Watson II Perceive?

Watson can detect miniscule variations in its input and, up to a point, understand their meaning in terms of English sentences and their relationship to other English sentences. Moreover, the sentences it detects are directly related to what is currently its primary need—its reason for being—coming up quickly with the right answer ("question") to the *Jeopardy* question ("answer") and learning by its mistakes to further refine its discrimination. Watson's perception of its electronic input, however efficient and refined, is also very constrained. That is because of the narrowness of its primary need (to answer questions).

But Watson currently has other needs: a steady supply of electric power with elaborate surge protection, periodic maintenance, a specific temperature range, protection from the elements, and protection from damage or theft of its hardware and software. I assume that currently there exist sensors, internal and external, that monitor the state of the systems supplying these needs. Some of the sensors are probably external to the machine itself, but let us imagine that all are located on Watson II's surface.

Watson currently has no way to satisfy its needs by its own behavior, but it can be given such powers. Watson II will be able to monitor and analyze his own power supply. He will have distance sensors to monitor the condition of his surroundings (his external environment) and to detect and analyze movement in the environment, as well as his own speech, in terms of benefits and threats to his primary and secondary functions. He will be able to organize his speech into patterns—those that lead to better functioning in the future and those that lead to worse. He will be able to act in such a way that benefits are maximized and threats are minimized by his actions. That is, he will be able to discriminate among (i.e., behave differently in the presence of) different complex situations that may be extended in time. He will be able to discriminate one from another of his handlers. He will be able to discriminate between a person who is happy and a person who is sad. He will be able to discriminate between a person who is just acting happy and one who truly is happy, between a person with hostile intentions toward him and a person with good intentions.

As indicated in Chapter 2, teleological behaviorism enables an observer to make such distinctions; they depend on narrow versus wide perspectives. Just as the difference between a person who is actually hearing a quartet and a deaf person behaving in the same way for a limited period depends on patterns of behavior beyond that period, so the difference between a person having a real perception, a real emotion, or a real thought and a great actor pretending to have the perception, emotion, or thought depends on patterns of behavior extending beyond the actor's current performance—before the curtain rises and after it goes down. I do not believe that a system that can learn to make such discriminations is beyond current technology. The most sophisticated, modern poker-playing computers currently bluff and guess at bluffs depending on the characteristics of specific opponents over extended periods.

These very subtle discriminations would extend to Watson II's social environment. Watson II will have the power to lie and to deceive people. Like other humans, he will have to balance the immediate advantages of a lie with the long-term advantage of having a reputation for truth-telling and the danger of damaging another person's interests that might overlap with his own interests. These advantages may be so ineffable that he may develop the rule: don't lie except in obvious emergencies. Like the rule: stop at red lights except in obvious emergencies, this might serve well to avoid difficult and complex calculations and may free up resources for other purposes.

With such powers, Watson II's perception will function for him as ours does for us. It will help him in his social interactions as well as his interactions with physical objects that make a difference in satisfying his needs. What counts for Watson II's humanity is not *what* he perceives, not even *how* he perceives, but *why* he perceives; his perception must function in the same way as ours does.

Will Watson II Be Able to Imagine?

Watson seems to have a primitive sort of imagination. Like any computer, it has internal representations of its input. But a picture in your head, or a coded representation of a picture in your head, while it may be part of an imagination mechanism, is not imagination itself. Imagination itself is behavior—acting in the absence of some state of affairs as you would in its presence. Such behavior has an important function in human life—to make perception possible. Pictures in our heads do not themselves have this function.

Recall the illustration of imagination from Chapter 2: Two people a woman and a man, are asked to imagine a lion in the room. The woman closes her eyes, nods, says, "Yes, I see it. It has a tail and a mane. It is walking through the jungle." The man runs screaming from the room. The man is imagining an actual lion. The woman would be imagining not a lion but a picture of a lion; in the absence of the picture, she is doing what she would do in its presence. An actor on a stage is thus a true imaginer, and good acting is good imagination—not because of any picture in the actor's head, but because he is behaving in the absence of a set of conditions as he would if they were actually present.

What would Watson need to imagine in this sense? Watson already has this ability to a degree. As a question is fed in, Watson does not wait for it to be completed. Watson is already guessing at possible completions and looking up answers. Similarly, we step confidently onto an unseen but imagined floor when we walk into a room. The outfielder runs to where the ball will be on the basis of the sound of the bat and a fraction of a second of its initial flight. We confide in a friend and do not confide in strangers on the basis of their voices on the telephone. On the basis of small cues, we assume that perfect strangers will either cooperate with us in mutual tasks or behave strictly in their own interests. Of course, we are often wrong. But we learn by experience to refine these perceptions. This tendency, so necessary for everyday human life, to discriminate on the basis of partial information and past experience, and to refine such discriminations based on their outcomes vis-à-vis our needs, will be possessed by Watson II.

Will Watson II Feel Pain?

In a classic article, Dennett (1978) took up the question of whether a computer could ever feel pain. Dennett designed a pain program that duplicated in all relevant respects what was then known about the human neural pain-processing system and imagined these located inside a robot capable of primitive verbal and non-verbal behavior. But in the end, he admitted that most people would not regard the robot as actually in pain. I agree. To see what the problem is, let us consider the "Turing test," invented by the mathematician Alan Turing (1912–1954) as a means for determining the degree to which a machine can duplicate human behavior.

The Problem with the Turing Test

Imagine the machine in question and a real human side by side behind a screen. For each there is an input device (say, a computer keyboard) and an output device (say, a computer screen) by which observers may ask questions and receive answers, make comments, and receive comments, and generally communicate. The observer does not know in advance which inputs and outputs are going to and coming from the human and which are going to and coming from the machine. If, after varying the questions over a wide range so that in the opinion of the observer only a real human can meaningfully answer them, the observer still cannot reliably tell which is the computer and which is the machine, then, within the constraints imposed by the range and variety of the questions, the machine is human—regardless of the mechanism by which the computer does its job.

What counts is the machine's behavior, not the mechanism that produced the behavior. Nevertheless, there is a serious problem with the Turing test—it ignores the function of the supposedly human behavior in human society. Let us agree that Dennett's computer would pass the Turing test for a person in pain. Whatever questions or comments typed on the computer's keyboard, the computer's answers would be no less human than those of the real person in real pain at the time. Yet the machine is clearly not really in pain, while the person is.

For Dennett, the lesson of the Turing test for pain is that certain mental states, such as pain, pleasure, and sensation, which philosophers call "raw feels," are truly private and are available only to introspection. That, Dennett believes, is why the Turing test fails with them—not, as I believe, because it cannot capture their functions—most importantly, their social functions. Dennett believes that other mental states, called "propositional attitudes," such as knowledge, thought, reasoning, and memory, unlike raw feels, may indeed be detectible in a machine by means of the Turing test. But, like raw feels, propositional attitudes have social functions. Thus, the Turing test is not adequate to detect *either* kind of mental state in a machine. Watson may pass the Turing test for logical thinking with flying colors but, unless the actual *function* of its logic is expanded in ways discussed here, Watson's thought will differ essentially from human thought.

The Turing test is a behavioral test. But as it is typically presented, it is much too limited. If we expand the test by removing the screen and allowing the observer to interact with the mechanisms in meaningful ways over long periods of time—say, in games that involve trust and cooperation, and the computer passed the test—we would be approaching the example of Dolly II. Such a Turing test would indeed be valid. Let us call it the *tough* Turing test.

Passing the Tough Turing Test for Pain

In an article on pain (Rachlin, 1985), I claimed that a wagon with a squeaky wheel is more like a machine in pain than Dennett's computer would be (although, of course, the wagon is not really in pain either). What makes the wagon's squeak analogous to pain? The answer lies in how we interact with wagons, as opposed to how we interact with computers. The wagon clearly needs something (oil) to continue to perform its function for our benefit. It currently lacks that something and, if it does not get it soon, may suffer permanent damage, may eventually, irreparably, lose its function altogether. The wagon expresses that need in terms of a loud and annoying sound that will stop when the need is satisfied. "You help me and I'll help you," it seems to be saying. "I'll help you in two ways," the wagon says. "In the short term, I'll stop this annoying sound; in the longer term, I'll be better able to help you carry stuff around."

To genuinely feel pain, Watson must interact with humans in a way similar to a person in pain. For this, Watson would need a system of lights and sounds (speech-like, if not speech itself), the intensity of which varied with the degree of damage and the quality of which indicated the nature of the damage. To interact with humans in a human way, Watson would need the ability to recognize individual people. Currently, Watson has many systems operating in parallel. If it became a general purpose advisor for medical or legal or engineering problems, it might eventually need a system for allocating resources, for acknowledging a debt to individual handlers who helped it, a way of paying that debt (say, by devoting more of its resources to those individuals, or to someone they delegate) and, correspondingly, to punish someone who harmed it. Additionally, Watson II would be proactive, helping individuals on speculation, so to speak, in hope of future payback. Furthermore, Watson II would be programmed to respond to the pain of others with advice from his store of diagnostic and treatment information and with the ability to summon further help—to dial 911 and call an ambulance, for example. In other words, to really feel pain, Watson would need to interact in an interpersonal economy, giving and receiving help, learning whom to trust and whom not to trust, responding to overall rates of events as well as to individual events. In behaving probabilistically, Watson II will often be "wrong"—too trusting or too suspicious. But his learning capacity would bring such incidents down to a minimal level.

Watson II will perceive his environment in the sense discussed previously—learning to identify threats to his well-being and refining that identification over time. He will respond to such threats by signaling his trusted handlers to help remove them, even when the actual damage is far in the future or only vaguely anticipated. Again, the signals could be particular arrangements of lights and sounds; in terms of human language, they would be the vocabulary of fear and anxiety. In situations of great danger, the lights and sounds would be bright, loud, continuous, annoying, and directed at those most able to help. The first reinforcement for help delivered would be the ceasing of these annoyances (technically, negative reinforcement). But, just as the wagon with the squeaky wheel functions better after oiling, the primary way that Watson II will reinforce the responses of his social circle will be his better functioning.

It is important to note that the question: Is Watson really in pain? cannot be separated from the question: Is Watson human? A machine that had the human capacity to feel pain, and only that capacity—that was not human (or animal) in any other way—could not really be in pain. A Watson that was not a human being (or another animal) could not really be in pain. And this is the case for any other individual human trait. Watson could not remember, perceive, see, think, know, or believe in isolation. These are human qualities by definition. Therefore, although we consider them one by one, humanity is a matter of all (or most) or none. Watson needs to feel pain to be human but also needs to be human before it can feel pain. But, a Watson that is human (that is, Watson II) in other respects *and* exhibits pain behavior, as specified above, would really be in pain.

What Do We Talk about When We Talk about Pain?

Once we agree that the word "pain" is not a label for a non-physical entity within us, we can focus on its semantics. Is it efficient to just transfer our conception of "pain" (its meaning) from a private undefined *spiritual* experience that no one else can observe to a private and equally undefined *physical* stimulus or response that no one else can observe? Such a shift simply assumes the privacy of pain (we all know it; it is intuitively obvious) and diverts attention from an important question: What is *gained* by insisting on the privacy of pain? Let us consider that question.

In its primitive state, pain behavior is the unconditional response to injury. Sometimes an injury is as clear to an observer as is the behavior itself; but sometimes the injury may be internal, such as a tooth cavity, or may be abstract in nature—such as being rejected by a loved one. In these cases the help or comfort we offer to the victim cannot be contingent on a detailed checking-out of the facts; there is no time; there may be no way to check. Our help, to be effective, needs to be immediate. So, instead of checking out the facts, we give the person in pain, and so should we give Watson II, the benefit of the doubt. Like the fireman responding to an alarm, we just assume that our help is needed. This policy, like the fireman's policy, will result in some false alarms. Watson II's false alarms might teach others to ignore his signals. But, like any of us, Watson II would have to learn to ration his pain behavior, to reserve it for real emergencies. Watson II's balance point, like our balance points, will depend on the mores of his society. That society might (like the fire department) find it to be efficient to respond to any pain signal, regardless of the frequency of false alarms; or that society, like a platoon leader in the midst of battle, might generally ignore less than extreme pain signals, ones without obvious causative damage.

Our social agreement that pain is an internal and essentially private event thus creates the risk that other people's responses to our pain will, absent any injury, reinforce that pain. This is a risk that most societies are willing to take for the benefit of quickness of response. So, instead of laying out a complex set of conditions for responding to pain behavior, we imagine that pain is essentially private, that only the person with the injury can observe the pain. We take pain on faith. This is a useful shortcut for everyday-life use of the language of pain (as it is for much of our mentalistic language), but it is harmful for the psychological study of pain and is irrelevant to the question of whether Watson II can possibly be in pain. Once Watson II exhibits pain behavior and other human behavior in all of its essential respects, we must acknowledge that he really is in pain. It may become convenient to suppose that his pain is a private internal event. But this would be a useful convenience of everyday linguistic communication, like the convenience of saying that the sun rises and sets, not a statement of fact.

Because Watson II's environment would not be absolutely constant, he would have to learn to vary his behavior to adjust to environmental change. *Biological evolution* is the process by which we organisms adjust over generations, in structure and innate behavioral patterns, as the environment changes. *Behavioral evolution* is the process by which we learn new patterns and adjust them to environmental change within our lifetimes. In other words, our behavior evolves over our lifetimes, just as our physical structure evolves over generations.

I say *behavioral evolution* rather than *learning,* to emphasize the relation of behavioral change to biological evolution. Just as organisms evolve in their communities and communities evolve in the wider environment, so patterns of behavior evolve in an individual's lifetime (see Chapter 7). Evolution occurs on many levels. In biological evolution, replication and variation occur mostly on a genetic level, while selection acts on individual organisms. In behavioral evolution, replication and variation occur on a biological level, while selection occurs on a behavioral level; we are born with or innately develop behavioral patterns. But those patterns are further shaped by the environment over an organism's lifetime and often attain high degrees of complexity. This is nothing more than a repetition of what every behavior analyst knows. But it is worth emphasizing that operant conditioning is itself an evolutionary process (see Staddon & Simmelhag, 1971, for a detailed empirical study and argument of this point). We hunt through our environment for signals that this adaptation is working. Similarly, Watson II will adjust its output in accordance with complex and temporally extended environmental demands. Watson II will signal that things are going well in this respect with lights and sounds that are pleasurable to us. With these signals he will not be asking his handlers for immediate attention, as he would with pain signals. But such pleasing signals will give Watson II's handlers an immediate as well as a long-term incentive to reciprocate—to give Watson II pleasure and to avoid giving him pain.

Giving Watson Self-Control and Altruism

People often prefer smaller-sooner rewards to larger-later ones. A child, for example, may prefer one candy bar today to two candy bars tomorrow. An adult may prefer $1,000 today to $2,000 five years from today. In general, the further into the future a reward is, the less it is worth today. A bond that pays you $2,000 in five years is worth more today than one that pays you $2,000 in ten years. The mathematical function relating the present value of a reward to its delay is called a *delay discount (DD) function*. Delay discount functions can be measured for individuals. Different people discount money more or less steeply than others (they have steeper or more shallow delay discount functions); these functions can be measured and used to predict degree of self-control. As you would expect: children have steeper DD functions than adults; gamblers have steeper DD functions than non-gamblers; alcoholics have steeper DD functions than non-alcoholics; drug addicts have steeper DD functions than non-addicts; students with bad grades have steeper DD functions than students with good grades; and so forth (Madden & Bickel, 2009). Watson's behavior, to be human behavior, needs to be describable by a DD function, too. It would be easy to build such a function (hyperbolic in shape, as it is among humans and other animals) into Watson II. But DD functions also change in steepness with amount, quality, and kind of reward. We would have to build in hundreds of such functions, and even then it would be difficult to cover all eventualities. A better way to give Watson II DD functions would be to first give him the ability to learn to pattern his behavior over extended periods of time. As Watson II learned to extend his behavior in time, without making every decision on a case-by-case basis, he would, by definition, develop better and better self-control. A Watson II with self-control would decide how to allocate his time over the current month or year or five-year period, rather than over the current day or hour or minute. Patterns of allocation evolve in complexity and duration over our lifetimes by an evolutionary process similar to the evolution of complexity (e.g., the eye) over generations of organisms. This ability to learn and to vary temporal patterning would yield the DD functions we observe (Locey & Rachlin, 2011). To have human self-control, Watson II needs this ability.

A person's relation with other people in acts of social cooperation may be seen as an extension of her relation with her future self in acts of self-control. That there is a relation between human self-control and human altruism has been noted in modern philosophy (Parfit, 1984), economics (Simon, 1995), and psychology (Ainslie, 1992; Rachlin, 2002). Biologists have argued that we humans inherit altruistic tendencies—that evolution acts over groups as well as individuals (Sober & Wilson, 1998). Be that as it may, altruistic behavior may develop within a person's lifetime by behavioral evolution—learning patterns (groups of acts) rather than individual acts. There is no need to build altruism into Watson. If Watson II has the ability to learn to extend his patterns of behavior over time, he may learn to extend those patterns over groups of individuals. The path from swinging a hammer to building a house is no different in principle than the path from building a house to supporting one's family. If Watson can learn self-control, then Watson can learn social cooperation. (See Chapter 8 for a more detailed discussion of delay and social discount functions and their relation to self-control and altruism.)

Watson in Love

Robots (or pairs or groups of them) may design other robots. But I am assuming that IBM or a successor will continue to manufacture Watson throughout its development. Previously in this chapter, I claimed that Watson has no interests different from IBM's. But that does not mean that Watson could not evolve into Watson II. IBM, a corporation, itself has evolved over time. If Watson's development is successful, it will function within IBM like an organ in an organism; as

Wilson and Wilson (2008) point out, organ and organism evolve together at different levels. The function of the organ subserves the function of the organism because if the organism dies, the organ dies (unless it is transplanted).

Watson II would not reproduce or have sex. Given his inorganic composition, it would be easier in the foreseeable future for IBM to manufacture his clones than to give him these powers. Would this lack foreclose love for Watson II? It depends what you mean by love. Let us consider Plato on the subject. Plato's dialogue *The Symposium* consists mostly of a series of speeches about love. The other participants speak eloquently, praising love as a non-material good. But Socrates expands the discussion as follows:

> "Love, that all-beguiling power," includes every kind of longing for happiness and for the good. Yet those of us who are subject to this longing in the various fields of business, athletics, philosophy and so on, are never said to be in love, and are never known as lovers, while the man who devotes himself to what is only one of Love's many activities is given the name that should apply to all the rest as well. (*Symposium*, 305d)

What Plato is getting at here, I believe, is the notion, emphasized by the twentieth-century Gestalt psychologists, that the whole is greater than the sum of its parts—that combinations of things may be better than the sum of their components. To use a Gestalt example, a melody is not the sum of a series of notes. The pattern of the notes is what counts. The melody is the same and may have its emergent value in one key and another—with an entirely different set of notes.

A basketball player may sacrifice her own point totals for the sake of the team. All else being equal, a team that plays as a unit will beat one in which each individual player focuses solely on her own point totals. Teams that play together, teams on which individuals play altruistically, will thus tend to rise in their leagues. In biological evolution, the inheritance of altruism has been attributed to natural selection on the level of groups of people (Sober & Wilson, 1998; Wilson & Wilson, 2008). In behavioral evolution, Locey and I claim, altruism may be learned by a corresponding group-selection process (Locey & Rachlin, 2011).

According to Plato, two individuals who love each other constitute a kind of team that functions better in this world than they would separately. The actions of the pair approach closer to "the good," in Plato's terms, than the sum of their individual actions. How might Watson II be in love in this sense? Suppose the Chinese built a robot—Mao. Mao, unlike Watson II, looks like a human and moves around. It plays ping-pong, basketball, and soccer, and of course swims. It excels at all these sports. It is good at working with human teammates and at intimidating opponents, developing tactics appropriate for each game. However, good as Mao is, wirelessly connecting him to Watson II vastly improves the performance of each. Mao gets Watson II's lightning-fast calculating ability and vast memory. Watson II gets Mao's knowledge of human frailty and reading of human behavioral patterns, so necessary for sports—not to mention Mao's ability to get out into the world. Watson II, hooked up to Mao, learns faster; he incorporates Mao's experience with a greater variety of people, places, and things. Watson II is the stay-at-home intellectual; Mao is the get-out-and-socialize extrovert. [One is reminded of the detective novelist Rex Stout's pairing of Nero Wolfe (so fat as to be virtually housebound, but brilliant) and Archie Goodwin (without Wolfe's IQ but full of common sense, and mobile). Together they solve crimes. It is clear from the series of novels that their relationship is a kind of love—more meaningful to Archie, the narrator, than his relationships with women.]

In an influential article (Searle, 1980), the philosopher John Searle argued that it would be impossible for a computer to understand Chinese. Searle imagines a computer that memorized all possible Chinese sentences and their sequential dependencies and simply responded to each Chinese sentence with another Chinese sentence as a Chinese person would do. Such a computer, Searle argues, would pass the Turing test but would not know Chinese. True enough. Searle's argument is not dissimilar to Dennett's argument that a computer cannot feel pain (although these two philosophers disagree in many other respects). But, like Dennett with pain, Searle ignores the *function*, in the world, of knowing Chinese. Contrary to Searle, a computer that could use Chinese in subtle ways to satisfy its short- and long-term needs—to call for help in Chinese, to communicate its needs to Chinese speakers, to take quick action in response to warnings in Chinese, to attend conferences conducted in Chinese, to write articles in Chinese that summarized or criticized the papers delivered at those conferences. That computer would know Chinese. That is what it *means* to know Chinese—not to have some particular brain state or pattern of brain states that happens to be common among Chinese speakers.

It is important that Watson II and Mao each understand the other's actions. Watson II will therefore know Chinese (in the sense outlined above) as well as English. Each will warn the other of dangers. Each will comfort the other for failures. Comfort? Why give or receive comfort? So that they may put mistakes of the past behind them and more quickly attend to present tasks. Mao will fear separation from Watson II and vice versa. Each will be happier (perform better) with the other than when alone. To work harmoniously together, each machine would have to slowly learn to alter its own programs from those appropriate to its single state to those appropriate to the pair. It follows that were they to be suddenly separated, the functioning of both would be impaired. In other words, such a separation would be painful for them both. Watson II, with annoying lights and sounds, and Mao, in Chinese, would complain. And they each would be similarly happy if brought together again. Any signs that predicted a more prolonged or permanent separation (for instance, if Mao should hook up with a third computer) would engender still greater pain. For the handlers of both computers, as well as for the computers themselves, the language of love, jealousy, pain, and pleasure would be useful.

But, as with pain, love *alone* could not make a computer human. Perception, thought, hope, fear, pain, pleasure, and all or most of the rest of what makes us human would need to be present in its behavior before Watson II's love could be human love.

What We Talk about When We Talk about Love

Let us consider whether Watson II might ever lie about his love, his pleasure, his pain, or other feelings. To do that, we need to consider talk about feelings separately from having the feelings themselves. In some cases they are not separate. In the case of pain, for example, saying "Ouch!" is both a verbal expression of pain and part of the pain itself. But you might say, "I feel happy," for instance, without that verbal expression being part of your happiness itself. We tend to think that saying "I feel happy" is simply a report of a private and internal state. But, as Skinner (1957) pointed out, this raises the question of why someone should bother to report to other people her private internal state, a state completely inaccessible to them, a state that could have no direct effect on them and no meaning for them. After all, we do not walk down the street saying "the grass is green, or "the sky is blue," even though that may be entirely the case. If we say those things to another person we must have a reason for saying them. Why then should we say, "I am happy," or "I am sad," or "I love you"? The primary reason must be to tell other people something about how we will behave in the future. Such information may be highly useful to them; it will help in their dealings with us over that time. And if they are better at dealing with us, we will be better at dealing with them. The function of talking about feelings is to predict our future behavior, to tell other people how we will behave. Another function of Watson II's language may be to guide and organize his own behavior—as we might say to ourselves, "this is a waltz," before stepping onto the dance floor. But how do we ourselves know how we will behave? We know because in this or that situation in the past we have behaved in this or that way and it has turned out for the good (or for the bad). What may be inaccessible to others at the present moment is not some internal, essentially private, state but our behavior yesterday, the day before, and the day before that. It follows that another person, a person who is close to us and observes our behavior in its environment from the outside (and therefore has a better view of it than we ourselves do), may have a better access to our feelings than we ourselves do. Such a person would be better at predicting our behavior than we ourselves are. "Don't bother your father, he's feeling cranky today," a mother might say to her child. The father might respond,

"What are you talking about? I'm in a great mood." But the mother could be right. This kind of intimate familiarity, however, is rare. Mostly we see more of our own (overt) behavior than others see. We are always around when we are behaving. In that sense, and in that sense only, our feelings are private.

Given this behavioral view of talk about feelings, it might be beneficial to us at times to lie about them. Saying "I love you" is a notorious example. That expression may function as a promise of a certain kind of future behavior on our part. If I say "I love you" to someone, I imply that my promised pattern of future behavior will not just cost me nothing but will itself be of high value to me. It may be, however, that in the past such behavior has actually been costly to me. Hence, I may lie. The lie may or may not be harmless but, in either case, I would be lying not about my internal state but about my past and future behavior.

You could be wrong when you say "I love you," and at the same time not be lying. As discussed previously, our perception (our discrimination) between present and past conditions may lack perspective. (This may especially be the case with soft music playing and another person in our arms.) Thus, "I love you" may be perfectly sincere but wrong. In such a case, you might be thought of as lying to yourself. The issue, like all issues about false mental states, is not discrepancy between inner and outer but discrepancy between the short term and the long term.

So, will Watson II be capable of lying about his feelings and lying to himself about them? Why not? Watson II will need to make predictions about his own future behavior; it may be to his immediate advantage to predict falsely. Therefore he may learn to lie about his love, as he may learn to lie about his pain as well as his other mental states. Moreover, it will be more difficult for him to make complex predictions under current conditions when time is short than to make them at his leisure. That is what it takes to lie to himself about his feelings.

Does the Mechanism Matter?

Let us relax our self-imposed restraint of appearance and bodily movement and imagine that robotics and miniaturization have come so far that Watson II (like Mao) can be squeezed into a human-sized body that can move like a human. Instead of the nest of organic neural connections that constitutes the human brain, Watson II has a nest of silicon wires and chips. Now suppose that the silicon-controlled behavior is indistinguishable to an observer from the behavior controlled by the nest of nerves. The same tears (though of different chemical composition), the same pleas for mercy, and the same screams of agony that humans have are added to the behavioral patterns discussed previously. Would you say that the nest of nerves is really in pain while the nest of silicon is not? Can we say that the writhing, crying man is really in pain while the similarly writhing, crying robot is not really in pain? I would say no. I believe that a comprehensive behavioral psychology would not be possible if the answer were yes; our minds and souls would be inaccessible to others, prisoners within our bodies, isolated from the world by a nest of nerves.

Nevertheless, many psychologists, and many behaviorists, will disagree. (They would be made uncomfortable with Dolly II, probably get a divorce, were she to reveal to them, perfect as she was, that she was manufactured, not born.) Why would such an attitude persist so strongly? One reason may be found in teleological behaviorism itself. I have argued that our status as rational human beings depends on the temporal extent of our behavioral patterns. The extent of those patterns may be expanded to events prior to birth—to our origins in the actions of human parents, as compared to Watson II's origins in the actions of IBM. Those who would see Watson II as non-human because he was manufactured, not born, might go on to say that it would be worse for humanity were we all to be made as Watson II may be made. To me, this would be a step too far. We are all a conglomeration of built-in and environmentally modified mechanisms anyway. And no one can deny that there are flaws in our current construction.

Acknowledgment

Copyright 2013 by the Association for Behavior Analysis. Reprinted with permission of the publisher. Because this chapter includes comments by others based on the reprinted article (Rachlin, 2012b), I have not made any changes in this version, other than stylistic and grammatical ones. The chapter therefore contains repetitions of arguments, examples, and analogies, some lifted directly from earlier chapters, for which I apologize to the careful reader.

Two Commentaries

1. *Minding Rachlin's Eliminative Materialism*

J. J. McDOWELL, EMORY UNIVERSITY

Evidently, Rachlin (2012b), like many other scientists and philosophers, finds problematic the internality, privacy, ineffability, and non-physicality of mental events such as consciousness of the external world, the subjective experience of pain, qualia, raw feels, and so on. Philosopher of mind Colin McGinn (1994) discussed various ways in which thinkers have tried to deal with this dilemma, one of which is to "eliminate the source of trouble for fear of ontological embarrassment" (p. 144). This is what Rachlin has done. By identifying mental events and states with extended patterns of behavior, he has dispatched the phenomenology of consciousness *tout de suite*, leaving behind a purely materialist account of human behavior. It follows immediately that a machine can be human, provided only that it can be made to behave as a human behaves over extended periods of time. The only problem that remains, then, is to determine what patterns of behavior constitute "behaving like a human," and this is what Rachlin addresses in his paper.

Thirty-two years ago, noted philosopher John Searle (1980) published a paper in *Behavioral and Brain Sciences* in which he presented his now famous Chinese Room argument against the computational theory of mind that is entailed by cognitive science and much artificial intelligence research. Rachlin was a commentator on that article and in his published remarks made arguments similar to those advanced in the paper currently under consideration. In Searle's response to Rachlin, he said "I cannot imagine anybody actually believing these [i.e., Rachlin's] views . . . . what am I to make of it when Rachlin says that 'the pattern of the behavior *is* the mental state'? . . . . I therefore conclude that Rachlin's form of behaviorism is not generally true" (p. 454). Rachlin's version of eliminative materialism will be regarded as not generally true by anyone who, like Searle, believes that an adequate account of human behavior must accept as real and deal with the phenomenology of consciousness. And their number is legion. In an earlier paper, Rachlin (1992) commented on widespread "anitbehaviorist polemics from psychologists of mentalistic, cognitive, and physiological orientations as well as from philosophers of all orientations" (p. 1381). This sentiment is directed toward behaviorism as philosophy of mind. It gives rise to charges that behaviorism is ludicrous (Edelman, 1990) and an embarrassment (Searle, 2004), and not generally true. Unfortunately, such sentiments and charges often generalize to behavior analysis, the science of behavior, which of course can be practiced in the absence of any commitment to a philosophy of mind, and probably usually is.

For most people, philosophers and scientists included, conscious experience with a first-person, subjective ontology is *prima facie* evident as a property of human existence. *Res ipsa loquitor*. Rachlin does not explicitly deny this, but neither does he assert it. To assert it, given his teleological behaviorism, it seems that he would have to revert to a form of dualism, probably epiphenomenalism. There would have to be something *in addition to* temporally extended patterns of behavior, which would be the conscious experience. On the other hand, if he denied it, well, then Searle and many others would continue to wonder how he, or anyone, could believe such a thing.

There are at least three alternatives to Rachlin's eliminative materialism. One is to practice the science and clinical application of behavior analysis without a commitment to a specific philosophy of mind. This is not a bad alternative. Philosophers, and perhaps some scientists, might eventually sort things out and develop an understanding of conscious experience that could inform the science and clinical practice of behavior analysis in a useful way. It is important to note that this alternative entails agnosticism about mind, not eliminativism. A second alternative is to revert to a form of dualism that acknowledges consciousness as *res cogitans*. This is probably not a good idea because dualism, like eliminative behaviorism (behaviorism that entails eliminative materialism), is roundly rejected by philosophers and scientists of all persuasions (e.g., Searle, 2004). In our scientifically minded world we do not like the idea that a substance could exist that is not matter (dualism), just as we do not like the idea of denying what appears to be right under our noses (eliminative behaviorism). A third alternative is to try to reconcile the first-person, subjective ontology of consciousness with the materialist science of behavior. This is a tall order, but philosophers of mind have been working on a general form of this problem for many years. This third alternative will be considered further in the remainder of this paper.

The Phenomenology of Consciousness

What is consciousness? Many philosophical treatises have been written to address this question. This vast literature cannot be reviewed fully here, but we can get at least a basic understanding of the nature of consciousness by considering what is called intentionality. This is an idea that was introduced by Franz Brentano (1874/1995) and was later developed by Edmund Husserl (1900–1901/2001) and Jean-Paul Sartre, among others. Intentionality refers to the phenomenal fact that consciousness always appears to have an object. Consciousness is not an entity that exists on its own, like, say, a chair. Instead, it is a process or action, a consciousness *of* something. It is a *relation* toward objects in the world. Consciousness is not a thing, as its nominative grammar misleadingly suggests (cf. Wittgenstein, 1953/1999). It will be helpful to keep in mind the Husserlian motto: consciousness is always consciousness *of* something.

In a remarkable paper, Sartre (1947/1970) rhapsodized that Husserl had delivered us from the "malodorous brine of the mind" in which contents of consciousness float about as if having been consumed. No, said Husserl, consciousness, or mind, cannot have contents because it is not a substance with, among other things, an inside. It is not a stomach. The objects of conscious experience are not assimilated into the mind, according to Husserl, they remain out in the world, the point that Sartre celebrated in his brief paper. Consciousness is always consciousness *of* these external objects, *tout court*. Importantly, Husserlian intentionality also extends to consciousness of ourselves:

> We are. . . delivered from the "internal life"... for everything is finally outside: everything, even ourselves. Outside, in the world, among others. It is not in some hiding-place that we will discover ourselves; it is on the road, in the town, in the midst of the crowd, a thing among things, a human among humans. (Sartre, 1947/1970, p. 5)

This understanding of conscious experience is echoed in Rachlin's view that extended patterns of behavior in the external natural and social world are constitutive of humanity (and consciousness). Hilary Putnam (1975) advanced an analogous, externalist, view of meaning, and Maurice Merleau-Ponty's (1942/1963) phenomenology and psychology likewise have a strong externalist cast (Noë, 2009).

Sartre (1957/1960) further developed his view of consciousness in *The Transcendence of the Ego: An Existentialist Theory of Consciousness*, in which he discussed what might be considered two classes of conscious experience. The first, which will be referred to as primary conscious experience, does not entail an "ego," that is, a reference to the person who is having the conscious experience:

> When I run after a street car, when I look at the time, when I am absorbed in contemplating a portrait, there is no *I*. There is consciousness of the streetcar-having-to-be-overtaken, etc . . . . In fact, I am then plunged into the world of objects; it is they which constitute the unity of my consciousnesses; it is they which present themselves with values, with attractive and repellent qualities—but *me*, I have disappeared . . . . There is no place for *me* on this level. (pp. 48–49, italics in the original)

It is possible, however, to reflect on having a conscious experience, which then creates, as it were, the ego as a transcendent object, according to Sartre. This will be referred to as secondary conscious experience. In an act of reflection, "the *I* gives itself as transcendent" (Sartre, 1957/1960, p. 52), that is, as an object of consciousness, and hence as an object in the world. Furthermore, "the *I* never appears except on the occasion of a reflective act" (p. 53). This represents a radical break with Husserl, who held that the *I* always stood on the horizon of, and directed, conscious experience. For Sartre, the ego does not exist except in an act of reflection, and then it is an object of consciousness just like any other.

If phenomenology is the study of consciousness, and if human consciousness is always consciousness of the external world in which humans are immersed at every moment of their waking lives, then the study of consciousness must be the study of human existence. In this way, for Sartre, phenomenology becomes existentialism. What is important is not what a human being has as a set of properties—that is, his essence—but what the human being does, his existence or being-in-the-world (Heidegger, 1927/1962). The resonance of this perspective with a behavioral point of view is noteworthy. I have discussed some of the common grounds between behavior analysis and existential philosophy in other articles (McDowell, 1975, 1977). The task of the existential phenomenologist is to describe human existence, a topic that Sartre (1956/1966) turned to in *Being and Nothingness*. The task of the behavior analyst is to understand human behavior, which is a different approach to what is, in many ways, the same thing.

The elements of Sartre's understanding of consciousness discussed here can be summarized in three statements: (a) Consciousness is always consciousness *of* something and hence it is a process or action, a relation to things in the world. It follows that consciousness is not a substance or object (i.e., it is not *res cogitans*), and consequently it is not something that can have contents, like a stomach, or that can be located in a part of space, such as the brain, the head, or elsewhere in the body. (b) The "ego" or *I* is not something that stands behind and directs consciousness, as Husserl supposed. Instead, the *I* is given as an object of consciousness in an act of reflection; it is an object of consciousness like any other. Furthermore, the *I* does not exist except in an act of reflection. It follows that at least two classes of conscious experience can be distinguished, namely, primary consciousness, which is consciousness of objects in the world that does not include a reference to the consciousness of the subject, and secondary consciousness, which entails an act of reflection and hence includes a reference to the consciousness of the subject. These types of consciousness are not fundamentally different inasmuch as both are conscious experiences *of* something. But in secondary consciousness, the something entails a reference to the consciousness of the subject and hence creates the Sartrean *I*. (c) If conscious experience always exists with reference to the world, then it is probably best to study and try to understand it in the context of the human being acting in the world, which is to say, in the context of human existence, action, and behavior in the natural and social environment.

No doubt some philosophers would take issue with some of these points. Searle (2004), for example, would probably want to include a few additional considerations. But I think most philosophers would agree that this is at least a good start to understanding the nature of consciousness. Before going any further, it might be worthwhile to consider a possible contradiction. Why, if consciousness is right under our noses and therefore is immediately apparent, do we need a phenomenological analysis of it? Why do we need philosophers to tell us about the nature of conscious experience? Don't we already know, because we have it? The answer to these questions is that the brute fact of consciousness is what is right under our noses. It is possible that a careful analysis could uncover something important about its properties and nature, or could refine our understanding of it. If, when a philosopher says something like "consciousness is always consciousness *of* something," we examine our own conscious experience and find that it is consistent with the philosopher's statement, then we have benefited from the philosophical analysis.

Since the work of Husserl and Sartre, the philosophy of mind has come to be influenced strongly by neuroscience. Many contemporary philosophers of mind seek a physical, that is, a materialist, account of consciousness, and most (maybe even all) look to brain function as the source of conscious experience. This focus on the brain is likely to be problematic in view of the foregoing analysis of consciousness as a property of human interaction with the natural and social environment. Nevertheless, there are some ideas in these brain-based philosophies that are worth considering.

Brain-Based Philosophies of Mind

Three points of view will be discussed in this section, namely, those advanced by John Searle, Thomas Nagel, and Colin McGinn. Searle puts forward the idea that conscious experience is a natural property of the material function of the brain, and therefore something that simply happens as the brain goes about its business of regulating commerce between the whole organism and its environment. Thomas Nagel's view is similar, except that he is wary of contamination by remnants of Cartesian dualism. A view like Searle's may be overreacting in a way, and hence too insistent on *res extensa*. An alternate possibility, according to Nagel, is that a new conceptual framework is required that would allow us to consider both brain function and conscious experience as a single type of thing, undercutting, as it were, the duality of Descartes. Colin McGinn likewise advances a point of view much like Searle's, but he concludes, pessimistically, that a full understanding of how brain processes give rise to conscious experience is, in principle, beyond human comprehension.

John Searle

Searle (2004) believes that much confusion was created by, and has persisted because of, the language of Cartesian dualism. *Res extensa* and *res cogitans* are too starkly bifurcated. What is needed is an expanded notion of the physical that permits a subjective element. Such a notion would allow conscious experience to be a part of the physical world. Consciousness, according to Searle (1992, 2004), is caused by brain processes and therefore is causally reducible to them. Conscious experience nevertheless retains its subjective, first-person ontology and therefore is not *ontologically* reducible to brain processes. The two, neural activity and conscious experience, are different aspects, or levels of description, of the same thing, in the same way that, say, the molecular structure of a piston and the solidity of the piston are different aspects, or levels of description, of a piston (Searle's example). Importantly, however, in the case of conscious experience and the brain processes that cause it, the two aspects have different ontologies, that is, the reduction of conscious experience to brain processes is causal but not ontological.

Thomas Nagel

Thomas Nagel's view falls somewhere between Searle's and McGinn's. Early on, Nagel expressed doubt about whether existing conceptual categories and schemes could be used to obtain an effective understanding of consciousness from a physicalist perspective (Nagel, 1974). Searle wanted to expand the concept of the physical to include subjective elements. In contrast, Nagel wants to expand the concept of the subjective to include elements of the physical (Nagel, 1998, 2002). The first step is to acknowledge that the manifest properties of conscious experience, such as its subjectivity and first-person ontology, do not exhaust its nature. In other words, there also may be physical properties that are not manifest in the conscious experience itself. This is an important and plausible idea, and it bears repeating. The manifest properties of conscious experience, in particular its first-person, subjective ontology, may not exhaust its nature. There may be other, perhaps physical, properties of consciousness that we do not experience directly. For example, as I type these words I experience the movement of my arms, hands, and fingers on and over the keyboard, but I do not experience the many neuron firings and electrochemical events that I know are occurring in my central and peripheral nervous system, and that in principle could be detected with appropriate instrumentation. It is possible that my conscious experience of my body *entails* these neuron firings and chemical events, rather than just going along with them.

While Searle expresses his view with assertive certainty, Nagel is more tentative. To say that the mental supervenes on the physical, which Nagel believes to be the case (Nagel, 1998), does not constitute a solution to the problem. Instead, it is "a sign that there is something fundamental we don't know" (p. 205). Nagel's (2002) view is that a radically different conceptual framework is required in order to understand these matters fully:

> If strict correlations are observed between a phenomenological and a physiological variable, the hypothesis would be not that the physiological state causes the phenomenological [which is Searle's view], but that

there is a third term that entails both of them, but that is not defined as the mere conjunction of the other two. It would have to be a third type of variable, whose relation to the other two was not causal but constitutive. This third term should not leave anything out. It would have to be an X such that X's being a sensation and X's being a brain state both follow from the nature of X itself, independent of its relation to anything else. (p. 46)

X would have to be something "more fundamental than the physical" (Nagel, 2002, p. 68). I understand this to mean that X must be something *conceptually* more fundamental than the physical, not a *substance* that is more fundamental than the physical. An example would be a field (Nagel's example), analogous to the electromagnetic, gravitational, and Higgs fields that have proved to be useful in physics. An appropriately conceived field might be understood to give rise to both brain processes and conscious experience, and also to explain their connection and interaction. Nagel (2002) goes on:

> ...we may hope and ought to try as part of a scientific theory of mind to form a third conception that does have direct transparently necessary connections with both the mental and the physical, and through which their actual necessary connection with one another can therefore become transparent to us. Such a conception will have to be created; we won't just find it lying around. A utopian dream, certainly: but all the great reductive successes in the history of science have depended on theoretical concepts, not natural ones—concepts whose whole justification is that they permit us to give reductive explanations. (p. 47)

Colin McGinn

While Nagel is hopeful that a true understanding of consciousness in the material world can be achieved, Colin McGinn (1993, 2002) has given up hope. Like Searle and Nagel, McGinn believes that conscious processes supervene on brain processes but are not ontologically reducible to them. Searle believes that this provides a reasonable understanding of consciousness, but Nagel finds this view incomplete. McGinn also disagrees with Searle, but unlike Nagel, believes it will never be possible, even in principle, to understand the relationship between conscious experience and material reality. There is a reason that efforts to understand this relationship for thousands of years have failed. It can't be done. This does not mean there is no relationship, it just means that the human intellect is too limited to understand it. McGinn refers to this as cognitive closure. Just as a dog can know nothing about quantum physics because of its intellectual limits, a human cannot fully understand conscious experience and its relation to the material world because of his or her intellectual limits (McGinn's example).

Making Sense of the Brain-Based Philosophies

Searle seems confident that an expanded notion of the physical, which includes a subjective element, together with the understanding that conscious experience is causally but not ontologically reducible to physical states in the brain, is a reasonable solution to the mind-body problem. But how can we be sure this is true? Is there an experiment that could conceivably produce results showing Searle's solution to be false, that is, that conscious experience can exist independently of brain states? If not, then McGinn's pessimism may be warranted. But we can't be sure that McGinn's idea of cognitive closure is true either, because it is not possible to prove the negative. In view of these uncertainties, it may be that Nagel has the best perspective. A new analytic framework that entails a conceptual X "more fundamental than the physical" may help us to understand in a transparent way how conscious experience is related to material reality.

Reconciling Conscious Experience with the Material World

Missing from all these philosophies, no doubt because they are so taken with contemporary neuroscience, is an understanding of how the natural and social environment figures into the workings of brain and consciousness. Where is consideration of the streetcar-having-to-be-overtaken, the watch-having-to-be-consulted, the portrait-having-to-be-understood? The earlier phenomenological analysis revealed the importance of such considerations, but even from a purely naturalistic perspective their importance is obvious; there would be no brain and no consciousness if there were no external environment. Indeed, the brain and consciousness are *for* the world of human existence, action, and behavior, they are *for* overtaking the streetcar, consulting the watch, and understanding the portrait. Contemporary philosopher of mind Alva Noë agrees:

> The conscious mind is not inside us; it is . . . a kind of attunement to the world, an achieved integration . . . . The locus of consciousness is the dynamic life of the whole, environmentally plugged-in person or animal. (Noë, 2009, p. 142)

Let us acknowledge that Nagel's view may constitute the beginning of a reconciliation, but that his unifying conceptual X should be sought not in the context of brain and consciousness alone, but in the context of brain, consciousness, and world. This may be our best hope for reconciling conscious experience with the material world of brain and behavior. Obviously, the reconciliation is far from complete—indeed, it has hardly begun. Furthermore, its ultimate achievement is far from certain. But this perspective at least allows us to talk about consciousness in a reasonable way from a materialist perspective.

Mental Causation

One problem a reconciliation like this poses is the possibility of mental causation. If we admit consciousness into our account of human action, then aren't we also admitting the possibility that mental events can cause physical events, such as bodily motion? The answer to this question is yes, but it is not a *necessary* feature of such a reconciliation. Searle (2004), for example, takes mental causation as a given because it is manifest in conscious experience. But recall that for Searle, a mental event is an aspect of, and is itself caused by, a physical event, specifically a brain process. Hence it is the brain process, which entails both a physical and a mental aspect, that is the actual cause. Given Searle's expanded understanding of the physical, mental causation really consists in a physical event causing another physical event. A brain process causes, say, behavior, and also the conscious experience of the mental aspect of the brain process causing the behavior. So far so good. But what causes the brain process in the first place? Searle entertains the possibility that the organism as an agent may initiate the brain process. This is the 2,400-year-old Aristotelian idea of an internal principle of movement, a principle that Aristotle used to explain the motion of all natural objects, including celestial and sub-lunary bodies, and animate beings and their parts (McDowell, 1988). But it could be that the causes of motion instead lie outside the bodies. In the case of celestial and sub-lunary bodies, the Aristotelian internal causes were abandoned in favor of external forces during the Middle Ages (for sub-lunary bodies) and during the Enlightenment (for celestial bodies; McDowell, 1988). Similarly, in the case of animate beings and their parts, classical behavior analysis has sought to replace the internal motive principle with an external cause, namely, the organism's past adaptive interaction with its environment. Evidently then, admitting consciousness, and with it the experience of mental causation, does not necessarily introduce agency into an account of human action and behavior. Instead, it is possible that mental causation is only an appearance, in the same way that the setting sun and the stationariness of the earth are appearances.

A Different Approach: Build a Conscious Artifact

The interesting work of thinker, neuroscientist, and Nobel laureate Gerald Edelman brings us back to a consideration of machine humanity. From a philosophy of mind similar to Searle's, Edelman (1990) goes on to develop an elaborate and detailed neurobiological theory of consciousness that is based on his theory of neuronal group selection (Edelman, 1987). Neuronal group selection is a theory about how the brain, understood as a selectional system, regulates the behavior of whole organisms in their environments. Briefly, neural circuits subserving behavior are selected by value systems in the brain, which are activated when the organism's behavior produces consequences in the environment. This is a theory about the functioning of whole brains in whole organisms that are actively engaged with their environments, and as such is a theoretical rarity in contemporary neuroscience. Interestingly, Edelman's theory is consistent with our understanding of the phenomenology of consciousness, and it shares features with a behavior analytic point of view, both in terms of its focus on whole organisms behaving in environments that may provide consequences for behavior, and in terms of its selectionist principles. The latter have been discussed extensively in behavior analysis (e.g., Skinner, 1981; Staddon & Simmelhag, 1971) and have been used explicitly in behavior-analytic theory building, which has met with some success (McDowell, 2004; McDowell, Caron, Kulubekova, & Berg, 2008). I have summarized Edelman's theory of neuronal group selection and discussed its connection to selectionism in behavior analysis in another article (McDowell, 2010).

Edelman believes that a machine built with a selectionist nervous system would have at least primary conscious experience. How can one know for sure? Build the machine. Edelman believes this is possible and, moreover, he is committed to making it happen. In a recent paper, he and two colleagues assert "that there is now sufficient evidence to consider the design and construction of a conscious artifact" (Edelman, Gally, & Baars, 2011, p. 1). Determining that such an artifact is conscious (no mean feat, as discussed below) would confirm that material objects and processes can in fact give rise to conscious experience.

Discussion

A reasonable alternative to Rachlin's eliminative materialism is to admit the reality of first-person subjective conscious experience, and seek to reconcile it with the material world by means of Nagel's X, understood in the context of the whole organism (brain included) behaving adaptively in the natural and social environment.

Machine Humanity

This alternative implies that for a machine to be judged human it must have conscious experiences that are characterized by a first-person subjective ontology, and it also must be able to do all the things that Rachlin said it must be able to do. Is this possible? We have seen that Edelman and his colleagues believe so. Among other philosophers and scientists, opinions vary. No doubt building a conscious machine would be a complicated and challenging task. At least as complicated and challenging would be the task of determining whether the machine really was conscious. A small start might be made by testing it in mental rotation experiments, and comparing the results to those obtained from human subjects (Edelman, Gally, & Baars, 2011). Koch and Tononi (2011) suggested a visual oddity test in which the artifact would be required to tell the difference between a sensible picture, for example, a person sitting in a chair at a desk, and a nonsense picture, such as a person floating in the air above the desk. A third method of testing for consciousness would be to observe extended patterns of behavior, which would tell us something about the artifact's conscious state. Rachlin, of course, would approve of this method (it is his tough Turing test), whether he thought the behavior *was* the consciousness or only indicative of it. He gave a good example of such testing in his commentary on Searle's (1980) Chinese Room article:

> [A conscious robot] might answer questions about a story that it hears, but it should also laugh and cry in the right places; it should be able to tell when the story is over. If the story is a moral one the robot might change its subsequent behavior in situations similar to the ones the story describes. The robot might ask questions about the story itself, and the answers it receives might change its behavior later (p. 444).

This is probably the best of the three methods of determining consciousness. The more behavior that is observed, and the more complicated, subtle, temporally organized, and teleological it appears to be, the more convinced we would be that the robot had conscious experience. But can we be *sure*? I suspect we could be no more or less sure than we can be about another person's consciousness. After lengthy experience with the machine (as in Rachlin's Dolly II example) we may interact with it as a matter of course as if it were conscious. If pressed, we would admit that we were not absolutely certain that it was. But at some point, after extended interaction, during which there was no behavioral indication that the machine was not conscious, the absence of absolute certainty probably wouldn't matter. At that point, for all intents and purposes, we would take the artifact to be sentient, which is what we do with other people. Does this mean that the extended behavior *is* the consciousness? No. According to the perspective developed here, it means that the existence of acceptable extended behavior necessarily implies the *other* aspect of its material realization, which is consciousness. The two go together. They are necessary co-manifestations of the more fundamental X of Nagel. In this sense, Nagel's X is like dark matter. We don't know what it is, but it helps us explain our observations of the world.

Consequences for Formal- and Efficient-Cause Behavior Analysis

Rachlin's emphasis on temporally extended and organized patterns of behavior is valuable and interesting. Would his teleological behaviorism change in any way if its elimination of conscious experience were rescinded, and were replaced by a view that acknowledged the existence and reality of consciousness? Of course, it would entail this new understanding of conscious experience, but other than that, it seems there would be little, if any, change. The use of utility functions, the assertion of correlation-based causality, and so on, would remain the same, and the science based on these tools and ideas could proceed as it always has. If Nagel's "utopian dream" were realized at some point, then Rachlin's program might be affected, depending on what the X was asserted to be. But then again, it might not. The discovery of synapses, for example, dramatically improved our understanding of how neurons worked, but this information does not affect the science of behavior analysis in any discernible way. The discovery of the dopaminergic value system in the brain comes a bit closer because it deals with the rewarding properties of external events. But this information also does not affect the science of behavior analysis, except insofar as it confirms what behavior analysts knew in more general terms had to be the case anyway.

The same can be said for classical, efficient-cause behavior analysis. Accepting the version of Nagel's theory discussed here probably would not change its practice or clinical application in any discernible way, depending again on what Nagel's X ultimately turned out to be. In view of these considerations, I feel confident in predicting that most (of the few?) behavior analysts who read these papers, when they return to their laboratories and clinics, will not give a second thought to the philosophy of mind that their science or clinical practice entails. However, if pressed by interlocutors who charge ludicrousness, embarrassment, or untruth, they may wish to call up some of these ideas as transcendent objects of consciousness and with them dispatch the naysayers forthwith.

Acknowledgment

I thank the Stadtbibliothek in Aschaffenburg, Germany, for providing a helpful and welcoming environment while I was working on this paper. I also benefited from interesting discussions with Andrei Popa about Howard Rachlin's point of view. Nick Calvin, Andrei Popa, and Giovanni Valiante made many helpful comments on an earlier version of this paper, for which I am grateful. Finally, I thank Howard Rachlin, who was my PhD mentor, for my initial schooling in matters of behavior and mind. I hope I have not disappointed him. Copyright 2013 by the Association for Behavior Analysis. Reprinted with permission of the publisher and author.

2. What Would It Be Like to Be IBM's Computer Watson?

HENRY D. SCHLINGER, JR., CALIFORNIA STATE UNIVERSITY, LOS ANGELES

Rachlin (2012a) makes two general assertions: (a) that "to be human is to behave as humans behave, and to function in society as humans function," and (b) that "essential human attributes such as consciousness, the ability to love, to feel pain, to sense, to perceive, and to imagine may all be possessed by a computer" (p. 1). Although Rachlin's article is an exercise in speculating about what would make us call a computer human, as he admits, it also allows us to contemplate the question of what makes us human. In what follows, I mostly tackle the second general assertion, although I briefly address the first assertion.

To Be or Not to Be Human

Without becoming ensnared in the ontological question of what it means to be human, let me just say that from a radical behavioral perspective, the issue should be phrased as: What variables control the response "human"? This approach follows from Skinner's (1945) statement of the radical behavioral position on the meaning of psychological terms. His position was that they have no meaning separate from the circumstances that cause someone to utter the word. Thus, when we ask what perception, imagining, consciousness, memory, and so on, are, we are really asking what variables evoke the terms at any given time. As one might guess, there are numerous variables in different combinations that probably evoke the response "human" in different speakers and at different times. Rachlin (2012a) claims that a "computer's appearance, its ability to make specific movements, its possession of particular internal structures—for example, whether those structures are organic or inorganic—and the presence of any non-material 'self,' are all incidental to its humanity" (p. 1). However, it could be argued that one's appearance and genetic (e.g., 46 chromosomes) and physiological structures (as behaviorists, we will omit the presence of any non-material "self") are not incidental to the extent that they, either alone or in some combination, evoke the response "human" in some speakers (e.g., geneticists, physiologists) at some times. For example, most people would probably call an individual with autism human because he or she has a human appearance and human genetic and physiological structures and behavior, even though he or she may lack language and the consciousness that is derived from it. But because the variables that control Rachlin's response "human" lie in the patterns of behavior of the individual organism or computer over time, we must wonder whether he could call this person "human." If this conception of humanity is at all troubling, as behavior analysts, we would have to at least agree with him that "[a] behavioral conception of humanity is better than a spiritual or neurocognitive conception. . . because it is potentially more useful." Once we accept his basic premise, we can move on to Rachlin's second general assertion: that a computer may possess all of the attributes listed above.

What Attributes Are Essentially Human?

Rachlin includes sensing, perceiving, consciousness, imagining, feeling pain, and being able to love as "essential human attributes" (later, he includes memory and logic in the list), but what does he mean by "essential"? There are two possibilities. The first meaning, which I would call the strong view, is that only humans possess these attributes; that is, the terms are applied only to humans. Thus, as Rachlin argues, the computer that possesses them would be human, The second meaning (the weak view) is that although other animals (or computers) might possess some of these attributes, to be called human, an individual must possess them all or must possess some (e.g., consciousness) that other organisms do not.

The term "strong view" (of essential human attributes) is meant to mirror, though not precisely, the term *strong AI* used by Searle (1980) to refer to one of two views of artificial intelligence (AI). According to Searle, in strong AI, "the appropriately programmed computer really is a mind, in the sense that computers given the right programs can be literally said to understand and have other cognitive states" (1980, p. 417). (*Weak AI* refers to using computers as a tool to understand human cognition, and it is therefore synonymous with the information-processing model of modern cognitive psychology; Schlinger, 1992.) Rachlin appears to support the strong view of human attributes (that only humans possess them) when he writes, "These are human qualities by definition." Thus, if a computer possessed these attributes, it would be human. (Of course, an alternate conception is that if a computer could possess them, then they are not essentially human.)

The strong view can be challenged simply by carrying out a functional analysis of terms such as *sensing, perceiving, consciousness*, and so on—that is, determining the variables that control our typical use of the terms (corresponding to the term's definitions), and then looking to see whether such variables occur in other organisms. Thus, without too much debate, I believe that we can at least eliminate sensation and perception from the strong view of essential human qualities. Sensation, as the transduction of environmental energy into nerve impulses, and perception, as behavior under stimulus control, are clearly present in most other species. The remainder of Rachlin's list of essential human attributes is trickier. Although some psychologists are willing to talk about animals being conscious and having feelings such as sadness and empathy, it is probably the case that such pronouncements are made based on some, but not all, of the behaviors exhibited by humans in similar situations. For example, regardless of any other behaviors, it is highly unlikely that other animals talk the way humans do when we are described as being empathetic. Describing non-humans with distinctly human-like terms is what leads some to level the charge of anthropomorphism.

Most behaviorists would probably not subscribe to the strong view of essential human attributes—that a computer possessing them would be human. The weak view, on the other hand, is more defensible, but not without its problems. Let us return to the question posed by Rachlin, about whether a computer—IBM's Watson—can possess these attributes.

Could Watson Possess Essential Human Attributes?

In what follows, I address each of the essential human attributes that Rachlin believes Watson could possess, and argue that the responses *sensation, perception, consciousness, feeling,* and *loving* as applied to Watson would be, at best, controlled by some, but not all, of the variables in humans that typically occasion the responses. Thus, the question of whether Watson can be made human may be moot. Perhaps a more relevant question is whether there is any justification to describe Watson, or any computer for that matter, with terms usually reserved for humans and some animals.

Before addressing the list of attributes, however, there is a more important issue to tackle, namely, the origin of almost all of the attributes listed by Rachlin. This issue is at the heart of Rachlin's statement that "[t]he place to start in making Watson human is not at appearance or movement but at human *function* in a human environment." This statement raises the question of just what a human function in a human environment is.

With the exception of sensation, which is built into biological organisms, the remaining attributes arise as a function of organisms interacting with their environment; and that environment consists of the natural environment as well as other organisms. In fact, one of the perennial problems in AI, at least for the first several decades of attempts to design and build computers that simulate human behavior, has been the failure on the part of researchers to recognize some important differences between computers and biological organisms, for example that organisms have bodies that sense and act upon the environment and their behavior is sensitive to that interaction; in other words, their behavior can be operantly conditioned (Schlinger, 1992). This is possible because organisms have bodies with needs and a drive to survive (Dreyfus, 1979). Of course, the "drive to survive" refers to the biological basis of staying alive long enough to increase the chances of passing on one's genes. Based on Dreyfus's critique of AI, Watson would need something akin to this drive. Moreover, from a behavioral perspective, a computer would have to be constructed or

programmed with unconditional motivation and, like humans and other animals, be capable of acquiring conditioned motivations and reinforcers through
learning. Rachlin's Watson II does have needs, but they are primarily to answer
questions posed to him by humans. In addition, he needs "a steady supply of
electric power with elaborate surge protection, periodic maintenance, a specific
temperature range, protection from the elements, and protection from damage or theft of its hardware and software." Getting needs met by acting on the
world presupposes another significant human attribute, the ability to learn in
the ways that humans learn. In other words, Watson II's behavior must be adaptive in the sense that successful behaviors (in getting needs met) are selected
at the expense of unsuccessful behaviors. Such operant learning is the basis of
behavior that we refer to as purposeful, intentional (Skinner, 1974), and intelligent (Schlinger, 1992, 2003); as I have argued, any AI device—and I would
include Watson—must be adaptive, which means "that a machine's 'behavior'
in a specific context must be sensitive to its own consequences" (Schlinger,
1992, pp. 129–130).

However, even if we grant Watson II's ability to get these needs met through
his "behavior" and his ability to "learn," the question remains of whether they
are functionally similar to those of biological organisms. Either way, would he
then be able to possess all the human attributes listed by Rachlin?

Sensation and Perception

As mentioned previously, sensation refers to the transduction of environmental
energy into nerve impulses, and perception refers to behaviors under stimulus
control (Schlinger, 2009; Skinner, 1953). Following from these basic definitions,
could Watson II sense and perceive? Obviously, unless Watson II was built dramatically differently from Watson, he would not sense in the same way that
organisms can. He would have no sense organs and sensory receptors that could
respond to different forms of environmental energy. Using the information-processing analogy, we can say that information could be input in auditory, visual,
or even, perhaps, in tactile form if he were constructed as a robot. And although
this type of input could become functionally related to Watson II's output, I do
not think we would want to call it sensation. At best, it is analogous to sensation.
On the other hand, if by "perception," all we mean is behavior under stimulus
control, I think we could describe Watson II as engaging in perceptual behavior
to the extent that his "behaviors" are brought under the control of whatever
input he is capable of and assuming, even more important, that his behavior is
sensitive to operant conditioning. However, even though describing Watson II
as perceiving may be more accurate than describing him as sensing, it is still only
analogous to what biological organisms do.

Speaking of Watson II behaving raises yet another problem. Will Watson
II really be behaving? As the behavior of biological organisms is the result of

underlying (physiological and musculoskeletal) structures, Watson II's behavior, like his sensing, would, at best, be an analogy to the behavior of organisms. Although I do not necessarily agree with Rachlin that mechanism is unimportant, I do agree with Rachlin that at least for most of our history it is not what has defined us as human, and that it might be possible to produce behavior with a different underlying mechanism that, for all practical purposes, we would call human.

Imagining

Even though constructing Watson II with attributes functionally similar to sensation and perception may be possible, arranging for the other attributes on Rachlin's list poses greater problems. First, however, let us agree with Rachlin by acknowledging that for the behaviorist, perception, imagining, consciousness, memory, and other so-called mental states or processes are really just words that are evoked by behaviors under certain circumstances (see also Schlinger, 2008, 2009a). As mentioned previously, to understand what we mean by these terms, we must look at the circumstances in which they are evoked.

With respect to imagining, the question is: What do we do when we are said to imagine and under what circumstances do we do it? (Schlinger, 2009a, p. 80). The answer is that when we are said to imagine either visually or auditorily, we are engaging in perceptual behaviors that are evoked in the absence of actual sensory experience, or as Rachlin put it, "[i]magination itself is behavior; that is, acting in the absence of some state of affairs as you would in its presence." For example, the behaviors involved in auditory imagining are most likely talking (or singing), to oneself, and in visual imagining, the behavior of "seeing" (Schlinger, 2009a). Note that the self-talk or "seeing" need not be covert (i.e., unobserved), but most often it is (Schlinger, 2009b).

Rachlin states that the behavior of imagining "has an important function in human life—to make perception possible" and that "[p]ictures in our heads do not themselves have this function," but I would argue that he has it backward: perception (as behavior under stimulus control) makes imagining possible. In other words, we must first act in the presence of certain stimulus events and have our behavior produce consequences before we can act in the absence of those events. We must first "see" a painting by Picasso before we can "see" the painting in its absence.

What would it take for Watson II to imagine? Simply speaking, Watson II would have to be able to behave in the absence of the stimuli. He would either have to "hear" (i.e., talk or sing to himself) in the absence of auditory stimuli or "see" in the absence of visual stimuli. In order to "hear" he would need a verbal repertoire like that of humans, and to "see" he would need some kind of visual system that would enable him to behave in the absence of the stimuli in ways similar to how he would behave in their presence. The verdict is still out as to whether this is possible.

Consciousness

Let me start by saying that I agree with Rachlin that, "[f]or a behaviorist, con-sciousness, like perception, attention, memory, and other mental acts, is itself *not* an internal event at all. It is a word we use. . ." In fact, I said as much in an article titled "Consciousness is Nothing but a Word" (Schlinger, 2008). (The rest of Rachlin's statement—"to refer to the organization of long-term behavioral patterns as they are going on"—is open to debate, and I think we can address the problem raised by Rachlin without either accepting or rejecting his teleo-logical behaviorism.) The critical point made by Rachlin is summed up in the fol-lowing: "A computer, if it behaves like a conscious person, would be conscious." This statement evokes at least two questions: (a) What does a conscious person behave like? and (b) Could a computer behave like a conscious person? If the answer to the second question is yes, then we might further ask whether the computer could behave like a conscious person without necessarily calling it "human." A third possible question is whether a person can be a person with-out being conscious. Answering these questions requires some agreement about what it means to be conscious.

What Does a Conscious Person Behave Like?

In answering this question, radical behaviorists ask what variables cause us to say that a person (or any other organism for that matter) is conscious. In the afore-referenced article (Schlinger, 2008), I listed at least three such situ-ations. The first is when an organism is awake rather than asleep. This use of "conscious," although not the most germane for our discussion, may still be applied, if only analogically, to Watson, just as it is to my Macintosh computer. A second situation that evokes the response "conscious" is when an organ-ism's behavior is under appropriate stimulus control. For example, I say that my cat is conscious of his environment if he avoids walking into things, jumps on the bed, plays with a toy mouse, and so on. In this sense, animals are obvi-ously conscious, and their behavior that leads us to say so has been operantly conditioned by interactions with the environment. (In this usage, the term is evoked by the same circumstances that the term "perceive" is. For example, saying "the cat perceives the mouse" is controlled by the same variables as "the cat is conscious of the mouse.") Notice that the environment does not have to be a human environment; it can consist of the animal's natural envi-ronment, including other animals. Presumably a computer could be conscious in this sense as well if its behavior could come under the stimulus control of events in its environment as a result of interactions with that environment. For Watson II, its environment would presumably consist entirely of humans. It is this sense of consciousness that interested Crick and Koch (2003) with their emphasis on visual perception.

A third circumstance that probably evokes the term "conscious" most often—and the one that is of most interest to consciousness scholars and laypeople alike—is the tendency to talk (i.e., describe) or imagine "to ourselves about both our external and internal environments, and our own public and private behavior" (Schlinger, 2008, p. 60). It is these behaviors that give rise to what consciousness scholars refer to as *qualia*, or subjective experience, and consists of what I believe a conscious person behaves like. That is, a conscious person is taught by his or her verbal community to answer questions about his or her own behavior, such as "What are you doing?" "Why did you do that?" and "What, or how, are you feeling?" (Schlinger, 2008; Skinner, 1957). As a result, we are constantly describing our behavior and private events both to others and to ourselves. Presumably, this is what Rachlin means by human function in a human environment.

As Skinner (1945) first suggested, we learn to talk about private (i.e., unobserved) events in the same way that we learn to talk about public (i.e., observed) events, that is, from others. In the case of private events, others only have access to the public events that accompany them. As a result, our descriptions come under the control, though not perfectly, of the private events. So, for example, we are taught to say "it hurts" when parents and others see either overt signs of injury, such as a cut or bruise, or when they observe us engaging in some kind of pain-related behavior, such as crying moaning, wincing, and so on. Later on, we say "it hurts" only to the private painful stimulation. (Of course, it is also possible to say "it hurts" in the absence of any painful stimulation. Rachlin would still call this pain.) I believe that it is only because we learned to say "ouch" or "it hurts" from others, that we actually are said to "feel" the pain, that is, the subjective experience of pain, as opposed to simply experiencing or reacting to the painful stimulation as my cat would. I think this is consistent with Rachlin's statement, "To genuinely feel pain, Watson must interact with humans in a way similar to a person in pain." This sense of consciousness is simply an extension of perception in that our verbal behavior is brought under the control of both public and private events dealing with ourselves.

Such self-talk is what I believe Descartes was experiencing that led him to state his famous *Cogito ergo sum* (I think, therefore I am) or, in behavioral terms, "I talk (to myself), about myself, therefore I am conscious of my existence." Although I might not agree with Rachlin about the details, I would agree with him that "consciousness is in the behavior not the mechanism."

Could a Computer Behave Like a Conscious Person?

Based on the brief analysis presented above, for Watson II to behave like a conscious person, he would have to behave appropriately with respect to his entire environment, including the environment inside his skin. But therein lies the rub. We can grant that the computer should be able to describe its public behavior, whatever that behavior is, but what about private events? Without a sensory system that, in addition to exteroception, also includes interoception or proprioception, Watson II would not be able to describe private stimulation or, in other words, how he feels. And, unless he is constructed such that the mechanisms that produce behavior proximally (motor neurons, muscles) can function at reduced magnitudes without producing overt behavior, he would also not be capable of covert behavior and, thus, would not be able to learn to describe such behavior. So, at best, Watson II would behave sort of like a human in that he could potentially be able to describe his overt behavior. But he would be handicapped in that he would have no private world to experience and, thus, to describe. But even if Watson II were able to describe his overt behavior, would we call him human? As I suggested previously, I think that question is moot. It is probably best to skirt the ontological question and concentrate on whether Watson II could engage in human-like behaviors.

What Would It Be Like to Be IBM's Computer Watson?

In addressing this issue of qualia, Nagel (1974) asked, "What is it like to be a bat?" Based on the discussion above, the answer has to be "nothing." It is like nothing to be a bat, or any other animal, including pre-verbal or non-verbal humans, without self-descriptive behavior. As I have stated, "For the bat there will never be any qualia because there is no language to describe experience" (see Schlinger, 2008, p. 60). Even Dennett (2005) came around to this view of consciousness when he wrote, "acquiring a human language (an oral or sign language) is a necessary precondition for consciousness."

Rachlin does not see it quite this way. According to him:

> Do we know what it is like to be our brothers, sisters, mothers, fathers, any better than we know what it is like to be a bat?. . . if "what it is like" is thought to be some ineffable physical or non-physical state of our nervous systems, hidden forever from the observations of others. The correct answer to "What is it like to be a bat?" is "to behave, over an extended time period, as a bat behaves." The correct answer to "What is it like to be a human being?" is "to behave, over an extended time period, as a human being behaves."

Or, as Rachlin states elsewhere in the target article, "*all* mental states (including sensations, perceptions, beliefs, knowledge, even pain) are rather patterns of *overt* behavior."

Although I understand Rachlin's point (after all, these are clear statements of his teleological behaviorism), I do not think such a position will be very palatable to traditional consciousness scholars. I believe that the position I have outlined here and elsewhere (Schlinger, 2008), while still perfectly behavioral, is closer to what consciousness scholars are getting at with their interest in qualia and subjective experience.

Conclusion

Even though it may be possible to construct a Watson (Watson II) with attributes that resemble those in humans, the question of whether the resulting computer would be human is moot. A more practical question, as I have suggested, is whether there is any justification to describe Watson II with terms usually occasioned by the behavior of biological organisms, especially humans. But even then, the critical question is: What is to be gained by talking about computers using terms occasioned by humans? If we had to choose between the weak view of AI (that the main goal in building smart computers is to try to understand human cognition or behavior) and the strong view (that the computer with the essential human attributes mentioned by Rachlin would, for all practical purposes, be human), the weak view seems to be more productive. In other words, it would challenge us to analyze attributes such as perception, imagination, and consciousness into their behavioral atoms and the history of reinforcement necessary to produce them, and then try to build a computer (Watson II) that would interact with its environment such that those repertoires would be differentially selected. If we were successful, would we then call Watson II human? Rachlin's thesis is that we would. My point in this commentary is that such a conclusion is, at the present time, too uncertain, and we would have to wait and see if Watson II would occasion the response "human." I'm not so sure.

A more likely scenario, in my opinion, is that Watson II may be human-like in some very important ways. Regardless, the questions posed by Rachlin should help to pave the way for thinking about how to construct a computer that is most human-like. Rachlin is correct that, in order to do so, the computer must function like a human in a human environment. However, some of the so-called human functions mentioned by Rachlin (e.g., sensation and perception) are also possessed by other animals. And the functions he does mention that may be most distinctly human (e.g., consciousness) do not arise from interactions that differ in any fundamental way from those that are responsible for other behaviors; in other words, the behaviors in question are selected by their consequences. Thus, the most important consideration in going forward in designing human-like computers is to build them with the ability for their "behavior" to be adaptive (Schlinger, 1992) and then see what happens.

Acknowledgment

Copyright 2013 by the Association for Behavior Analysis. Reprinted with permission of the publisher and author.

Response to Commentaries

Our Overt Behavior Makes Us Human

The commentaries both make excellent points; they are fair and serve to comple-ment the target article. Because they are also diverse, it makes sense to respond to them individually rather than topically.

McDowell

Before discussing McDowell's (2012) thoughtful comments, I need to clarify his categorization of my position on consciousness as "eliminative materialism." He is correct that I would eliminate the *phenomenology* of consciousness from scien-tific discourse. However, I also claim that the concept of consciousness itself is extremely useful and has an important place in behavior analysis. So I would not eliminate the *concept* of consciousness from scientific discourse. The theory of consciousness implied by Watson II is a physical theory, like the neural identity theories to which McDowell refers. However, neural identity theorists believe that consciousness occurs within the organism and is identical to some pattern of nervous behavior. I claim that consciousness occurs in the world outside the organism and is identical to abstract patterns of overt behavior. The difference between my identity theory and theirs is not one of physical versus mental; we agree that the mental is real, and it is identical to an abstract pattern of activ-ity of the organism. The difference is that, for them, the pattern occurs (wholly or mostly) over some spatial extent in the brain, whereas for me the pattern occurs over time in the organism's overt behavior. It is not the word *conscious-ness* that I would eliminate from scientific discourse—still less from everyday speech. Contrary to what McDowell says, I *do* "acknowledge the existence and reality of consciousness." Abstract entities, such as behavioral patterns, are as real as or more real than their components. [Both Plato and Aristotle believed that abstract entities may be in a sense more real (because they are directly con-nected to their function) than their components. For Aristotle, a chair is more real than the parts that make it up, and for Plato, the user of the chair knows the chair better than does its maker—again because the user is directly involved in its function as a chair (Rachlin, 1994).] It is rather phenomenological intro-spection or internal "reflection" as a means of psychological investigation that I would eliminate. I recognize the importance of a kind of reflection (contingen-cies of reinforcement are essentially reflections from overt behavior to the world and back), but not a reflection that takes place wholly within the organism. Introspection, as a psychological technique, has been tried for at least a century and has produced little of value. [Nevertheless, introspection may be useful in everyday life. I may say, "I am angry," or "I love you," but not merely to report an internal state, any more than I would say, "the grass is green," or "the sky is blue," merely to report an external state. Any statement must be made for a reason. The reason, in the case of "I am angry," and so on, is to predict one's own future behavior on the basis of one's own past behavior in similar circumstances. Such a prediction enables the hearer (it could be just one's own self) to react appropriately. A person (who is less observant of his own behavior than is someone close to him or her) may be wrong about an introspective statement. I might say, "I am angry," and truly believe it, and my wife may say, "No you're not," and she may be right. It is introspection as a scientific method, not introspection as a useful kind of everyday behavior, to which I object.]

One argument I take very seriously is that my view of the mind is bad for behavior analysis. But I cannot abandon that view because non-behaviorists or anti-behaviorists like John Searle are not able to understand why I have it. The history of science is full of *prima facie* facts proven to be less useful than their contraries. Especially suspicious are those facts that put humans at the center of the universe (physical or spiritual). The sorts of existence postulated by the phenomenologists arguably come under this heading. From a pragmatic viewpoint (my viewpoint), something is true because it is useful in the long run to behave as if it were true. The burden is on us behaviorists to show that our account is more useful than others. Once that happens, what seems obvious will change accordingly. Searle's objection, quoted by McDowell, rests on the implicit premise that what Searle cannot imagine or understand must be false. If the research based on teleological behaviorism by me and others turns out to be unfruitful or useless, then such objections will have weight. It is perhaps fair to say that there has not yet been enough research on behavioral patterns, or acceptance and understanding, even within behavior analysis, to give teleological behaviorism a fair test. One purpose of the target article is to correct this lack. Meanwhile, I will have to take my chances with Searle. He may be beyond convincing, but hopefully not every philosopher is that closed-minded. McDowell and others have reached across disciplines to make contact with philosophers and neuroscientists, and that gives one hope. If teleological behaviorism does not result in an improved behavioral technology, then that is why it will fail—not because it contradicts a philosopher's entirely subjective certitudes.

McDowell's summary of the views of Brentano, Husserl, and Sartre is interesting and enlightening. There is certainly a commonality between behaviorism and their philosophy, perhaps coming to a head in Ryle (1949) and the later Wittgenstein (1958), who said, "If one sees the behavior of a living thing, one sees its soul" (p. 357). More relevant to the current topic is McDowell's discussion of the modern philosophers John Searle, Thomas Nagel, and Colin McGinn. It seems to me that, at least as McDowell presents their views, all three are dancing around the mind-body problem and coming no closer to solving it than did the European philosophers of the eighteenth and nineteenth centuries. But modern philosophy is not as negative about behavioristic thought (or, more aptly, not as positive about phenomenology) as McDowell implies. According to Alva Noë (2009):

> After decades of concerted effort on the part of neuroscientists, psychologists, and philosophers, only one proposition about how the brain makes us conscious—how it gives rise to sensation, feeling, subjectivity—has emerged unchallenged: we don't have a clue. (p. xi)
>
> Consciousness is not something that happens inside us. It is something we do or make. Better: it is something we achieve. Consciousness is more like dancing [overt behavior] than it is like digestion [covert behavior] . . . . The idea that the only genuinely scientific study of consciousness would be one that identifies consciousness with events in the nervous system is a bit of outdated reductionism. (p. xii)

Searle, as quoted by McDowell, claims that "neural activity and conscious experience are different aspects, or levels of description, of the same thing, in the same way that, say, the molecular structure of a piston and the solidity of the piston are different aspects, or levels of description, of a piston." Amazingly, Searle has it almost right. Substitute *behavioral activity* (overt) for *neural activity* (covert) and I would completely agree. But Searle, despite his intention to rid philosophy of Cartesian remnants, has not completely eliminated Cartesian dualism from his own philosophy. If mental (or conscious) activity is an abstract version of physical activity, what is that physical activity? Why is it any more plausible for Searle, and the many philosophers who have considered this question, that conscious physical activity has to occur inside the head than that it occur in overt behavior? I understand why Descartes saw things this way. Because Descartes believed that the soul was located deep in the brain, and the physical motions had to directly influence the soul, and vice versa, the physical motions also had to be in the brain. But Searle presumably does not believe that there is a non-physical soul located deep within the brain interacting with our nerves. Nor, as McDowell points out, is this inherently obvious. Some societies and some ancient philosophers believed that our minds as well as our souls were in our hearts. I would guess that if you name a vital organ, there will be or have been some society that believed it to be the seat of the soul; there may even have been some who identified the soul with the whole organism. So if the mind is a molar or abstract conception of some physical activity (as Searle and I seem to agree), and there is no *a priori* reason (such as connectivity with an internal, non-physical soul) to assume that the physical activity occurs in the brain, where does it occur?

In answering this question, usefulness is paramount, especially as consciousness, and talk of consciousness, must have evolved along with the rest of our human qualities. Organisms may die without reproducing because their *behavior* is maladaptive, not (directly) because their *nerves* are maladaptive. Our nerves would be in direct contact with our souls if our souls, as the sources of consciousness, were inside us. But if our environment is seen as the source of our consciousness (as it would have to be if consciousness were a product of biological evolution), then it would be our overt behavior, not neural behavior, which is in direct contact with the source. Group selection (selection at the level of classes or patterns) may act at the level of nervous function, as Edelman and colleagues (e.g., Tononi & Edelman, 1998) have shown. It may act as well at the level of innate behavioral patterns across generations (Wilson & Wilson, 2008). And it may act as well at the level of learned patterns within the lifetime of a single organism (Rachlin, 2011).

Consciousness is therefore not an epiphenomenon or a faint halo that wafts up from a certain degree of complexity in our nervous systems, but is a vital property of our overt behavior with a vital function in our complex world. Our long-term patterns of behavior—sobriety, moderation, cooperation with others, morality, rationality, as well as the language that reflects (and at the same time imposes) their organization, all evolved. These patterns are what we would have to create in Watson II for him to leap over those eons of biological evolution and be human. The mechanism that could create those patterns may very well turn out to resemble our actual nervous mechanism. Or it may not. But it is behavioral evolution, not neural evolution, that counts for Watson II's consciousness.

Searle, Nagel, and McGinn, as presented by McDowell, all have double-aspect theories of mind: Body and mind are two aspects of the same thing. The traditional question to ask two-aspect theorists is: Two aspects of what? Searle gives the correct answer: The body is to the mind as the molecular ("molecular structure of a piston") is to the molar ("solidity of a piston"). This is a spatial analogy, but it could just as well be a temporal one: as the notes are to the melody; as the steps are to the dance. But Nagel and McGinn both posit a third entity that the two aspects are aspects *of*. For Nagel it is Factor X and for McGinn it is "unknowable." Are these answers to the traditional question any more enlightening than the traditional answer to that question—two aspects of God? I do not believe so.

A view of consciousness proposed by Noë (2009) holds (as I do) that the mind cannot be understood except in terms of the interaction of a whole organism with the external environment. Nevertheless, for Noë, the brain remains an important component of mental activity. He retains a neurocognitive view of the mind while expanding its reach, beyond the brain, into the peripheral nervous system and the external environment. According to Noë, "My consciousness now—with all its particular quality for me now—depends not *only* on what is happening in my brain but *also* on my history and my current position and interaction with the wider world" (p. 4, italics added).

I believe that this is a step in the right direction, but its problem is that it mixes levels of explanation. Consider (the following transcription of) Searle's distinction between physical activity and conscious experience: "[Behavioral] activity and conscious experience are different aspects, or levels of description, of the same thing, in the same way that, say, the molecular structure of a piston and the solidity of the piston are different aspects, or levels of description, of a piston." If conscious experience is analogous to the solidity of the piston, then it cannot *also* be analogous to its molecular structure. Noë's conception of conscious activity blurs the distinction between conscious and non-conscious activity. Extended cognition theory extends the domain of consciousness *spatially* beyond the brain, into the peripheral nervous system and out into the world. But it does not consider a *temporally* extended view of cognition, which extends behavior beyond the present moment into the past and future. It is this temporal extension, I believe, that gives Watson II his humanity.

Finally, McDowell proposes a mental rotation test and a visual oddity test as possible alternatives to the tough Turing test I proposed in the target article. The problem with these alternatives is that it would be extremely easy to build a machine that would pass these tests with flying colors. I believe the current Watson, with a little tweaking, could easily do it. Suppose Watson did pass these tests but failed the tough Turing test. Would anyone believe that it was human? Suppose Watson passed the tough Turing test (for sensation, perception, imagination, cognition, as well as the emotions of love, anger, hope, fear, etc.), but failed the mental rotation and visual oddity tests. Would it not be a violation of our common morality not to consider it human?

Schlinger (2012) claims that "Watson would be handicapped if he had no private world to experience and thus to describe" (p. 43). But he also agrees with me that "consciousness is in the behavior not the mechanism" (p. 42). The question I would like to address in this reply is: Do covert talking and covert picturing properly belong to the class of movements we call *behavior*, or are they themselves, like the chemical and electrical events involved in neural transmission, part of a *mechanism* underlying behavior? If the latter, then, by Schlinger's own reasoning, Watson's private world would be irrelevant to whether or not he could be conscious; we would then have to look, as I do in the target article, for Watson's and our own consciousness in our overt rather than covert behavior.

The nub of Schlinger's views is best captured by the following passage:

> A. . . circumstance that probably evokes the term "conscious" most often—and the one that is of most interest to consciousness scholars and laypeople alike—is the tendency to talk. . . to ourselves about both our external and internal environments, and our own public and private behavior. . . . It is these behaviors that give rise to what consciousness scholars refer to as *qualia*, or subjective experience, and consist

of what I believe a conscious person behaves like. That is, a conscious person is taught by his or her verbal community to answer questions about his or her own behavior, such as "What are you doing?" "Why did you do that?" and "What, or how, are you feeling?"...As a result, we are constantly describing our behavior and private events.

Let us start from the back of this statement. Why does our verbal community want to know what we are doing, how we are feeling, why we do this or that? What's in it for them to know? Or more precisely, what reinforces these requests of theirs? The answer is that we are interacting with our verbal community in a social system, our future behavior impacts on their welfare, and they would benefit by the ability to predict better than they currently can what our future behavior will be. [There may, of course, be other reasons. It may be idle curiosity. Or the questioner might be a neighbor saying "how are you?" and I answer, "fine," even if I happen to be rushing to the doctor. But I think that the reasons for such interchanges, like the reasons for those Schlinger cites, are reducible to a mutual interest in greasing the wheels of our current and future interactions.] So when we answer their questions, we are essentially making predictions about our future behavior. Now let us consider the reverse question: Why should we bother to answer these questions? Why should we bother to make such predictions? The answer, again, must be that the questioners are interacting with us in a social system; their future behavior affects our welfare, and we are trying as best we can to maximize the value to us of their behavior, both now and in the future. In other words, we are engaged with them in a joint venture and it is to our interests to refine the flow of discriminative stimuli back and forth between us and them. Schlinger may agree so far.

Now let us consider to what we may refer when we answer their questions. We could be referring, as Descartes believed, to a spiritual state, a state in a non-physical world with its own rules, located somewhere inside us (perhaps in our pineal glands), to which our questioners have no access but to which we have direct and unimpeachable access through introspection. Or we could be referring to a state of our nervous systems (the chemicals and electrons running through our nerves), or to a kind of organization of those chemicals and electrons in which they mimic the executive function of a computer program. I assume that Schlinger agrees with me that such neurocognitive events are interesting and valuable objects of study but are mechanisms rather than behaviors and are not what we refer to when we answer questions such as "How are you feeling?" (Moreover, why, unless they are neurologists, should other people be interested in the state of our nervous systems?)

Or, when we answer such questions, we could be referring to what we say to ourselves. According to this scenario, if my wife asks me, "What did you think of those people we met for dinner last night?" and I say, "I think they were a pair of creeps," I must actually be referring not to the people themselves, nor to their actual behavior, nor to my interaction with them, but to some sentences I was saying to myself or some image of them undetectable (to my wife) that I created in my muscles between her question and my answer. But even that implausible scenario would not be getting at my consciousness. According to Schlinger, it is not the covert words or images that constitute my consciousness but my proprioceptive feedback from these words and images. Schlinger claims that "...the tendency to talk or imagine [to ourselves] give[s] rise to what consciousness scholars refer to as *qualia* or subjective experience..." (p. 42) and, "Without a sensory system that in addition to exteroception, also includes interoception or proprioception, Watson would not be able to describe private stimulation or, in other words, how he feels" (p. 42). But, aren't interoception and proprioception chemical and electrical events in our nerves? You can't have it both ways. Covert movements cannot just "give rise" to consciousness; if they are to explain consciousness, they must be consciousness itself. And, if covert behavior is consciousness itself, consciousness cannot also be the *perception* of covert behavior. But let us suppose for a moment that consciousness is perception of internal speech by our proprioceptive nervous system. What exactly would that perception be? Is it identical to the entirely physical activity in our proprioceptive nerves? Or, do we need a still more covert activity (the perception of the perception) to explain the perception. And so, on until we get to the center of the brain, where the only remaining possibility is a non-physical soul, and we are back to Descartes' model. Moreover, what a waste it seems for such an important functional property as consciousness to have evolved to rely on the relatively impoverished proprioceptive system when our exteroceptive system is so exquisitely accurate. It is our past behavior (our reinforcement history) that best predicts our future behavior. If, as I claim, the purpose of answering Schlinger's questions is to predict our overt behavior, the part of our behavior that will affect them, why would our answer refer to our unreliable inner speech? There is no denying that we talk and picture things to ourselves. I believe that these covert acts, when they occur, are part of the *mechanism* by which our overt behavior is sometimes organized. But I do not believe that they can be usefully identified as thinking, perceiving, sensing, imagining, and so on. There is insufficient room between our central and peripheral nervous systems, on the one hand, and our overt behavior, on the other, for a massive covert behavioral system, a system that, if the covert-behavior view of consciousness is right, would have to be the referent for our entire mental vocabulary.

In the face of this unlikelihood, bordering on impossibility, what is a behaviorist to do? One tactic would be for behaviorists to join many philosophers and to declare that the mind is simply inaccessible to scientific study. Such an attitude is understandable coming from philosophers, because by implication *they* would be the experts on mental life. But, for a psychologist, to give up on the scientific study of the mind and consciousness is to give up on what psychology is supposed, by the people who support our research, to be all about. Such a tactic, if adopted, would marginalize behaviorism still further within psychology. But these are just extrinsic reasons. The intrinsic reason for a behavioral science of mind, the reason that I wrote the target article [and this book], is that a view of the mind as overt behavior is the best, the most logically consistent, the most satisfying (try it and see) view of the mind that one can take.

To take this view, however, we need to give up on the strict efficient-cause, mechanical, interacting billiard-ball view of causation in which each cause must lie temporally as well as spatially up against its effect, and to adopt a teleological view of causation. From a teleological viewpoint, abstract patterns of movements are (final) causes of the particular acts that make them up. Instead of efficient causes prior to their effects, final causes are more abstract and extended in time than their effects. For example, fastening a board is a final cause of hammering a nail, building a floor a final cause of fastening a board, building a house a final cause of building a floor, sheltering a family a final cause of building a house, and so on. Each final cause is an answer to the question WHY. Efficient causes are answers to the question HOW. Thus, final causes are more appropriate than are efficient causes for Skinnerian behaviorists who are focused on explaining behavior in terms of reinforcement. Skinner's notion, that a contingency of reinforcement (that takes time to occur) can be a cause, and that a response rate (that takes time to occur) can be an effect, is an example of departure from efficient causation. We do not need to justify the effect of contingencies by imagining miniature contingencies represented in the brain efficiently causing behavior. Physics long ago gave up the billiard-ball view of the connection between cause and effect (gravity, magnetism, electric fields, not to mention all of quantum physics). In economics, utility functions are viewed as causes of the particular economic exchanges that make them up. A utility function need not be represented in the brain or anywhere except in the economist's observations. Aristotle believed that final causes are actually more scientific than efficient causes because they are more abstract (Randall, 1960). In the target article I tried to demonstrate that our mental vocabulary fits like a glove on patterns of overt behavior over time. It is in that (teleological) sense and in that sense only that, as Aristotle claimed, the mind can cause behavior (Rachlin, 1992, 1994).

11

Shaping the Coherent Self: A Moral Achievement

As the previous chapters have emphasized, a person's self is an abstract pattern of the person's actions. This chapter, from an article by Marvin Frankel (MF) and myself (HR), takes this conception and applies it to a clinical problem—the development of incoherent patterns in a person's life. The self becomes incoherent, the chapter claims, when different situations come to serve as signals for different, sometimes incompatible, behavioral patterns. From this viewpoint, self-examination or understanding another person is accomplished not by probing deeply within the self or another person for hidden motives but rather by exploring widely over time for superordinate signals in the person's life (meta-discriminative stimuli) that can make behavioral patterns coherent. The implications of this perspective are explored in the contexts of moral accountability, self-deception, and psychotherapy.

Here is a passage from the novel *The Crossing* by Cormac McCarthy (1994):

> By day he sits in the park. . . . He watches passersby. He has become convinced that those aims and purposes with which they imagine their movements to be invested are in reality but a means by which to describe them. He believes that their movements are the subject of larger movements in patterns unknown to them and these in turn to others. He finds no comfort in these speculations. . . . (p. 14)

For the character in McCarthy's book and, for all we know, McCarthy himself, this view of human motives as a series of interwoven behavioral patterns, however true it may be, is bleak and soulless. We quote the passage here because we believe that this view is not only true but also not at all bleak or soulless. It forms the basis for teleological behaviorism—a useful, meaningful, rich, and philosophically sustainable psychology (Rachlin, 1992, 1994, 1997). Teleological behaviorism identifies people's mental lives with the wider and more abstract

180

patterns of their actual lives (their habits). It differs from other ways of under-standing mental life in that it refuses to consider the mind as a prisoner within the body, a prisoner with whom only that person can communicate. On the con-trary, the patterns that comprise a person's mental life are there to be seen by anyone as they occur.

Like McCarthy's character, the teleological behaviorist sees aims and purposes as patterns of movements. But the teleological behaviorist goes further. For her, all mental terms—*sensation, perception, imagination, thought, belief, knowledge,* and so forth—refer to patterns in overt behavior. Any superiority of a person's perception of his own mind over another person's perception of his mind lies in the *quantity* of his observations of his own behavior (he is always there when he is behaving), not in their *quality*. There is nothing inherently superior in a first-person perspective on the mind over a third-person perspective. In fact, because your behavior is more clearly seen by an observer than by you, a third-person perspective may be more accurate. The meanings of mental terms (*expectancy, belief, purpose, feeling,* etc.) are, after all, socially learned (Gergen, 1991). For example, a child of five informs his father that surely it will stop raining and he will be able to go out and play. The father replies, smiling, "You *are* an optimistic little fellow aren't you?" whereupon the child asks, "Am I?" learning the meaning of that concept.

Sounds and sights correlated with behavior are, in the behaviorist's lan-guage, called *discriminative stimuli*. For the behaving person they serve as signals for valuable behavioral patterns. A red traffic light is a discriminative stimulus for stopping the car because, in the red light's presence, it is safer to stop than go. The actor who acts one way while on the stage and another way off the stage is responding in complex ways to two complex sets of discrimi-native stimuli. Good actors are able to turn on and off entire personalities (that is, behavioral patterns) in different situations as one or another situ-ation presents itself. This art takes a great deal of skill. Good acting is good imagining (see discussion of imagination in Chapter 2). Actors often complain that their "real" personalities become lost among the roles they play. That is, the off-stage discriminative stimuli fail to control the actor's behavior as they should—resulting in neglect of family and friends—and the actor feels "alive" only on the stage. The same might happen to a businessperson. The set of discriminative stimuli controlling her behavior at work comes to overlap in harmful ways with the set of discriminative stimuli controlling her behavior at home. We often fail to make the subtle behavioral adjustments constitut-ing discrimination among complex, overlapping everyday-life situations. In such cases we need to discover, in our environments, still more complex and abstract sets of rules (moral rules) that may guide our behavior both in busi-ness and among our families and friends—both on stage and off, as it were. We call these rules *meta-discriminative stimuli*.

Teleological Behaviorism and Other Psychologies

In its emphasis on the externality of mental life and in its view of the mind as existing in patterns of behavior, teleological behaviorism differs from both neurocognitive and modern holistic psychologies. Neurocognitive psychologies are molecular and materialistic. They see the mind as a machine, like a computer; neuroscientists study its hardware, cognitive scientists study its software. Whether cognitive science is potentially reducible to brain physiology or whether cognitive psychology and neuroscience are, in principle, separate spheres of investigation is a matter of debate in both psychology and philosophy (Dennett, 1978). But, whatever the ferocity of their differences, cognitive psychologists and neuroscientists are as one in their antagonism to behaviorism. The ultimate object of both is to understand the workings of the nervous system (however it may be conceived). And the nervous system is, without question, *inside* the organism. This tendency to *internalize* concepts, to identify mental terms with internal organs or internal physical or spiritual actions, is the common attribute of all non-behavioral psychologies (Stout, 1996). Overt behavior (verbal and non-verbal) of the person as a whole is important to non-behavioral psychology only to the extent that it reveals the workings of an internal organ or the actions of an internal entity. For the behaviorist, it is just the opposite. For the behaviorist, sympathy, pity, joy, rage, and other emotional states are characterized by their distinct behavioral trajectories rather than the place or places in the brain activated during their expression (see Figure 6.1 in Chapter 6).

In its non-mechanistic character, teleological behaviorism may seem to resemble modern "holistic" psychology (Miller, 1992). However, teleological behaviorism differs from holistic psychology in exactly the same way that it differs from cognitive psychology and neuroscience—that is, in its ultimate object, which is to understand the mind as overt behavior, observable in principle by another person. For the modern holistic psychologist, behavior is only a byproduct of the mind, which can be understood only by phenomenological observation—not by *wide* behavioral observation (observation over an extended time period) but by *deep* observation within yourself (Rogers, 1951).

The language of teleological behaviorism is not only different from that of neurocognitive and holistic psychologies, but it is also different from folk psychology—the way people understand their own minds. We generally locate motives, feelings, and beliefs within ourselves; we see ourselves as causal agents; we believe that our mental motives precede and produce our actions. Our everyday language has a great affinity with the holistic psychologies and may explain the wide acceptance of the psychotherapies that emerge from holistic perspectives (Norcross, 2002, p. 6). Teleological behaviorism, on the other hand, requires a radical shift in perspective and argues instead that thinking is a way of acting over time, rather than a prologue to action. We will discuss everyday mentalistic language and implications for psychotherapy in later sections.

The Self

From a teleological-behavioral viewpoint, a person's self is that person's pattern of interactions with the world, particularly interactions with other people—social interactions. It is common to claim that our selves are separate entities inside our bodies—cognitive entities, such as the totalitarian self that permits only self-serving data to become conscious, or physiological or spiritual entities—existing independently of overt behavior and responsible for that behavior as well (Shrum & McCarthy, 1992). The postulation of an internal self, however common, is what the philosopher Gilbert Ryle (1949) called a category mistake. [Of course, physiological mechanisms exist. The organism is not literally empty. But the framework offered here suggests that there is no unified internal module, no introspecting cause of behavior, which could be identified as a self. The self is the socially behaving organism, not something within the organism.]

To take the simplest example of a category mistake, a three- or four-year-old child might say, "Daddy, Mommy, what is a dog?" And let us say the parent has on her bookshelf a book of photographs of dogs. So she takes out the book and shows the child: "Here's a dog and it's a collie, here's a dog and this is a corgi, here's a dog and this is a dachshund." The child looks and says, "Oh, that's a collie, that's a dachshund, that's a corgi. Where's the dog? I don't see the dog." There is, of course, no abstract dog that could be placed alongside a group of particular dogs. By assuming that there is, the child is making a category mistake. Now substitute "self" for "dog." To say that a person's self is independent of the pattern of the person's interactions with therapist, teacher, friend, stranger, is to commit a category mistake in the same way as the child who said, "Show me a picture of the dog." It is a category mistake to consider the self as an entity independent of the behavioral patterns of that person. If you were able to categorize all of a person's actions into the patterns they form, you would know all there is to know about that person's self (Frankel & Sommerbeck, 2005).

The Coherent Self

How can a self, seen as pattern of social interactions, be coherent or incoherent? Imagine that a woman, let us call her Xenia, gathers together all of the people she has ever encountered in her life, everyone living or dead (the dead are briefly resurrected) who has had an influence on her, for a three-day symposium on the subject of Xenia's life. She tells them, "I want you to give an exhaustive account of me to each other. Exhaustive, every love affair, everything I've ever said or done, as you know it." When the symposium participants tell each other everything they know about her, what common behavioral patterns will be found? There might be very little that they could all agree on. Some participants might be appalled when they hear what the others have to say. Some of them might say, "I can't imagine Xenia, the Xenia I know, doing that! That's just unbelievable!" Those participants would be saying, in essence, "This person is incoherent." The incoherence is the inability of an observer to explain the logic or the consistency of Xenia's various social interactions. The newspapers abound with such examples. Recently a medical student in Boston was arrested and charged with murdering a woman he had met through a website. His fiancée, fellow students, parents, none of them, could believe him to be capable of such an act. [Friends and relatives of the recent Boston marathon bombers cannot reconcile the boys they thought they knew with their crime.]

Some symposium participants might be disaffected from Xenia because some of the things they heard were about them: "Xenia said this about me? I thought she was my friend. I'm not going to talk to her anymore." *The incoherence therefore is in the judgment of the observer.* It may be surprising that the observer, rather than Xenia herself, should determine her own coherence or incoherence. But it is the thesis of this chapter that if we were to place Xenia in the room with the other symposium participants, she might be as likely as any of them to be appalled by what she heard. She might say things like, "Oh my God, I forgot that... you're right." On the other hand, she may well understand the coherence of her actions, even if friends and members of her family do not.

The Incoherent Self

Let us consider two examples of incoherent selves. The first is a composite of numerous cases in the literature on World War II and its aftermath. Herr Stauffen, as we will call him, was a mailman in a small town in eastern Prussia. He was known for his warmth, his friendliness, and his consideration. People liked him. During World War II he had been an SS officer; as an SS officer, he was known by his victims as imperious, arrogant, and greedy. He wore his cap in such a way that a shadow was cast half down his face. There is a photograph of Herr Stauffen as the SS officer, and you can see in his features a cruel, smug look of superiority. It is important to note that Herr Stauffen was perfectly content as a mailman, husband, and father. It would never have occurred to anyone to suggest that he see a psychotherapist. Similarly, when he was an SS officer, he was perfectly content, and again it would never have occurred to anyone to suggest that he see a psychotherapist. However, when the picture of Herr Stauffen the SS officer was shown to Herr Stauffen the mailman, he could not bear to look at it. He became extremely distressed. He said, "This is not me. This person is horrible. I cannot stand the sight of him." But now imagine going back to 1943, locating the SS officer, and saying to him, "Herr Stauffen, you were my mailman. I have a picture of you as a mailman." We suspect he would have been embarrassed. Herr Stauffen as the SS officer would likely look at the face in the picture, see its ingratiated expression of weakness, and say, "That cannot be me. I could not have been so weak." The SS officer and the mailman cannot bear the sight of each other. As a couple, they would be incompatible. The two social interactions are incoherent. The mailman cannot understand the SS officer, and the SS officer cannot understand the mailman.

Hans Frank, the governor-general of German-occupied Poland during World War II, stated: "We must obliterate the Jews. We cannot kill them with poison. But somehow or other we will achieve their extermination" (Perisco, 1994, p. 22). Frank did achieve considerable success in implementing this program of extermination. Less than four years later, on trial for his life, Frank made a serious suicide attempt and stated: "It's as though I am two people. . . . The Frank you see here (he was supposedly a repentant and born-again Christian) and Frank, the German leader. I wonder how that other Frank could do those things. This Frank looks at the other and says, Hans what a louse you are" (Perisco, 1994, p. 85). Lifton (1986), in his study of Nazi doctors who performed medical experiments on concentration camp inmates, takes people like Frank seriously and refers to such incoherence as the product of "mental doubling." Lifton assumes that people are generally coherent but on occasion incoherent. For him, incoherence requires an explanation, rather than coherence. In the story this book is telling, the reverse is the case. The coherent self is the achievement and incoherence the general rule.

Consider a more complicated example. MF was living in Prague for a year, a few years ago. Billy, whom MF had known in college, was visiting Prague for a week. They were in Billy's hotel room, and they got into a conversation, the topic of which was Billy's dissatisfaction with his current life. At one point MF asked him a critical question—a very critical question, MF thought—and then the phone rang. Billy picked up the phone. It was his wife, Leslie. He started to speak to her. MF began to read a magazine but could still follow the tone of the conversation. Billy was speaking to Leslie in a warm, caring, confident way. He was asking about the children. There was every sign of contentment and, clearly, a sustained commitment to family. Billy then hung up and turned to MF; MF looked up from the magazine and said, without missing a beat, "So?" and again put that critical question to him.

Billy said, "What are you talking about?" He was angry.
"Billy, I just asked you this question, don't you remember?"
"No, no," Billy responded, his voice rising in evident agitation.

In an effort to calm Billy down, MF asked, in as compassionate a tone as he could command, "Look, may I review the entire conversation with you?" Billy agreed and MF started to review. Together, they went over the 10- to 15-minute conversation to the point where the question came up. As they reached that point, Billy got pale. He does not usually get pale. He is generally the life of the party; anxiety is alien to his character. But here he was, vulnerable and fragile and anxious. Then MF said, "Remember, Billy. . ." and again asked the question. Billy covered his face and anxiously—hysterically—cried, "Am I going crazy? Am I going crazy? Something's wrong with me." He had no explanation for this sudden loss of memory. "What's wrong with me?" he asked. He went on in this vein for about a minute. Finally, MF took him by his elbow and said, "Relax, relax, you're not going crazy." But MF was seriously concerned. Billy was looking to him now for help, to save him from this blatant and terrifying incoherence. "No, no you're not crazy. Relax. Here's what happened. . . ."

A mark of the incoherence in Billy's life is the fact that his wife calls him William. She hates the name Billy. She thinks it is a child's name, and she resents the fact that his old friends call him Billy; to her, it is like calling him Junior. Her husband, whom she would like to see as a masculine presence, should be William. MF said, "Look, here's what happened. Nothing more than this. When you're with Leslie, you're William. And William is a businessman, a good husband and father, not deeply religious perhaps but certainly willing to go through the motions for the sake of his wife and children. When you're talking to Leslie you love her. Whatever doubts you have, they're normal, and therefore okay, and that's you, that's William. Billy is different. Billy is an outspoken atheist, does all sorts of things that if Leslie were to know she'd go bananas. When Billy is talking to me he is ambivalent about Leslie. In fact, Leslie didn't marry Billy, she married William. As for me, I'm not interested in William at all. And what happened here is that when you got off the phone you were William, but I was talking to Billy. It was as if Leslie were in the room with us. So, when I resumed the conversation, you wanted to say, 'How could you tell me this in front of Leslie? She'll leave me!' You didn't recognize Billy, he came on you too quickly; you didn't have a month to recuperate from being with me."

The similarity of these two examples should be clear. Billy and William are unfamiliar to each other, just as the SS officer and the mailman are unfamiliar to each other. They are parts of an incoherent self, an incoherence that neither of them can explain. MF and Billy were discriminative stimuli for each other in that their mutual presence signaled the general rules in which their relationship would be enacted. For example, they enjoyed challenging each other to take social risks that could have embarrassing consequences. They were also discriminative stimuli for one another in that their comments and gestures served as signals to act in certain ways. In the case of Billy/William, MF was a discriminative stimulus and provided the social rewards that created Billy—just as Billy created MF. However, the rewards that people provide for each other are complex; they are not arranged in 1:1 fashion with a simple pattern of behavior as they are in an experiment.

There are multiple social rewards and multiple social discriminative stimuli signaling social actions. Imagine, for example, Billy/William, Leslie, and MF all present at the same party. Normally this would be a problem for Billy/William. How to act? But suppose that, at the party, Leslie had too much to drink. Billy could then act as Billy because an inebriated Leslie might actually be amused by Billy and even, in that context, prefer him to William. Billy might even come to believe that his wife had changed, that he could be Billy all of the time, only to discover the following day that she preferred William at the breakfast table— because Billy eats his breakfast too rapidly.

If one person acts in one way, another person might or might not react in another way, and might or might not do it next week, or next month, or next year. A consequence of this complexity is that the individual may lose a sense of who he is. Billy emerges at a party with his wife, and William emerges at the breakfast table. It is as if each of us is looking at our own behavior through a peephole in time. We see what happens at one time and place and must remember and infer the rest. This is not an easy task. This is why people are often unaware of their own motives—not because they cannot look deeper into themselves, but because they do not piece together the discriminative stimuli and rewards that control their patterns of behavior. As an outside observer, MF could see the contrasting behavioral trajectories of Billy and William, whereas William and Billy were in an either/or position.

Now consider a much less severe example, familiar to teachers. Recently, one of MF's students at Sarah Lawrence College, a woman about 21 years old, asked him if he was going to graduation. MF said, "Well, I may, I may not, I don't know."

> "I'd like you to come and meet my father, but I hope he doesn't embarrass me."
> "No, you hope you don't embarrass yourself."
> "What do you mean by that?"

What MF meant was that in a situation such as graduation, when a Sarah Lawrence student brings her parents face to face with a teacher with whom she has studied, the student often faces an uncomfortable dilemma. At Sarah Lawrence the relationship between students and teachers is fairly egalitarian. Teachers are encouraged to treat students as adults. But, at graduation, 21-year-old women and men become about 14. In other words, they become daughters and sons. Parental pride in their achievement overwhelms them. They are thrilled that their parents are proud of them, but also ashamed of it. They are ashamed to care so much that their parents are proud of them because when you

get to be an adult your pride is supposed to be in your achievement, not in someone else's pleasure in your achievement. What happens at graduation is that the
parent/child relationship clashes with the teacher/student relationship. In such
a situation, students do not know how to behave. If they relate to their teacher
as they always do, their parents suddenly see a woman or a man. If they relate
to their parents as sons or daughters, they are uncomfortable with the teacher.

The student may have been perfectly consistent in her actions as a student
and equally consistent in her actions as a daughter, but inconsistent across the
two patterns. At graduation the two patterns come painfully into conflict. From
a behavioral viewpoint, the problem with inconsistent behavior lies not in its
internal causes but in its potential external consequences. For the student, a
childish display at graduation in front of a valued teacher or seemingly cold conduct before her beloved parents could put either of these relationships at risk.
The consequences, in the case of Billy, may be the loss of his wife or friend. In
the case of Herr Stauffen, the consequences could be loss of his life. Some pedo-
philiac priests seem able to live comfortably with their inconsistencies so long as
there is no threat of being discovered.

It may be argued that a person can have both insight and outsight to differing
degrees and that we are creating a false dichotomy between them. But "insight"
and "outsight" stand for two explanations of a *single* phenomenon. From a teleological-behavioral viewpoint, attributing some specific act to an internal cognition or emotion (apparent insight) is actually attributing that act to a temporally
extended pattern of interaction with the environment (actual outsight). There is
only one thing to explain, not two things. For the teleological behaviorist, cogni-
tions and emotions *are* such patterns and not internal events at all.

Confusion among discriminative stimuli is common in a psychotherapeutic
relationship. The client may have a profound outsight in the therapeutic context; that is, he recognizes a currently operative discriminative stimulus (such
as the imperious nature of his spouse), but fails to bring the implications of that
outsight into the currents of his life (and remains a victim of that spouse's bul-
lying). This may happen because the client is not the spouse, friend, or parent of
the therapist. When the client is confronted with the discriminative stimuli of
spouse, friend, or parent, the outsight may simply dissolve.

Resolution of Conflicting Behavioral Patterns

Aristotle's golden mean is not a midpoint between two extremes, as is often
understood, but rather a wider perspective (a final cause) different from either
of the extremes. For example, the extremes of rashness and cowardice are
resolved by courage. The extremes of surliness and obsequiousness are resolved
by friendliness. Similarly, justice is a mean between too much for one person and

too much for another. ["Actions. . . are called just and temperate when they are such as the just and temperate man would do; but it is not the man who does these that is just and temperate but the man who does them *as* just and temperate men do them" (*Nicomachean Ethics*, chap. 4, 1105b, 5; italics in original). For example, two people may perform the same just act (say they are storekeepers who return an overpayment to a customer), but both acts are not necessarily just. To be just, the act has to appear in the context of a series of other acts that form a pattern—a habit. A particular act done merely to win praise (as determined by other acts in the pattern), or in the context of a promotional campaign, or by compulsion, or by accident, would not be just—no matter how closely it resembled a particular act within a just pattern.]

MF's friend Billy had an impulsive devil-may-care attitude and for this reason was fun to be around; William was stodgy, conventional, somewhat ingratiating, and less fun to be around. The resolution to this incompatibility would be a new identity rather than a little less or more of William and/or Billy. *In effect, coherence is an achievement, rather than a given.* The individual may be in search of a meta-discriminative stimulus to resolve a conflict.

It is important to note that the person who broke down was neither William nor Billy; neither of them was inclined to hysterical breakdown. The person who broke down was a new person who was no longer with his old friend MF but instead with his momentary therapist. William/Billy would have had to orient himself to a new and broader discriminative stimulus to navigate his relationships with both Leslie and MF. But he did not do this. In fact, as stated above, MF became friends with William, thus ending the life of Billy.

Accountability

If people are literally the pattern of their social interactions, then the more you act one way, the more you are that person. Had Hitler and the fascist government not come along, the mailman may very well have lived all his life and died a nice, considerate, normal person. Suppose that after the war this person returned to his mailman job and lived exactly as before. If evidence were brought forward that he committed crimes when he was an SS officer, should the mailman be held accountable? You might say, "Well, too bad we couldn't catch him when he was the SS officer, then we'd be punishing the person who did the crimes. He's no longer that person." If a dog had rabies and bit someone, and if we could cure rabies and the dog were cured, would you kill it? No, you would say the dog is not the same dog anymore. But most people feel, quite correctly, that human beings should be held accountable for nearly all of their non-compelled actions. The question of whether we can hold the mailman accountable is fundamental to the concept of a coherent self. We should indeed hold the mailman accountable because the rules (the meta-discriminative stimuli) that governed his behavior were too narrow (or too concrete or too affected by immediate rewards); they did not disallow the behavior of the SS officer. The mailman is responsible because his behavior was not governed by available meta-discriminative stimuli. Christianity, for example, could conceivably have rendered the SS social interaction inoperable. The mailman is guilty, in essence, of having an incoherent self.

None of us can predict how he would act under drastically altered circumstances. For some of us, perhaps for most of us, this is fortunate. As many studies in social psychology have shown, behavior tends to be more sensitive to immediate social reinforcement than to the abstract meta-discriminative stimuli that might have controlled coherent patterns.

Consider Billy/William on this issue. In that Prague hotel, after the events described above, MF explained to Billy what the discriminative stimuli were— Leslie was one and MF was one. Once this split was (compassionately) made explicit, Billy's confusion abated; MF showed Billy that he could be William and there would be no aversive consequences to the relationship; given that 95 percent of his life was spent as William, the choice was easy to make. Billy was destroyed, at that moment at any rate. The dissonance (incoherence) between Billy and William was rendered irrelevant because there were no harmful consequences resulting from the incoherence.

Should Billy/William be held responsible for his anger? After all, it is William who is angry at MF; Billy is not there. If MF should say, "William, I'm holding you responsible for this," he would be talking not to his friend, but to Leslie's husband. In the mirror-image situation, Leslie would be talking not to her husband but to MF's friend. The same moral issue exists here as with the mailman/SS officer, although the magnitude here is much less. MF can hold Billy responsible for not learning a rule that allows him to be Billy for an entire evening. Leslie can hold him responsible for not learning a rule that allows him to be William for a life. In other words, Billy and William, like the SS officer and the mailman, are responsible because they failed to learn a rule that makes their different social interactions coherent. Consequently, their actions as husband and friend were inconsistent and unreliable. An angry William was not a good friend and an angry Billy was not a good husband. [We hope the reader understands that neither MF nor HR is holding himself aloof in this regard.]

Psychotherapy

Recall the example of a three-day symposium in which people were asked to say all they knew about Xenia. It would be a sign that Xenia was living an incoherent life if people in that room were shocked. Moreover, if Xenia herself were in that room, and if she were living an incoherent life, she might well have been more shocked than some of those people. Why? Because they, or at least some of them, know her better than she knows herself. They have a bird's-eye view of her behavioral path, while she is like a passenger in a car, driven this way and that. From the teleological-behavioral perspective, it is a myth to think that we necessarily know ourselves better than the people who observe us, especially the significant people in our lives. The therapist is also an observer. She may attain a bird's-eye view of the client's behavioral patterns. It is the therapist's job to discover, and put before the client, the incoherent social interactions of his life.

The emergence of the talking cure at the end of the nineteenth century was an effort to deal with a new kind of person, a person who was no longer living in apparent continuity with his past. That the past of the individual had become invisible can be illustrated with the following thought experiment. Imagine Freud entering a small village in Poland and meeting a peasant. The peasant might invite Freud to dinner that evening; there at the head of the table would be the peasant's mother and at the other end the peasant's father; if the grandparents were alive they would be seated there as well. The peasant is living in his history. He does not require Freud to recreate it for him. The life of the peasant was a continuous whole; clear, natural discriminative and meta-discriminative stimuli guided the peasant from one period of his life to another. For employment he would probably do what his father did. He would marry a woman raised in the same village and taught by the same schoolmaster. Most relevant, the peasant would be known by nearly everyone with whom he came in contact. The notion of a compartmentalized life was not conceivable under the watchful eyes of the villagers and under a heaven inhabited by a God whose commandments had the power of law. But Freud did not treat this person. The patients he encountered felt that they had left their pasts behind. Freud had to tell them that, while the objects in their lives might be novel, their relationships to those objects were shaped by historical forces. In this context, Freud agreed with Wordsworth that "the Child is father of the Man," with the important qualification that for Freud the child was charged with sexuality; so the relevant history of the man, for Freud, was his sexual history. Freud argued that the modern man was more historically anchored than he knew and more bound by his biological nature than he realized.

Let us consider, then, how Freud approached the task of creating historical coherence (and how his conception of its nature may be compared and contrasted to teleological behaviorism). In Freud's analysis of hysteria—the case of Dora—he describes Dora's relationship to Herr K., a friend of the family and her companion on weekend walks (Freud, 1959). On one particular weekend afternoon, Herr K. invited Dora and his wife to meet with him to view a church festival from the window of his business office. Dora alone showed up because Herr K. had managed to dissuade his wife from coming. During this time he "…suddenly clasped the girl to him and pressed a kiss upon her lips." (p. 36).

But Dora would have none of it and fled with a "violent feeling of disgust." Freud then proceeds with his diagnosis:

> ...the behavior of this child of fourteen was already entirely and completely hysterical. I should without question consider a person hysterical in whom an occasion for sexual excitement [a "natural" discriminative stimulus for sexual behavior] elicited feelings that were predominantly or exclusively unpleasurable [from which she violently escaped] .... The elucidation of the mechanism of this reversal of affect is one of the most important and at the same time one of the most difficult problems in the psychology of the neuroses. (p. 37)

Critics of Freud's analysis have stressed his failure to understand the sexuality of a young woman, but they have not offered alternative explanations for her conduct. Dora herself did not offer an explanation for her revulsion since, like Freud's critics, she did not think any explanation was necessary (Rieff, 1959). In her eyes it was self-evident that Herr K's sexual overture was wrong and she was, in effect, a simple victim. But Freud recounts a number of her actions that suggest she was attracted to Herr K. For example, she blushed at one point in the presence of Herr K., and her friend commented that she seemed to be in love with him; she took weekly walks with Herr K. and accepted the flowers he brought to her each weekend.

Freud's case history allows us to view Dora's behavior as resulting from a conflict between two different patterns of behavior, rather than simply repressed sexuality. With the right questions, Dora might have confessed that she was flattered by Herr K.'s interest in her and was playfully flirtatious. She might have also acknowledged that such conduct was not befitting a young woman and that was why she blushed. But she may have added that playing the coquette was a far cry from wanting to be sexually engaged. If, for the moment, we imagine that this were Dora's explanation of her conduct, it would be apparent that for her there is incoherence between the coquette and the middle-class young woman. From a teleological behavioral perspective, Dora is not only a failed coquette, but she does not have a moral stance that would permit compatibility between acting as a respectable young woman and being occasionally coquettish. We can say that the culture failed to provide Dora with meta-discriminative stimuli that would allow her to be a respectable young woman and a coquette at the same time. In these terms, Dora suffered from a conflict between selves.

In contrast, Freud's theory of normal infantile sexuality attributes Dora's "hysteria" to her sexual feelings for her father. Freud approaches Dora as a divided self, pushed by the passionate strivings of the id and restrained by the puritanical conscience of the super-ego (all occurring internally). For Freud, the conflict between the coquette and the young woman is due to the repression of her strong physical affection for her father (expression of which would certainly have been punished in her middle-class, Victorian family). Consequently, Freud would expect Dora to be sexually frigid if she were married. Freud was a sexual reductionist. For him, a failed performance of coquetry would not be the result of poor (that is, narrowly based) behavioral control, but of sexual repression. Freud viewed Dora's problem as intra-personal whereas, from a behavioral perspective, Dora suffered from an incompatibility between two behavioral trajectories. Dora, the vain coquette, was in conflict with Dora, the innocent and dutiful daughter. The conflict was actually interpersonal.

Why, in Freud's terms, does Dora reject the sexual advance of the man she is attracted to? The sexual overture of Herr K. was, according to Freud, "an occasion for sexual excitement" (a discriminative stimulus for an intrinsically pleasurable act). But Dora failed to respond with sexual pleasure in the presence of her desire because the repressed incest with her father short-circuited what Freud deemed her natural and healthy response. Freud hoped that, by simply bringing such deeply buried motives into consciousness, patients would discover *within themselves* guidelines that would render their lives more coherent.

Despite his claim that psychoanalysis was not a *Weltanschauung*, a particular view of the world, but should be judged as a science in no less a way than biology, Freud did offer a way of looking at the human condition and a way to live comfortably in it. In this particular case, Dora did not accept Freud's view of her conduct and left her analysis. She insisted that she did not love Herr K. She insisted even more strongly that she did not incestuously love her father. We will never know what her fate would have been if Freud had treated Dora as suffering from incoherent selves rather than an internal divided self and had entered into a therapeutic reconciliation of the various behavioral patterns she exhibited. Such reconciliation would be, we argue, a *moral* achievement.

Finding Coherence

In contrast to the psychoanalyst and the cognitive therapist, a teleological behaviorist would not shy away from directly aiding patients in finding meta-discriminative stimuli in the *external,* temporally extended environment (ethics, religion, moral codes, examples from literature) that might guide their behavior. The relationship between therapist and client would be similar to the relationship between a graduate student and his thesis advisor. George Kelly (1955) claimed that to be of any help the therapist, like a thesis advisor, had to possess a more complex construct system (a higher meta-discriminative rule) than the student.

Insofar as a teleological understanding requires an appreciation of complex and possibly conflicting narrative trajectories over time, an understanding of literature may be an important aspect of clinical training and treatment; this is what authors do in presenting us with lives over time. Incoherent lives have been a central concern of nineteenth- and twentieth-century literature. How much more instructive (or outsightful) for Dora would have been a discussion that compared the seeming pattern of her life to the lives of Elizabeth and her sister Lydia in *Pride and Prejudice* or Amy in *Little Women*?

From the teleological perspective, self-knowledge requires an understanding of present and future reinforcement contingencies. People may fail to change because, despite an understanding of the historical sources of their current behavior, they do not see an alternative future pattern. A liberated slave may understand the historical basis of his difficulties, but this does not help him to live as a free man. A person may understand and prefer a new pattern to the old one and yet not know how to act in specific cases. In *The Psychology of Personal Constructs*, George Kelly did in fact describe a therapy in which clients rehearsed novel roles to play in their lives in their therapeutic hour before enacting these roles for a two-week period (Kelly, 1955). Indeed, in the current psychotherapeutic climate it is not uncommon for therapists to give homework to their clients to enable them to transfer their therapeutic learning to other settings.

These psychotherapeutic implications of teleological behaviorism may be further illustrated by the moral education of Dickens's character Ebenezer Scrooge. *A Christmas Carol* opens with Scrooge as utterly lacking in Christmas spirit, a selfish materialist incapable of any kind of fraternity not leading to a profitable material exchange. At the end of the story, "He became as good a friend, as good a master, and as good a man as the good old City knew, or any other good old city, town, or borough in the good old world." The transformation comes about through the intervention of three therapeutic agents: ghosts of Scrooge's Christmas past, Christmas present, and Christmas yet to come. In the pattern of his life, Scrooge is able to see the full spectrum of his social engagement; thus he is able to see himself. But most important, he is also allowed to see the pattern of the life of his clerk, Bob Cratchit; by contrast Scrooge cannot help but see the emptiness of his own life unless he changes. Perhaps unwittingly, perhaps indirectly, therapists who may not take kindly to a teleological behavioral perspective succeed because they facilitate the "outsight" necessary for the change. The mystery is less deep than it appears. Actually, society provides Bob Cratchits for us all, and the wise therapist makes excellent use of such models. In this chapter I have simply tried to provide a theoretical rationale for doing so.

Teleological Behaviorism and Psychotherapeutic Discourse

As an example of people's difficulty in accepting a teleological behavioral view of their lives, let us return to the case of Scrooge. He was not a willing voyager. He did not want to see his past, present, and alternative future patterns. But what did he fear? He insists again and again that he cannot change. He is what he is. But he does change. How? Scrooge is compelled to see that he did indeed choose his fate, though that fate was unforeseen by him when he made a series of individual choices (as alcoholism is unforeseen by the person who consumes drink after drink). Just prior to his journey to the past and future, Scrooge is confronted by the ghost of his former partner Marley. Marley is in evident anguish as he displays himself in chains.

> "You are fettered," said Scrooge, trembling. "Tell me why?"
> "I wear the chain I forged in life," replied the Ghost. "I made it link by link, and yard by yard; I girded it on of my own free will, and of my own free will I wore it. Is its pattern strange to you?"

Marley was unable to see, as it was being forged, the pattern he was creating in his daily life, the pattern he implores Scrooge to recognize before it is too late. It is only after Marley's ghost's visit that Scrooge comes to understand the pattern his own life is taking—the misery of which is more than the simple sum of his individual selfish acts. With this knowledge, as we have seen, Scrooge is confronted with a future pattern of life much better in all respects than the one he had been living.

The opportunity to behave in a new pattern, a new fate, is what makes teleological behaviorism threatening. The less threatening nature of insight therapies becomes apparent if you consider the many women who accepted the notion of an inner, unconscious penis envy to explain both their professional ambitions and their inability to completely submerge themselves in the lives of their husbands and children. These women of the twentieth century could accept an inner unconscious motive because it seemed to explain their discontent. They could not have what men had in the social world because they were not men! The unconscious cause or motive of their despair was hardly their fault, and the remedy was vague with regard to subsequent action. Instead, therapeutic attention was centered on the historical causes of the over-determined penis envy. If that could only be resolved, the despair would dissipate. With a teleological behavioral analysis, a woman's behavior would be able to conform to a larger (and possibly risky) pattern. She may verbalize the ultimate value of that pattern but still not be willing to pay the immediate social and economic price or take the risk of failing.

The teleological behavioral perspective also poses a threat to the client's authenticity. Consider, for example, a client, let us call him Harry, who suffers from morbid thoughts of illness and dying and who regards the slightest ailment as a sign of cancer or heart disease. Harry would be instructed by an analyst or a cognitive psychotherapist to attend to the inner-self, to examine what repressed motives (psychoanalysis), mistaken beliefs (cognitive therapy), or denied and distorted feelings (person-centered) serve as the mental context for these anxieties. Once these are identified and accepted by the client, a causal inference connects these internal workings of the self to the public suffering self.

In contrast, the teleological behaviorist attempts to illuminate a system of social contingencies connecting the person to the community. Consequently, the client is informed that almost all of his actions, words, and even expressive behavior (facial and postural) serve as a form of social currency historically designed to elicit reinforcement (immediate and short-term) from the community. Many clients might feel they are being judged as insincere or inauthentic because the therapist is informing them that they are outer-directed and manipulative. Such a view goes against the grain of their experience. Their sufferings are unquestionably real; for such clients, being real means existing in their inner selves, not their public selves. How can one explain to a client that the inner self may be viewed as a pattern of social behavior? How can one explain to a client that the thoughts of Rodin's *Thinker* might more productively be conceptualized as a presently unseen pattern of overt actions over time than an equally unseen internal physiological or spiritual state? How can one explain to a client that genuineness or congruence does not need to be conceptualized only as harmony between experience (inner) and behavior (outer) but also, or rather, as harmony between the pattern of his behavior and that of the world around him—"A Dance to the Music of Time," in the words of Anthony Powell (1951) [from the title of a painting by Nicolas Poussin (1594–1665)]. To be a genuine husband or wife or parent is to do all the actions demanded by these tasks. To be truly in love is to act consistently in a loving way, rather than to say or do any one thing; still less is being in love being in one or another internal physiological state.

If this perspective can be successfully explained, the teleological behavioral therapist would urge Harry, as a start, to cease presenting to the public a face and manner that suggests morbid concern. In this way, the client eschews immediate social reinforcement. Dewey (1922) stated that all thinking is problem solving. Hypochondria solves the problem of exacting attention and concern from significant others. Once that outlet is eliminated, the therapist may help the client to discover less destructive ways of securing such concern. But, of course, a given behavioral pattern may involve many different kinds of reinforcement (may be "over-determined"). Harry may disarm people when speaking to them of his vulnerabilities; it may be his way of maintaining intimate relationships. To give up such confessions would require alternative ways of creating intimate bonds. Moreover, the people who previously offered care and sympathy would have to find alternative ways of relating to Harry. It would not be surprising if these people objected to a therapy that forced them to find new ways of being significant to Harry. In offering clients interpretations that illuminate behavioral patterns, a clinical teleological behaviorist would empower the client. But such power inevitably requires the giving up of historical reinforcement for novel, unknown reinforcement and in so doing would upset the social cocoon of which he is a part. Clients may also object that by censoring their health concerns they are in effect lying by omission. In fact, they are creating a new truth of fearlessness. Would we say that a person on a diet is lying when he refuses a piece of cake that he craves?

The immediate consequences of outsight, as we have defined it here, typically involve the giving up of immediate social reinforcement and engaging in behavior historically reinforced only as part of highly abstract patterns. This is what makes clarity of outsight so threatening. In contrast, insight therapists draw an ambiguous line from thought to action and an even more ambiguous prescription for appropriate action. Thus, the client is able to enjoy the social reinforcement of his verbal behavior as a client while contemplating possible changes in his behavior. However in need of reflection and refinement the theory behind insight therapy may be, it can yield positive results when the patient goes beyond verbal behavior to other social actions. Some women must have benefited from resolving their nonexistent penis envy. Unfortunately, such therapies also reinforce the division between mind and body, experience and behavior and, most unfortunately, the split between the individual and the community. It is my hope that the perspective here offers an opportunity for reconciling such incoherence in self, other, and the world at large.

Acknowledgment

Chapter 11 is a revised version of Frankel and Rachlin (2010), Shaping the Coherent Self: A Moral Achievement, *Beliefs and Values*, 2, 66–79. Reprinted with permission of The International Beliefs and Values Institute.

REFERENCES

Ainslie, G. (1992). *Picoeconomics: The strategic interaction of successive motivational states within the person*. New York: Cambridge University Press.

Ainslie, G. (2001). *Breakdown of will*. New York: Cambridge University Press.

Aristotle (1941). *The basic works of Aristotle*. R. McKeon (Ed.). New York: Random House.

Augustine (ca. 395/1953). On free will. In J. H. S. Burleigh (Ed. & Trans.), *Augustine: Earlier writings* (pp. 113–218). Philadelphia: Westminster.

Baars, B. J. (1988). *A cognitive theory of consciousness*. New York: Cambridge University Press.

Baum, W. M. (2005). *Understanding behaviorism: Behavior, culture, and evolution*. Second Edition. Oxford: Blackwell.

Baum, W. M., & Rachlin, H. (1969). Choice as time allocation. *Journal of the Experimental Analysis of Behavior, 12*, 861–874.

Bax, C. (2009). *Subjectivity after Wittgenstein: Wittgenstein's embodied and embedded subject and the debate about the death of man*. Amsterdam: Institute for Logic, Language, and Computation.

Beakley, B., & Ludlow, P. (1992). *The philosophy of mind: Classical problems/Contemporary issues*. Cambridge, MA: MIT Press.

Bennett, M. R., & Hacker, P. M. S. (2003). *Philosophical foundations of neuroscience*. Oxford: Blackwell.

Blanshard, B., & Skinner, B. F. (1967). The problem of consciousness—a debate. *Philosophy and Phenomenological Research, 27*, 317–337.

Christensen, B. (2005, June 28). New robot looks strikingly human. *LiveScience*. Retrieved from http://www.livescience.com/.

Block, N. (1981). Psychologism and behaviorism. *Philosophical Review, 90*, 5–43.

Block, N. (2001). Behaviorism revisited. *Behavioral and Brain Sciences, 24*, 997.

Boring, E. G. (1957). *A history of experimental psychology*. Second Edition. New York: Appleton-Century-Crofts.

Boyd, H., Gintis, H., Bowles, S., & Richerson, P. J. (2005). The evolution of altruistic punishment. In H. Gintis, S. Bowles, R. Boyd, and E. Fehr (Eds.), *Moral sentiments and material interests: The foundations of cooperation in economic life* (pp. 215–228). Cambridge, MA: MIT Press.

Brentano, F. (1874/1995). *Psychology from an empirical standpoint*. London: Routledge.

Calvino, I. (1988). *Six memos for the next millennium*. Cambridge, MA: Harvard University Press.

Camerer, C. F. (2003). *Behavioral game theory: Experiments in strategic interaction*. Princeton, NJ: Princeton University Press.

Castro, L., & Rachlin, H. (1980). Self-reward, self-monitoring, and self punishment as feedback in weight control. *Behavior Therapy, 11*, 38–48.

Catania, A. C. (1975). The myth of self-reinforcement. *Behaviorism, 3*, 192–199.

Churchland, P. (1986). *Neurophilosophy*. Cambridge, MA: MIT Press.

Clark, A. (1997). *Being there: Putting brain, body and world together again*. Cambridge, MA: MIT Press.

Corsini, R. (2002). *Dictionary of Psychology*. New York: Brunner/Routledge.

Crick, F., & C. A. Koch. (2003). A framework for consciousness. *Nature Neuroscience 6*, 119–126.

Dawkins, R. (1989). *The selfish gene*. Second Edition. New York: Oxford University Press.

De la Piedad, X., Field, D., & Rachlin, H. (2006). The influence of prior choices on current choice. *Journal of the Experimental Analysis of Behavior, 85*, 3–21.

Dennett, D. (1978). *Brainstorms: Philosophical essays on mind and psychology*. Montgomery, VT: Bradford Books.

Dennett, D. (1978). Why you can't make a computer that feels pain. *Synthese, 38*, 415–416.

Dennett, D. (2005). Edge: The world question center. http://www.edge.org/q2005/q05_10.html#dennett24.

Descartes, R. (1637/1971). Discourse on method. In E. Anscombe & P. T. Geach (Eds. & Trans.), *Descartes' philosophical writings* (pp. 5–58). Indianapolis, IN: Bobbs-Merrill.

Descartes, R. (1641/1971). Meditations. In E. Anscombe & P. T. Geach (Eds. & Trans.), *Descartes' philosophical writings* (pp. 59–124). Indianapolis, IN: Bobbs-Merrill.

Descartes, R. (1664/1965). L'Homme. In R. J. Herrnstein & E. G. Boring (Eds.), *A source book in the history of psychology* (pp. 266–271). Cambridge, MA: Harvard University Press.

Dewey, J. (1896). The reflex arc concept in psychology. *Psychological Review, 3*, 357–370.

Dewey, J. (1922). *Human nature and conduct*. New York: Henry Holt.

Dreyfus, H. L. (1979). *What computers can't do: The limits of artificial intelligence*. Revised Edition. New York: Harper Colophon.

Edelman, G. M. (1987). *Neural Darwinism: The theory of neuronal group selection*. New York: Basic Books.

Edelman, G. M. (1990). *The remembered present: A biological theory of consciousness*. New York: Basic Books.

Edelman, G. M., Gally, J. A., & Baars, B. J. (2011). Biology of consciousness. *Frontiers in Psychology, 2*, 1–6.

Fearing, F. (1930). *Reflex action*. New York: Hafner Publishing Company.

Fehr, E., & Fischbacher, U. (2003). The nature of human altruism. *Nature, 425*, 785–791.

Frankel, M., & Rachlin, H. (2010). Shaping the coherent self: A moral achievement. *Beliefs and Values, 2*, 66–79.

Frankel, M., & Sommerbeck, L. (2005). Two Rogers and congruence: The emergence of therapist-centered therapy and the demise of client-centered therapy. In B. Levitt (Ed.), *Embracing non-directivity* (pp. 40–62). Ross-on-Wye: PCCS Books.

Freud, S. (1959). Fragment of an analysis of a case of hysteria (Dora). In *The collected works of Sigmund Freud*, vol. 4. New York: Basic Books.

Friedlander, P. (1958, 1964, 1969). *Plato*. 3 vols. Princeton, NJ: Princeton University Press.

Gadamer, H-G. (1986). *The idea of the good in Platonic-Aristotelian philosophy*. New Haven, CT: Yale University Press.

Gazzaniga, M. S. (1998). *The mind's past*. Berkeley: University of California Press.

Geach, P. T. (1957). *Mental acts*. New York: Humanities Press.

Gergen, K. J. (1991). *The saturated self*. New York: Basic Books.

Gintis, H., Bowles, S., Boyd, R., & Fehr, E. (Eds.) (2005). *Moral sentiments and material interests: The foundations of cooperation in economic life*. Cambridge, MA: MIT Press.

Graham, G. (2010). Behaviorism. *The Stanford encyclopedia of philosophy* (Fall 2010 Edition), E. N. Zalta (Ed.), http://plato.stanford.edu/archives/fall2010/entries/behaviorism/.

Gray, J. (2004). *Consciousness: Creeping up on the hard problem*. Oxford: Oxford University Press.

Grunow, A., & Neuringer, A. (2002). Learning to vary and varying to learn. *Psychonomic Bulletin and Review, 9*, 250–258.

Hamilton, W. D. (1964). The genetical evolution of social behaviour. I. *Journal of Theoretical Biology, 7*, 1–16.

Hardin, G. (1968). The tragedy of the commons. *Science, 162*, 1243–1248.

Heidegger, M. (1927/1962). *Being and time*. New York: Harper & Row.

Herrnstein, R. J. (1961). Relative and absolute frequency of response as a function of frequency of reinforcement. *Journal of the Experimental Analysis of Behavior, 4,* 267–272.

Herrnstein, R. J., and Hineline, P. N. (1966). Negative reinforcement as shock frequency reduction. *Journal of the Experimental Analysis of Behavior, 9,* 421–430.

Hinde, R. A. (1966). *Animal behaviour: A synthesis of ethology and comparative psychology* (pp. 331–360). New York: McGraw-Hill.

Hocutt, M. (1974). Aristotle's four becauses. *Philosophy, 49,* 385–399.

Homme, L. E. (1965). Perspectives in psychology XXIV. Control of coverants, the operants of the mind. *Psychological Record, 15,* 501–511.

Honig, W. K., & Staddon, J. R. (Eds.). (1977). *Handbook of operant behavior.* New York: Prentice-Hall.

Husserl, E. (1900–1901/2001). *Logical investigations.* London: Routledge.

Irwin, T. H. (1980). The metaphysical and psychological basis of Aristotle's ethics. In A. O. Rorty (Ed.). *Essays on Aristotle's ethics.* Berkeley: University of California Press.

James, W. (1890/1950). *The principles of psychology.* New York: Dover Publications.

James, W. (1907/1964) *Lectures on pragmatism.* New York: Meridian Books.

Jones, B. (2007). Social discounting: Social distance and altruistic choice. Dissertation, Psychology Department, Stony Brook University.

Jones, B. A., & Rachlin, H. (2006). Social discounting. *Psychological Science, 17,* 283–286.

Jones, B. A., & Rachlin, H. (2008). Altruism among relatives and non-relatives. *Behavioural Processes, 79,* 120–123. PubMed Central #56111.

Joyce, J. (1922/1986). *Ulysses.* New York: Random House.

Kahneman, D., & Tversky, A. (1979). Prospect theory: An analysis of decisions under risk. *Econometrica, 47,* 263–291.

Kantor, J. R. (1963, 1969). *The scientific evolution of psychology.* 2 vols. Chicago: Principia Press.

Kelly, G. A. (1955). *The psychology of personal constructs,* vols. 1 & 2. New York: Norton.

Koch, C., & Tononi, G. (2011). A test for consciousness. *Scientific American,* June, 44–47.

Koffka, K. (1955). *Principles of Gestalt psychology.* Oxford: Routledge & Kegan Paul, 1955.

Lifton, R. J. (1986). *The Nazi doctors.* New York: Basic Books.

Locey, M. L., Jones, B. A., & Rachlin, H. (2011). Real and hypothetical rewards in self-control and social discounting. *Judgment and Decision Making, 6,* 552–564. (online journal of Society of Judgment and Decision Making.) NIHMS 370506.

Locey, M. L., & Rachlin, H. (2011). A behavioral analysis of altruism. *Behavioural Processes, 87,* 25–33. NIHMS 260711.

Locey, M. L., & Rachlin, H. (2012). Commitment and self-control in a prisoner's dilemma game. *Journal of the Experimental Analysis of Behavior, 98,* 89–104.

Locey, M. L., & Rachlin, H. (2013). Shaping behavioral patterns. *Journal of the Experimental Analysis of Behavior, 99,* 245-259.

Locey, M. L., Safin, V., & Rachlin, H. (2013). Social discounting and the prisoner's dilemma game. *Journal of the Experimental Analysis of Behavior, 99,* 85–97.

Loewenstein, G. (1996). Out of control: Visceral influences on behavior. *Organizational Behavior and Human Decision Processes, 65,* 272–292.

Logue, A. W. (1985). The origins of behaviorism: Antecedents and proclamation. In C. Buxton (Ed.), *Points of view in the modern history of psychology* (pp. 141–167). New York: Academic Press.

Logue, A. W. (1988). Research on self-control: An integrating framework. *Behavioral and Brain Sciences, 11,* 665–679.

Madden, G. J., & Bickel, W. K. (Eds.) (2010). *Impulsivity: The behavioral and neurological science of discounting.* Washington, DC: APA Books.

Mahoney, M. (1974). *Cognitive behavior modification.* Cambridge, MA: Ballinger.

Marr, M. J. (2011). Has radical behaviorism lost its right to privacy? *The Behavior Analyst, 34,* 213–219.

McCarthy, C. (1994). *The Crossing.* New York: Vintage.

McDowell, J. J. (1975). Behavior modification's existential point of departure. *Behaviorism, 3,* 214–220.

McDowell, J. J. (1977). Behavior, existence, and ethics. *Behavior Therapy*, 8, 103–104.

McDowell, J. J. (1988). Behavior analysis: The third branch of Aristotle's physics. *Journal of the Experimental Analysis of Behavior*, 50, 297–304.

McDowell, J. J. (2004). A computational model of selection by consequences. *Journal of the Experimental Analysis of Behavior*, 81, 297–317.

McDowell, J. J. (2010). Behavioral and neural Darwinism: Selectionist function and mechanism in adaptive behavior dynamics. *Behavioural Processes*, 84, 358–365.

McDowell, J. J. (2012). Minding Rachlin's eliminative materialism. *The Behavior Analyst*, 35, 17–28.

McDowell, J. J, Caron, M. L., Kulubekova, S., & Berg, J. P. (2008). A computational theory of selection by consequences applied to concurrent schedules. *Journal of the Experimental Analysis of Behavior*, 90, 387–403.

McGinn, C. (1993). *Problems in philosophy: The limits of inquiry*. Hoboken, NJ: Wiley-Blackwell.

McGinn, C. (2002). *The mysterious flame: Conscious minds in a material world*. New York: Basic Books.

McKeon, R. (1941). *The basic works of Aristotle*. New York: Random House.

Melser, D. (2004). *The act of thinking*. Cambridge, MA: MIT Press.

Merleau-Ponty, M. (1942/1963). *The structure of behavior*. Boston, MA: Beacon.

Miller, G. (1962). *Psychology: The science of mental life*. London: Penguin Books.

Miller, R. B. (1992). The philosophy of humanistic approaches. In R. B. Miller (Ed.), *The restoration of dialogue*. Washington, DC: American Psychological Association.

Moyer, M. (2011). Watson looks for work. *Scientific American*, 304, 19.

Muraven, M., & Baumeister, R. F. (2000). Self-regulation and depletion of limited resources: Does self-control resemble a muscle? *Psychological Bulletin*, 126, 247–259. doi:10.1037/0033-909.126.2.247.

Nagel, T. (1974). What is it like to be a bat? *The Philosophical Review*, 83, 435–450.

Nagel, T. (1998). Conceiving the impossible and the mind-body problem. *Philosophy*, 73, 337–352.

Nagel, T. (2002). The psychophysical nexus. In *Concealment and exposure and other essays*. New York: Oxford University Press.

Nagel, T. (2013). *Mind and cosmos: Why the materialist, neo-Darwinian conception of nature is almost certainly false*. New York: Oxford University Press.

Neuringer, A. (2004). Reinforced variability in animals and people. *American Psychologist*, 59, 891–906.

Noë, Alva. (2009). *Out of our heads: Why you are not your brain, and other lessons from the biology of consciousness*. New York: Hill and Wang.

Norcross, J. C. (2002). Empirically supported therapy relationships. In J. C. Norcross (Ed.), *Psychotherapy relationships that work* (pp. 3–16). Oxford: Oxford University Press.

O'Regan, J. K., & Noë, A. (2001). A sensorimotor account of vision and visual consciousness. *Behavioral and Brain Sciences*, 24, 939–1031.

Parfit, D. (1984). *Reasons and persons*. Oxford: Oxford University Press.

Perisco, J. (1994). *Nuremberg infamy on trial*. New York: Viking.

Plato (trans. 1961). *The collected dialogs*. E. Hamilton & H. Cairnes (Eds.). Princeton, NJ: Princeton University Press.

Plato (trans. 1874). *The Republic*. Benjamin Jowett (Trans.). (http://classics.mit.edu/Plato/republic.html).

Powell, A. (1951). *A question of upbringing*. Boston: Little, Brown.

Premack, D. Reinforcement theory. In D. Levine (Ed.), *Nebraska symposium on motivation*. Lincoln: University of Nebraska Press, 1965.

Putnam, H. (1975). Meaning of "meaning," in K. Gunderson (Ed.), *Language, mind, and knowledge* (pp. 131–193). Minneapolis: University of Minnesota Press.

Quine, W. V. O. (1960). *Word and object*. Cambridge, MA: MIT Press.

Rachlin, H. (1977). A review of M. J. Mahoney's cognition and behavior modification. *Journal of Applied Behavior Analysis*, 10, 369–374.

Rachlin, H. (1985). Pain and behavior. *The Behavioral and Brain Sciences*, 8, 43–52.

Rachlin, H. (1989). *Judgment, decision, and choice*. New York: W. H. Freeman.

Rachlin, H. (1992). Teleological behaviorism. *American Psychologist, 47*, 1371–1382.

Rachlin, H. (1994). *Behavior and mind: The roots of modern psychology*. New York: Oxford University Press.

Rachlin, H. (1995a). Self-control: Beyond commitment. *Behavioral and Brain Sciences, 18*, 109–159.

Rachlin, H. (1995b). The value of temporal patterns in behavior. *Current Directions, 4*, 188–191.

Rachlin, H. (1997). The self and self-control. In G. Snodgrass & R. L. Thompson (Eds.), *The self across psychology: self-recognition, self-awareness, and the self-concept. New York Academy of Science Annals, 818*, 85–98

Rachlin, H. (2000). *The science of self-control*. Cambridge, MA: Harvard University Press.

Rachlin, H. (2002). Altruism and selfishness. *Behavioral and Brain Sciences, 25*, 239–296.

Rachlin, H. (2005). What Muller's law of specific nerve energies says about the mind. *Behavior and Philosophy, 33*, 41–54.

Rachlin, H. (2010a). How *should* we behave: A review of "Reasons and Persons" by Derek Parfit. *Journal of the Experimental Analysis of Behavior, 94*, 95–111.

Rachlin, H. (2010b). Teleological behaviorism and the problem of self-control. In R. R. Hassin, K. N. Ochsner, & Y. Trope (Eds.), *Self-control in society, mind, and brain* (pp. 506–521). New York: Oxford University Press.

Rachlin, H. (2012a). Is the mind in the brain? A review of: "Out of our heads: Why you are not your brain, and other lessons from the biology of consciousness" by Alva Noë. *Journal of the Experimental Analysis of Behavior, 98*, 131–137.

Rachlin, H. (2012b). Making IBM's computer Watson human. *The Behavior Analyst, 35*, 1–16.

Rachlin, H. (2012c). Our overt behavior makes us human. *The Behavior Analyst, 35*, 49–58.

Rachlin, H., & Jones, B. A. (2008). Social discounting and delay discounting. *Journal of Behavioral Decision Making, 21*, 29–43.

Rachlin, H., & Jones, B. A. (2010). The extended self. In G.J. Madden & W. K. Bickel (Eds.), *Impulsivity: The behavioral and neurological science of discounting* (pp. 411–432). Washington, DC: APA Books.

Rachlin, H., & Locey, M. L. (2011). A behavioral analysis of altruism. *Behavioural Processes, 87*, 25–33. NIHMS 260711.

Raineri, A., & Rachlin, H. (1993). The effect of temporal constraints on the value of money and other commodities. *Behavioral Decision Making, 6*, 77–94.

Ramachandran, V. S. (2011). *The tell-tale brain: A neuroscientist's quest for what makes us human*. New York: W. W. Norton.

Randall, J. H., Jr. (1960). *Aristotle*. New York: Columbia University Press.

Rieff, P. (1959). *Freud: The mind of the moralist*. New York: Viking Press

Rogers, C. R. (1951). *Client-centered therapy: Its current practice, implications, and theory*. Boston: Houghton Mifflin.

Ryle, G. (1949). *The concept of mind*. London: Hutchinson House.

Salter, J. (2013). Bill Styron: The ups and downs. *The New York Review of Books, 60*, 32–34.

Sartre, Jean-Paul. (1947). Intentionality: A fundamental idea of Husserl's phenomenology. Joseph P. Fell (Trans.). In *Situations, I*. Paris: Gallimard.

Sartre, Jean-Paul. (1957/1960). *The transcendence of the ego: An existentialist theory of consciousness*. New York: Hill and Wang.

Sartre, Jean-Paul. (1956/1966). *Being and nothingness*. New York: Washington Square Press.

Satel, S., & Lilienfeld, S. O. (2010). Singing the brain disease blues. *AJOB Neuroscience, 1*, 46–47.

Schlinger, H. D. (1992). Intelligence: Real or artificial? *The Analysis of Verbal Behavior, 10*, 125–133.

Schlinger, H. D. (2003). The myth of intelligence. *The Psychological Record, 53*, 15–32.

Schlinger, H. D. (2008). Consciousness is nothing but a word. *Skeptic, 13*, 58–63.

Schlinger, H. D. (2009a). Auditory imagining. *European Journal of Behavior Analysis, 10*, 77–85

Schlinger, H. D. (2009b). Some clarifications on the role of inner speech in consciousness. *Consciousness and Cognition, 18*, 530–531.

Schlinger, H. D. (2012). What would it be like to be IBM's computer, Watson? *The Behavior Analyst, 35*, 37–44.

Searle, J. R. (1980). Minds, brains and programs. *Behavioral and Brain Sciences, 3*, 417–456.

Searle, J. R. (1992). *The rediscovery of the mind*. Cambridge, MA: MIT Press.

Searle, J. R. (1997). *The mystery of consciousness*. New York: New York Review Books.

Searle, J. R. (2004). *Mind: A brief introduction*. Oxford: Oxford University Press.

Seligman, M. E. P., Railton, P., Baumeister, R. F., & Sripada, C. (2013). Navigating into the future or driven by the past. *Perspectives on Psychological Science, 8*, 119–141. doi: 10.1177/1745691612474317.

Shaffer, J. (1963). Mental events and the brain. *Journal of Philosophy, 60*, 160–166.

Shrum, L. J., & McCarty, J. A. (1992). Individual differences in differentiation in the rating of personal values: The role of private self-consciousness. *Personality and Social Psychology Bulletin, 18*, 223–230.

Siegel, E., & Rachlin, H. (1995). Soft commitment: Self-control achieved by response persistence. *Journal of the Experimental Analysis of Behavior, 64*, 117–128. doi: 10.1901/jeab.1995.64-117.

Simon, J. (1995). Interpersonal allocation continuous with intertemporal allocation. *Rationality and Society, 7*, 367–392.

Skinner, B. F. (1938). *The behavior of organisms*. New York: Appleton-Century.

Skinner, B. F. (1945). The operational analysis of psychological terms. *Psychological Review, 52*, 270–277, 291–294.

Skinner, B. F. (1953). *Science and human behavior*. New York: Macmillan.

Skinner, B. F. (1957). *Verbal behavior*. New York: Appleton-Century-Crofts.

Skinner, B. F. (1966). Preface to the seventh printing. *The behavior of organisms*. New York: Appleton-Century-Crofts.

Skinner, B. F. (1969). *Behaviorism at fifty*. New York: Appleton-Century-Crofts.

Skinner, B. F. (1974). *About behaviorism*. New York: Knopf.

Skinner, B. F. (1981). Selection by consequences. *Science, 213*, 501–504.

Skinner, B. F. (1987). Whatever happened to psychology as the science of behavior? *American Psychologist, 42*, 780–786.

Smart, J. J. C. (2011), The mind/brain identity theory. *The Stanford encyclopedia of philosophy* (Fall 2011 Edition), E. N. Zalta (Ed.), http://plato.stanford.edu/archives/fall2011/entries/mind-identity/.

Sober, E., & Wilson, D. S. (1998). *Unto others: The evolution and psychology of unselfish behavior*. Cambridge, MA: Harvard University Press.

Soltis, J., Boyd, R., & Richerson, P. J. (1995). Can group-functional behaviors evolve by cultural group selection? An empirical test. *Cultural Anthropology, 36*, 473–494.

Square, A. (1884/2006). Flatland: A romance in many dimensions. Oxford: Oxford University Press.

Staddon, J. E. R. (1973). On the notion of cause with applications to behaviorism. *Behaviorism, I*, 25–64.

Staddon, J. E. R. (2001). *The new behaviorism: Mind, mechanism, and society*. Philadelphia: Taylor & Francis.

Staddon, J. E. R., & Simmelhag, V. (1971). The "superstition" experiment: A reexamination of its implications for the principles of adaptive behavior. *Psychological Review, 78*, 3–43.

Stout, R. (1996). *Things that happen because they should*. Oxford: Oxford University Press.

Teitelbaum, P. (1977). Levels of integration of the operant. In W. K. Honig & J. E. R. Staddon (Eds.), *Handbook of operant behavior* (pp. 7–27). Englewood Cliffs, NJ: Prentice-Hall.

Thorndike, E. L. (1911/2000). *Animal intelligence*. New Brunswick, NJ: Transaction Publishers.

Titchener, E. B. (1909). *Elementary psychology of the thought process*. New York: Macmillan.

Tononi, G., & Edelman, G.M. (1998). Consciousness and complexity. *Science, 282*, 1846–1851.

Watson, J. B. (1913). Psychology as the behaviorist views it. *Psychological Review, 20*, 158–177.

Weiscrantz, L. (1986). *Blindsight*. Oxford: Oxford University Press.

Wilson, E. O. (2012). *The social conquest of Earth*. New York: Liveright Publishing Corporation.

Wilson, D. S., & Wilson, E. O. (2008). Evolution "for the good of the group." *American Scientist, 96*, 380–389.

Wittgenstein, L. (1958). *Philosophical investigations.* Third Edition. G. E. M. Anscombe (Trans.). New York: Macmillan.

Wojik, K., & Chemero, A. (2012). Nonneurocognitive extended consciousness. *The Behavior Analyst, 35,* 45–48.

Wolff, P. H. (1968). The serial organization of sucking in the young infant. *Pediatrics, 42,* 943–956.

Yourgrau, W., & Mandelstam, S. (1968). *Variational principles in dynamics and quantum theory.* New York: Dover.

Zuriff, G. E. (1979). Ten inner causes. *Behaviorism, 7,* 1–8.

INDEX